MAKING
FEDERALISM
WORK

JAMES L. SUNDQUIST
with the collaboration of
DAVID W. DAVIS

MAKING FEDERALISM WORK

A Study of Program Coordination
at the Community Level

THE BROOKINGS INSTITUTION
Washington, D.C.

Copyright © 1969 by

THE BROOKINGS INSTITUTION

1775 Massachusetts Avenue, N.W., Washington, D.C. 20036

SBN 8157 8218–7 (cloth)
SBN 8157 8217–9 (paper)

Library of Congress Catalog Card Number 78–104334

THE BROOKINGS INSTITUTION is an independent organization devoted to nonpartisan research, education, and publication in economics, government, foreign policy, and the social sciences generally. Its principal purposes are to aid in the development of sound public policies and to promote public understanding of issues of national importance.

The Institution was founded on December 8, 1927, to merge the activities of the Institute for Government Research, founded in 1916, the Institute of Economics, founded in 1922, and the Robert Brookings Graduate School of Economics and Government, founded in 1924.

The general administration of the Institution is the responsibility of a self-perpetuating Board of Trustees. The trustees are likewise charged with maintaining the independence of the staff and fostering the most favorable conditions for creative research and education. The immediate direction of the policies, program, and staff of the Institution is vested in the President, assisted by an advisory council chosen from the staff of the Institution.

In publishing a study, the Institution presents it as a competent treatment of a subject worthy of public consideration. The interpretations and conclusions in such publications are those of the author or authors and do not purport to represent the views of the other staff members, officers, or trustees of the Brookings Institution.

Foreword

IN THE AUTUMN OF 1966, the National Public Advisory Committee on Regional Economic Development, a body established by law to advise the Secretary of Commerce, became concerned about the proliferation of federal agencies and programs in the field of economic development and the problem of coordination among them. A community needing assistance encountered difficulty, the committee found, in determining which federal agency could best serve its needs, and the planning requirements imposed upon the communities by the various agencies seemed unnecessarily complex and at times inconsistent. The communities most needing help, particularly the smaller ones, experienced the greatest difficulty.

Through a subcommittee, the advisory committee requested the Brookings Institution to undertake a study of the problem of program coordination at the community level. Brookings designed such a study, and the Economic Development Administration of the Department of Commerce agreed to underwrite most of the cost. This volume presents the findings and conclusions of that undertaking.

James L. Sundquist and his collaborator, David W. Davis, examined the processes and problems of coordination, through interviews with participants in those processes, in a representative sample of American communities, large and small, and in state capitals, federal regional centers, and Washington. Assisted by Steven D. Lebowitz, they visited thirteen states and a representative group of communities within eight of those states during the last four months of 1967, and Mr. Sundquist paid a return visit to some of the communities in February 1969. In all, some seven hundred persons were interviewed.

Messrs. Sundquist and Davis collaborated in collection of data, preliminary analysis of findings, and drafting of tentative conclusions. In June 1968 Mr. Davis left Brookings to enter the employ of the City of Boston, where he is now director of the Office of Public Services, and Mr. Sundquist assumed responsibility for refining the analysis, reviewing the findings and conclusions with responsible program administrators and nongovernmental experts, and writing the volume. Mr. Davis, however, reviewed all of the drafts and concurs in the conclusions and recommendations.

The Brookings Institution acknowledges the excellent cooperation of persons whose views were sought. Almost without exception, persons associated with every type of program, at every level, gave generously of their time, and many were willing in addition to read parts of the manuscript and offer comments.

The study was planned and initiated under the direction of Franklin P. Kilpatrick, then acting director of the Governmental Studies Program at Brookings, and completed under the guidance of Gilbert Y. Steiner, as program director. Mr. Steiner, Charles E. Gilbert, and Allen Schick, also of the Brookings staff, read the entire manuscript and offered valuable criticisms and suggestions. Constance Holden and Judith Nissley transcribed with utmost patience the endless tapes of interview notes, and Grace Dawson endured the labor of typing successive drafts of the manuscript, in addition to double-checking names, dates, facts, and figures. The book was edited by Alice M. Carroll and indexed by Florence Robinson.

Neither the Economic Development Administration nor the National Public Advisory Committee on Regional Economic Development took any part in the direction of the study, and the conclusions do not necessarily represent their views, nor do they necessarily represent the views of the trustees, the officers, or other staff members of the Brookings Institution.

KERMIT GORDON
President

September 1969
Washington, D.C.

Contents

CHAPTER ONE

The Problem of Coordination in a Changing Federalism

IN THE NINETEEN-SIXTIES the American federal system entered a new phase. Through a series of dramatic enactments, the Congress asserted the national interest and authority in a wide range of governmental functions that until then had been the province, exclusively or predominantly, of state and local governments. The new legislation not only established federal-state-local relations in entirely new fields of activity and on a vast scale but it established new patterns of relationships as well.

The massive federal intervention in community affairs came in some of the most sacrosanct of all the traditional preserves of state and local authority—notably education and, in 1968, local law enforcement. It included major national programs in new fields of activity like manpower training and area economic development, as well as new aid for established functions of local government like mass transportation, water systems, and sewage treatment plants. Moreover, in the Economic Opportunity Act of 1964 and again in the model cities program of 1966, the Congress for the first time authorized aid to local communities for a virtually unrestricted range of functions, subject only to a general definition of purpose in the former case and a limitation by geographical area in the latter.

The transformation of the federal system in the 1960s can be seen in the dramatic rise in the number of federal grant-in-aid programs. The Advisory Commission on Intergovernmental Relations lists ninety-five areas of state and local activity for which federal grants-in-aid were available during the period 1966–68. In only ten of these areas had federal aid been initiated prior to 1930. Another seventeen areas were opened during the New Deal years. Twenty-nine more were added in the first fifteen years of the postwar period. But thirty-nine—or 41 percent of the total—were added in just six years, from 1961 to 1966.[1]

The transformation is reflected also in the expanded volume of federal grants to states and local communities under both new and old legislation. Table 1 shows the growth in federal aid since 1958. In a dozen years it has risen more than fivefold, from less than $5 billion to an estimated $25 billion in the 1970 fiscal year. It has risen also as a proportion of federal expenditures and of state-local revenue.

Table 1. Growth in the Volume of Federal Aid Expenditures, 1958–70

| Fiscal year | Amount of federal aid (in millions of dollars) | Federal aid as percentage of | | |
		Total federal expenditures	Domestic federal expenditures[a]	State-local revenue[b]
1958	4,935	6.1	14.6	12.0
1959	6,669	7.4	16.6	14.6
1960	7,040	7.8	17.2	13.8
1961	7,112	7.4	15.7	13.2
1962	7,893	7.5	16.4	13.5
1963	8,634	7.7	16.4	13.7
1964	10,141	8.6	18.2	14.8
1965	10,904	9.3	18.8	14.8
1966	12,960	9.9	20.3	15.7
1967	15,240	9.9	20.7	16.7
1968	18,599	10.4	20.9	17.8
1969[c]	20,813	11.3	22.0	17.9
1970[c]	25,029	12.8	23.6	n.a.

Source: *Special Analyses, Budget of the United States, Fiscal Year 1970*, Table O.3, p. 209.
n.a. Not available.
a. Excluding expenditures for national defense, space and international affairs and finance.
b. Based on compilations published by Governments Division, Bureau of Census. Excludes state-local revenue from publicly operated utilities, liquor stores, and insurance trust systems.
c. Estimate. The 1970 estimate is that of President Johnson's final budget and does not take account of President Nixon's revisions.

1. Advisory Commission on Intergovernmental Relations, *Fiscal Balance in the American Federal System* (1967), Vol. 1, Table 22, pp. 140–44. The entire list is included as the Appendix of this study. The 95 areas included 379 separate categorical grant offerings, by the Advisory Commission's Jan. 1, 1967, count. Of these, 219 had been added in the four-year period 1963–66, 109 of them in 1965 alone. Additional programs have, of course, been enacted since then, including assistance for crime prevention and control in the Omnibus Crime Control and Safe Streets Act of 1968.

Finally, the changing character of the federal system is evidenced in a shift of emphasis in the pattern of federal-state-local relationships in grant-in-aid programs. Characteristic of the legislation of the 1960s are forthright declarations of national purpose, experimental and flexible approaches to the achievement of those purposes, and close federal supervision and control to assure that the national purposes are served. Some earlier grant-in-aid programs are in this pattern too—urban renewal, for example—but typically the pre-1960 programs were cast in a different mold.

Before 1960 the typical federal assistance program did not involve an expressly stated *national* purpose. It was instituted, rather, as a means of helping state or local governments accomplish *their* objectives. It was the states that set the goal of "getting the farmers out of the mud" through improved state highway networks; federal highway aid was made available simply to help them reach that goal sooner. Communities needed hospitals and sewage treatment plants and airports; the leading lobbyists for expansion of federal assistance for community activities were the national organizations of municipal officials, and they sought it for specific and accepted functions of local government.

Policy making for the established functions, in the older model, remained where it resided before the functions were assisted—in the state and local governments. Federal review and control, accordingly, sought primarily the objectives of efficiency and economy to safeguard the federal treasury, and did not extend effectively to the substance of the programs. Even controls for purposes of assuring efficiency could be loose, because the programs called for a substantial state or local contribution—usually 50 percent—and it could be assumed that the sponsoring governments, in their vigilance against waste of their own money, would automatically protect the federal government too. Funds were distributed among the states on a formula basis, and the states—within broad statutory guidelines—determined the allocation among communities within the states. Where state plans had to have federal approval they were rarely rejected. The federal agencies saw their role as one of technical assistance rather than control. They would offer advice, and "work with" the states to improve their programs, but they would not substitute their policy judgment for that of the recipient agencies. Moreover, the state agencies organized potent national associations with the dual mission of lobbying for more federal money and resisting every suggested extension of federal control, through appeals to the Congress if necessary.

In the newer model the federal grant is conceived as a means of enabling the federal government to achieve *its* objectives—national policies defined, although often in very general terms, by the Congress. The program remains a *federal* program; as a matter of administrative convenience, the federal government executes the program through state or local governments rather than through its own field offices, but the motive force is federal, with the states and communities assisting—rather than the other way around. Following are some statements of national objective contained in recent laws (italics added):

> The Congress declares that the maintenance of the national economy at a high level *is vital to the best interests of the United States*, but that some communities are suffering substantial and persistent unemployment and underemployment; that such unemployment and underemployment cause hardship to many individuals and their families and *detract from the national welfare by* wasting vital human resources.... [Area Redevelopment Act (1961), Section 2.]

> *It is in the national interest* that current and prospective manpower shortages be identified and that persons who can be qualified for these positions through education and training be sought out and trained, *in order that the Nation may meet* the staffing requirements of the struggle for freedom. [Manpower Development and Training Act of 1962, Section 101.]

> *The United States can achieve its full economic and social potential as a nation* only if every individual has the opportunity to contribute to the full extent of his capabilities and to participate in the workings of our society. It is, therefore, *the policy of the United States* to eliminate the paradox of poverty in the midst of plenty in this Nation.... [Economic Opportunity Act of 1964, Section 2.]

> The Congress hereby finds and declares that improving the quality of urban life is *the most critical domestic problem facing the United States*....
> The Congress further finds and declares that cities, of all sizes, do not have adequate resources to deal effectively with the critical problems facing them, and that *Federal assistance* in addition to that now authorized ... *is essential* to enable cities to plan, develop, and conduct programs.... [Demonstration Cities and Metropolitan Development Act of 1966, Section 101.]

Achievement of a *national* objective requires close federal control over the content of the program. Projects are therefore individually approved; the state or community is not assured of money automatically through a formula apportionment.[2] On the other hand, in order to accomplish the national objective the federal government must make certain—through one means or another—that sufficient and appropriate proposals are initiated. Accordingly, federal agencies aggressively promote the program, solicit applications, and provide extensive technical assistance, either directly or by financing the employment of consultants. As further inducement, the federal contribution is raised well above the 50 percent that was characteristic earlier; it commonly begins at 100 percent and often remains there.[3] Since the states and communities have little or no financial stake in the undertaking, the expenditures must be closely supervised by the federal government from the standpoint of economy as well as substance.

Where the federal objectives are broadly defined and highly experimental—for example, the war on poverty—the federal agencies are given leeway as to what state or local agencies they will deal with and what specific activities they will finance. In these circumstances the federal government may find it expedient to deal with established organs of local government; or to foster the creation of wholly new bodies at the community level whose loyalty will be primarily to the federal agencies that finance them and who can be counted on to adhere to federal policies; or even to use private organizations as the local instrumentalities for the execution of federal programs. The money is thus put "more precisely on target" than it would be if distributed in the older fashion, through the state.[4]

The transition from the older to the newer model was not, of

2. Of the 379 grant-in-aid authorizations in effect on Jan. 1, 1967, 280 were project grants, by the definitions of the Advisory Commission on Intergovernmental Relations; 99 were formula grants. Well over half of the project grant authorizations—160 of the 280—were enacted in the three-year period 1964–66. In contrast, more than half of the formula grant authorizations—53 of the 99—were enacted before 1963. Advisory Commission on Intergovernmental Relations, *Fiscal Balance in the American Federal System*, Vol. I, Table 23, p. 151.

3. See *ibid.*, Table 24, pp. 156–57, for tabulation of program matching ratios by years of origin of programs.

4. Charles E. Gilbert and David G. Smith, "The Modernization of American Federalism," in Murray S. Stedman, Jr. (ed.), *Modernizing American Government: The Demands of Social Change* (Prentice-Hall, 1968), p. 140. In pp. 135–41 they review the changing character of federal grant programs.

course, an abrupt one. Before the 1960s, as already noted, programs like urban renewal were devised on the second model; and some statutes of the 1960s embodied more features of the former model than the latter—notably Title I of the Elementary and Secondary Education Act of 1965, under which funds are distributed among the states by formula and projects are approved at the state rather than the federal level (although the federal grant is 100 percent). In both periods, individual programs might incorporate elements of both models. Nevertheless, in the 1960s the mix changed. Before that decade, new programs characteristically embodied more features of the early model; in the 1960s, more features of the latter.

The Irreversible Trend

The dramatic expansion of the range of concern of the federal government in the 1960s can be seen as the culmination of a historic trend—the final burial, perhaps, of traditional doctrines of American federalism that, for a long time, had been dying hard.

In the traditional view of federalism that prevailed in the first hundred and fifty years of American history, commonly called dual federalism, the federal and state governments were seen as essentially separate sovereignties, with clearly demarked and independent spheres of activity. Chief Justice Taney expressed the doctrine in these words in a Supreme Court decision of 1859:

> The powers of the General Government, and of the State, although both exist and are exercised within the same territorial limits, are yet separate and distinct sovereignties, acting separately and independently of each other, within their respective spheres.[5]

A leading authority on nineteenth century federalism, Daniel J. Elazar, contends that the jurists' constitutional concepts were not an accurate picture of reality even at that time.[6] The federal and state governments were acting cooperatively, not separately and independently, in a number of governmental fields—internal improvements, banking, railroad construction, and so on. In any case, what Elazar and others call cooperative federalism, as distinct from dual

---

5. *Ableman* v. *Booth*, 21 How. 506 (1859), cited by Daniel J. Elazar, *The American Partnership* (University of Chicago Press, 1962), p. 20.

6. *Ibid.*, especially pp. 23–24. See also Morton Grodzins, *The American System*, ed. Daniel J. Elazar (Rand McNally, 1966), particularly pp. 10–12, 56–57.

federalism, has developed steadily from that time on. Toward the end of the century came the first of the modern permanent grant-in-aid programs—teaching materials for the blind, to begin with, and then the cooperative agricultural experiment stations, and aid for veterans' homes and land grant colleges. During the Wilson administration, federal aid was initiated for highway construction, for agricultural extension services, for vocational education and vocational rehabilitation. Then, in the 1930s, the national government accepted a major share of responsibility for public welfare, entered the field of housing, and on a temporary basis subsidized local public works of all kinds. By this time, academicians were writing of a "new federalism," in which responsibility was *shared* between federal and state governments rather than *divided*. The continuing growth of grant-in-aid programs after the war confirmed the new concept of federalism, and when Morton Grodzins dramatized the changing concept with his much-quoted metaphor calling the federal system not a layer cake but a marble cake, few political scientists disputed him.

The twentieth century extensions of federal responsibility were, however, almost all of Democratic origin. The Republican party and its leadership attacked the expansion of federal power, and much of the political debate from Woodrow Wilson to Lyndon Johnson centered upon that issue. In Republican rhetoric, the aggrandizement of the federal government was part of the Democrats' effort "to achieve their goal of national socialism"—in the words of the 1952 Republican platform—and its result, in the mixed metaphor of that same document, was "weakened local self-government which is the cornerstone of the freedom of men."

President Eisenhower, who ran on that platform, entered office with a deep personal and public commitment to reverse the centralizing trend. "I am here," he told the National Governors' Conference in 1953, "because of my indestructible conviction that unless we preserve, in this country, the place of the State government, its traditional place—with the power, the authority, the responsibilities and the revenue necessary to discharge those responsibilities, then we are not going to have an America as we have known it; we will have some other form of government."[7] Eisenhower's instrument of decentralization was his Commission on Intergovernmental Relations, which

7. Remarks at the Governors' Conference, Seattle, Wash., Aug. 4, 1953, *Public Papers of the Presidents, 1953*, p. 536.

became known as the Kestnbaum commission, after its chairman, Meyer Kestnbaum. Its purpose, he had told the governors at an earlier meeting, was "to find a logical division between the proper functions and responsibilities of the State and Federal government."[8] In proposing the commission to the Congress, he had said "the right areas of action for Federal and state government [must be] plainly defined" and to that end governmental activities should be "reallocated."[9] In other words, dual federalism should be restored.

The commission itself took no such view. In a sophisticated report it explicitly rejected the notion that the expansion of federal activity was a "usurpation of State rights" and a threat to freedom, and it accepted the doctrine of cooperative federalism. "The National government and the States should be regarded not as competitors for authority but as two levels of government cooperating with or complementing each other in meeting the growing demands on both," the commission wrote. "In the light of recent Supreme Court decisions and in our present highly interdependent society, there are few activities of government indeed in which there is not some degree of national interest, and in which the National Government is without constitutional authority to participate in some manner."[10] The commission offered no general plan for dividing federal and state functions and responsibilities, and on balance it proposed more expansion than contraction of federal activity.

That did not deter President Eisenhower from trying again. Speaking to the governors' conference at Williamsburg, Virginia, in 1957, the President echoed his dual federalism philosophy of four years earlier:

> I believe deeply in States' rights ... the States can regain and preserve their traditional responsibilities and rights.... Not one of us questions the governmental concepts so wisely applied by the framers of our Constitution ... we can revitalize the principle of sharing of responsibility, of separation of authority, of diffusion of power, in our free government.... I have a competent man and his assistants trying to identify those things where we believe the Federal government has im-

8. Excerpts from President's Remarks at the Closing of the White House Conference of Governors, May 5, 1953, *ibid.*, p. 260.

9. Special Message to the Congress Recommending the Establishment of a Commission To Study Federal, State, and Local Relations, March 30, 1953, *ibid.*, p. 141.

10. *Final Report of the Commission on Intergovernmental Relations*, H. Doc. 198, 84 Cong. 1 sess. (1955), pp. 2, 5.

properly invaded the rights and responsibilities of States . . . we must see that . . . each level of Government performs its proper function—no more, no less. . . . And so, America will continue to be a symbol of courage and hope for the oppressed millions over the world who, victimized by powerful centralized government, aspire to join us in freedom.[11]

Eisenhower proposed creation of a joint federal-state committee to identify federal functions that could be assumed by the states, along with federal revenue sources that could be relinquished to enable the states to assume responsibility. The governors agreed to participate. Yet even with the full support of the administration and the governors' conference, the committee did not come up with much; it proposed that the federal government eliminate grants-in-aid for vocational education and for sewage treatment plants, and that a portion of the tax on local telephone service be made available to the states. But there was no considerable public support for these modest proposals, the interest groups that would have been affected mobilized against them, and they were rejected by a hostile Congress.

If the trend toward national leadership and national decision making on domestic matters could be reversed, surely Dwight D. Eisenhower would have reversed it. No President has approached the issue with a sterner moral conviction nor tried harder. He sought for eight years to find a way to transfer to the states some federal functions— *any* function would have suited him. Yet even in his term the extension of federal responsibility moved, if more slowly, still inexorably on—occasionally, as in the establishment of the interstate highway system, under his own leadership.[12] Should another President share Eisenhower's deep personal convictions on the subject—which is itself improbable—there is little reason to believe he would be more successful. Indeed, a better prediction would be that no candidate for President, on either ticket, is likely to run for office in the future without commitments to thrust the federal government even further into domestic matters. The Republican platform on which Richard

11. Address to the Governors' Conference, Williamsburg, Va., June 24, 1957, *Public Papers of the Presidents, 1957*, pp. 494, 496.

12. An Eisenhower appointee to the Joint Federal-State Action Committee, Robert E. Merriam, has observed that the committee "perhaps put to rest for all time the notion that some neat sorting out of governmental functions could be made." "Federalism in Transition: The Dynamics of Change and Continuity" (speech delivered at the Graduate School, U.S. Department of Agriculture, April 16, 1969). Merriam was the "competent man" to whom the President referred in his Williamsburg address.

Nixon ran for President in 1968 promised to meet "the crisis of the cities" through "a vigorous effort, nationwide" and "effective, sustainable action enlisting new energies by the private sector and by governments at all levels." While Nixon, in his campaign, promised "a return to the states, cities, and communities of decision-making powers rightfully theirs," he expressed what he called "an activist view of his office." The President, he said "must articulate the nation's values, define its goals and marshal its will." Under his administration, he went on, "the Presidency will be deeply involved in the public concerns."[13] Just as Democratic administrations and Congresses have taken national action to help communities cope with their problems, so—it seems clear—will Republican administrations and Congresses.

The pattern of Washington-initiated and Washington-led programs may be simplified through consolidation of grants and other ways, and their administration may be decentralized—and means for doing so are suggested in later chapters. But the pattern itself will not be supplanted. National goals will continue to be defined in Washington, as President Nixon has reiterated, and they will be embodied in national programs. When and as unrestricted grants to the states and local communities (such as revenue sharing) are authorized, they will be a supplement to, not a substitute for, the programs of aid for special purposes. The same social, economic, and political forces that thrust the federal government into its new fields of concern will continue to press upon the nation's leadership, and with an intensity more likely to grow than to diminish.

The nation for decades has been steadily coalescing into a national society; the advance of communications and transportation, the nationalization of the economy, and the sheer physical congestion of population have destroyed the isolation of states and communities. Time was when the opponents of federal aid to education, for example, could take the view that if schools were substandard in some states and communities, the problem was a *local* problem for those states and communities. But nobody now says that if Los Angeles and Detroit and Newark and Cleveland have riots the problem is *local*; when the President appointed the National Advisory Commission on Civil Disorders, after the 1967 disturbances, no one

13. Radio speech on his conception of the office of president, as reported in *New York Times*, Sept. 20, 1968.

was heard even to suggest that he was invading state and local prerogatives. The mobility of agitators alone has been enough to make "law and order" a national problem and bring about the enactment of federal antiriot legislation.

The forces underlying the trend toward national decision making are mutually reinforcing. Given the present scope of responsibility assumed by Washington, people come to look to Washington when new problems arise. When Watts rioted, people turned to the governor of California but they also turned to the President. The President could not have remained indifferent to the causes and consequences of Watts even if he had been so inclined; if his own party had not propelled him into a position of interest and concern, the opposition party would have.

As a major internal problem develops—or comes to public attention—public attitudes appear to pass through three phases. As the problem begins to be recognized, it is seen as local in character, outside the national concern. Then, as it persists and as it becomes clear that the states and communities are unable to solve it unaided (partly because the same political groups that oppose federal action are wont to oppose state and local action too), the activists propose federal aid, but on the basis of helping the states and communities cope with what is still seen as *their* problem. Finally, the locus of basic responsibility shifts: the problem is recognized as in fact not local at all but as a *national* problem requiring a national solution that states and communities are mandated, by one means or another, to carry out—usually by inducements strong enough to produce a voluntary response but sometimes by more direct, coercive means. By now, the first phase has become a matter of history in virtually every field of governmental action save a few remnants like fire protection and sidewalk construction—and even in those fields, federal public works funds are from time to time available. But in matters relating to the fundamental nature of society—educational and economic opportunity for all citizens, equal rights for all, the quality of the human environment, health, welfare, housing—the country has been moving rapidly into the final phase.

There are no longer any constitutional barriers to the assertion of federal responsibility. Not for a generation has the Supreme Court invalidated a law of Congress as an invasion of states' rights. "The question of whether the Federal lawmakers have the power to do

something depends upon whether the Federal lawmakers want something done," concluded the *Wall Street Journal* reporter who covered the Senate debate on the 1968 open housing and antiriot bill.[14]
And not since Williamsburg has much been heard about dual federalism as a political, if not a constitutional, principle. In the ensuing
dozen years, the Congress has affirmed in statute after statute that
community problems are national problems, that the Congress has
a right and a duty to assist in the solution of those problems, and that
therefore there need be no limitations upon the extension of federal
responsibility except those imposed by the fiscal and administrative
circumstances that may prevail at any given time.[15] The climax and
symbol of that philosophy was President Johnson's concept of the
Great Society, enunciated in 1964. The Great Society was, by definition, one society; the phrase was singular, not plural. The Great Society was to be designed by national leadership and achieved on a
national scale. The means were to be local (or state and local) programs, locally initiated and carried out, but brought into being and
made possible by national leadership and national assistance. The
President had a name, too, for this structure of intergovernmental
cooperation—"creative federalism."

But the questions of how to design and operate a structure of
creative federalism were not resolved. The basic dilemma of the
Great Society—or, for that matter, one with humbler aspirations—
is how to achieve goals and objectives that are established by the
national government, through the action of other governments, state
and local, that are legally independent and politically may be even
hostile. Those state and local governments are subject to no federal
discipline except through the granting or denial of federal aid. And
that is not very useful, because to deny the funds is in effect to veto
the national objective itself. Coercive measures, like court action in
the case of civil rights or enforcement procedures under water pollution control legislation, are limited in their applicability. For the
most part, the federal government must depend upon the competence, and the motivation, of government officials whom it can in-

14. Arlen J. Large, "Federal Power and 'Flexible' Senators," *Wall Street Journal*,
March 13, 1968.

15. The political conflict surrounding the extension of national responsibility in the
1950s and 1960s, and the evolution of the legislation extending that responsibility, are
traced in James L. Sundquist, *Politics and Policy: The Eisenhower, Kennedy, and
Johnson Years* (Brookings Institution, 1968).

fluence or induce but cannot directly control. This has always been the dilemma of the federal system, but it is a dilemma many times intensified in the 1960s by the centralization of objective-setting. The country—and that means especially the federal government—must learn how to manage a federal system far more complex than it has known before. So far the country and the government have not learned to manage the system—first of all, perhaps, because they have not yet even come to look upon it as *a single system*.

The Demand for Coordination

When the federal structure was transformed in the 1960s, it was not recast according to anybody's master plan. Nobody had one. Indeed, in the enactment of the new programs of federal assistance, scant attention was paid to the pattern of federal-state-local relations that was emerging. At every level—in the executive department, in the White House, in the Congress—the concentration was upon the substance of the legislation; the administrative language was inserted almost incidentally. "We have no organizational philosophy, only a program philosophy," one high federal official put it. In the absence of a common doctrine, the structure of federalism embodied in a particular bill reflected the ideas of whatever particular group of legislative draftsmen worked on that particular measure and what laws they used as precedents. Each statute had its own administrative strategy. Some programs followed the older model of federalism; most were patterned on the new. Formula grants coexisted with project grants. Established agencies vied with new ones as the recipients of the federal funds, in a welter of relationships and patterns that varied from agency to agency and from program to program.

By the mid-1960s, governors, mayors, and federal officials alike began raising their voices against the "proliferation" of federal programs and agencies and the "confusion" and "lack of coordination" in the administration of the grant-in-aid programs. The rise in criticism coincided with the peak years of enactment of new grant authorizations and particularly with the gathering momentum of the war on poverty. Under that banner a host of new programs was being launched and a new institution—the community action agency (CAA)—was being created in each community, with uncertain relations to local governments and to other existing institutions.

In the summer of 1965 the U.S. Conference of Mayors organized a series of consultations to assess the first year's experience with the community action program. Reporting on the consultations, the mayors' conference dwelt heavily upon the problem of coordination:

> The local CAA's are continuing to encounter difficulties in getting comprehensive programs underway because of a serious and continuing lack of coordination at the federal level. . . .
>
> . . . Most of the CAA Directors reported that they had not encountered meaningful coordination between OEO and . . . the Department of Labor, the Department of Health, Education, and Welfare and various other departments. Neighborhood Youth Corps projects, work-study programs and others have frequently been approved by federal agencies without any involvement of the local CAA.
>
> If local communities are expected to achieve any effective program development of a comprehensive and coordinated sort, the OEO must take the initiative among the federal agencies which local CAA's are powerless to affect . . . if coordination is to become a reality in the community, someone needs to be able to say that when inter-agency conflict occurs one practice or project is to prevail over another. This is not now possible. . . .
>
> . . . many community action directors at the consultation sessions cited numerous examples of their attempts to achieve local coordination being frustrated by unilateral action between federal and existing state or local agencies without reference to the new community action agency. Closer coordination at the federal level of all grant-in-aid programs which can be used in anti-poverty efforts is essential for the coming year.[16]

At the same time that the mayors' consultations were proceeding, the President's principal management agency, the Bureau of the Budget, appointed a group of consultants as a task force on intergovernmental program coordination, under the chairmanship of Stephen K. Bailey. Its report, submitted in December, was not released, but Bailey soon afterward, in an article entitled "Coordinating the Great Society," referred to "the need for new administrative methods" as "urgent." "Federal programs," he wrote, "must be more effectively related to each other and must complement state and local programs without the sacrifice of initiative, experimenta-

16. U.S. Conference of Mayors, "Special Report: The Office of Economic Opportunity and Local Community Action Agencies" ([1965]; processed), pp. 3–5. The consultations on which the report was based were organized in cooperation with the Office of Economic Opportunity and the National Association for Community Development and involved 93 local government representatives along with federal officials and private social welfare, education, housing, and manpower experts.

tion, and momentum."[17] In January 1966, President Johnson observed that "we must strengthen the coordination of Federal programs in the field,"[18] and announced that he would appoint a commission made up of "the most distinguished scholars and men of public affairs" to examine the federal system and "move on to develop a creative federalism."[19] (The President subsequently changed his mind—preferring, presumably, to rely upon the Advisory Commission on Intergovernmental Relations, a permanent body established by statute in 1959. The commission, during this period, conducted its own study of intergovernmental relations in the poverty program.)

In March 1966, Senator Edmund S. Muskie of Maine, chairman of the Senate subcommittee on intergovernmental relations, presented a detailed analysis of the coordination problem at all levels of government and a series of proposed remedial measures, which he said had grown out of a three-year subcommittee study. He told the Senate:

> We found substantial competing and overlapping of Federal programs, sometimes as a direct result of legislation and sometimes as a result of empire building. Similar competition and duplication were found at the State and local levels. We learned that too many Federal aid officials are not interested in, and in fact are even hostile to coordinating programs within and between departments, and that they are reluctant to encourage coordination and planning at State and local levels. These conditions frequently and predictably result in confusion and conflicting requirements which discourage State and local participation, and adversely affect the administrative structure and fiscal organization in these jurisdictions. . . .
>
> In short, we found conflict between professional administrators at the Federal level and less professional administrators at the State and local levels, between line agency officials and elected policymakers at all levels, between administrators of one aid program and those of another, between specialized middle-management officials and generalists in the top-management category, and between standpat bureau heads and innovators seeking to strengthen the decision-making process at all levels.
>
> The picture, then, is one of too much tension and conflict rather than coordination and cooperation all along the line of administration—

17. *Reporter*, Vol. 34, No. 6 (March 24, 1966), p. 41.
18. Budget Message, Jan. 24, 1966, *Public Papers of the Presidents, 1966*, p. 66.
19. State of the Union Message, Jan. 12, 1966, *ibid.*, p. 7.

from top Federal policymakers and administrators to the State and local professional administrators and elected officials.[20]

The senator proposed new coordinating mechanisms at every level of the federal government. At the top, he proposed a national intergovernmental affairs council, patterned after the National Security Council, to serve as "an operating mechanism for developing the President's policies of program coordination, and overseeing their implementation." At the departmental level, he called for a deputy undersecretary or his equivalent in each department with "full-time responsibility for coordinating aid programs on a departmental, interdepartmental, and inter-governmental basis." At the regional level, he endorsed a suggestion for a federal regional coordinator who would be responsible directly to the executive director of the national council. At the local level, he noted, an administration bill then pending provided for an office of federal coordinator in each city.[21] In introducing a bill embodying some of these proposals, in June, Senator Muskie warned, "We are headed for trouble in the building of the Great Society if we do not pull the Federal Establishment together and develop a more positive attitude of helping State and local governments meet their increasing public needs."[22] In hearings in November he drew admissions from members of the Cabinet and the budget director that the problem of coordination was serious. "In almost every domestic program we are encountering crises of organization," Secretary of Health, Education, and Welfare John W. Gardner told the Muskie subcommittee. "Coordination among Federal agencies leaves much to be desired. Communication between the various levels of government—Federal, State and local—is casual and ineffective. State and local government is in most areas seriously inadequate."[23]

The criticism continued throughout the remainder of the Johnson administration. In March 1968, for example, Mayor Henry W. Maier of Milwaukee, appearing on a national television show, protested that "a whole maze of some thirty possible agencies involving

20. *Congressional Record,* Vol. 112, 89 Cong. 2 sess. (1966), p. 6834.
21. The demonstration cities and metropolitan development bill. Protests from mayors led to elimination of the office by the Congress before the bill was passed.
22. *Congressional Record,* Vol. 112, 89 Cong. 2 sess. (1966), p. 13228.
23. *Creative Federalism,* Hearings before the Subcommittee on Intergovernmental Relations of the Senate Government Operations Committee, 89 Cong. 2 sess. (1966), p. 267.

the city, the county, the state, and the Federal Government, and yes, the private sector" might be dealing with the welfare problems of a single family, and went on: "The thing is duplicated from top to bottom. We have now a general in HUD, we have a general in OEO, we have a general in HEW, at the top, and each one of these generals goes down the line to deal with the generals at the county level, the city level, the private sector. And I think that what we ought to have is . . . something that parallels a Joint Chiefs of Staff, starting at the top, some models of coordination going down to the bottom. . . ."[24] And later in that year both party platforms took cognizance of the administrative problems. The Republicans promised "a complete overhaul and restructuring of the competing and overlapping jumble of Federal programs to enable state and local governments to focus on priority objectives." The Democrats pledged to "give priority to simplifying and streamlining the processes of government, particularly in the management of the great innovative programs enacted in the 1960s." Acknowledging the existence of "duplication, administrative confusion, and delay," the platform pledged to "seek to streamline this machinery by improving coordination and management of federal programs."

A Definitional Digression

In all the discussion the constantly recurring objective has been "coordination." The word, however, is one of many definitions, and it has been used in many senses. Coordination is sometimes a process, sometimes a result. Federal agencies are coordinated, so are levels of government, so are programs and projects.

In terms of process, coordination may be lateral—consultation, sharing of information, and negotiation among equals, a type of coordination that has been labeled "mutual adjustment."[25] Or it may be the settlement of a conflict by the decision of a "coordinator."

24. Comments on Meet the Press, National Broadcasting Co., March 3, 1968.
25. Charles E. Lindblom, *The Intelligence of Democracy* (Free Press, 1965), p. 24, offers a tentative definition of coordination: "A set of interdependent decisions is coordinated if each decision is adapted to the others in such a way that for each adjusted decision, the adjustment is thought to be better than no adjustment in the eyes of at least one decisionmaker." His book is an analysis of the methods, and comparative advantages in various circumstances, of two general types of coordination processes—"central coordination," or coordination by a decision maker, and "mutual

Or it may be a combination of these—a process in which lateral coordination is expedited, facilitated, and even coerced by leadership and pressure from an independent or higher level coordinator.

Coordination may take place during the planning stage of a project or program, particularly if the planning process is a comprehensive one. By definition the elements of a properly drafted comprehensive plan are mutually consistent, mutually reinforcing, and hence coordinated. Through the planning process, conflicts can be defined early and resolved before, rather than after, programs go into operation. In some discussions, therefore, the words "planning" and "coordination" may be used almost interchangeably. The planning process itself can be either lateral or hierarchical or both; the plan can be assembled by equals who mutually adjust its elements, or it can be centrally drawn by planners and then adopted and enforced by those with authority to decide, or it can grow out of a combination of these. But coordination takes place in operations, too, after the plans are finished. Thus, training, job development, and placement organizations coordinate their handling of the same trainees; and welfare, health, rehabilitation, and other agencies coordinate their work by arranging for the cross referral of clients. The coordination may be lateral and voluntary or, if the agencies report to a common superior, it may be achieved through central direction.

In terms of result, coordination means consistency, harmony, mutual reinforcement, the absence of conflict and duplication. It may mean the consolidation of separate projects or programs into single undertakings serving the purposes of more than one program, agency, or government. It may mean, conversely, the division of single programs into clearly demarked segments that do not overlap, as in the apportionment of a training program among training agencies. Coordination may be spatial—the optimum physical relation of activities with one another, as in the assembly of related service agencies in a common neighborhood center, or the coordination of

---

adjustment," or lateral adaptation in the absence of a central decision maker (plus, of course, combinations of the two). His sympathies lie with mutual adjustment.

The San Francisco Federal Executive Board, Oakland Task Force, *An Analysis of Federal Decision-Making and Impact: The Federal Government in Oakland* (August 1968), pp. 181–88, offers three coordinative models, called "central direction," "mutual interaction," and "adaptation." The last two models appear to be subtypes of Lindblom's "mutual adjustment" model.

shoreline recreation and access road development with reservoir construction, or the expansion of transportation systems to serve new employment areas. It may be sequential, as in the scheduling of training of employees to coincide with the opening of a new plant. It may pertain to both space and time, as in the concentration of services in an urban renewal area when residents are displaced.

Given all these usages of the word, the objective of coordination has come to embrace in public discussion a wide range of improvements in interagency, intergovernment, interprogram, and interproject relationships—indeed, almost any change in organization, relationships, policies, practices, projects, or programs that will resolve whatever conflict or hiatus in the federal-state-local chain of relationships the user of the term may happen to be concerned with. A term whose meanings are so broad, so loose, and so varied may seem virtually without meaning at all. But there *is* a problem—recognized by Presidents, Cabinet members, governors, mayors, and observers of every station. The use of a single term to describe the problem is a recognition that, in all its many and varied aspects, it is still a *single* problem. It should be described, then, by a single word; another might be used, but "coordination" serves the purpose. In this study the term is used—as in contemporary jargon—as a convenient shorthand for any or all of a range of related concepts. Usually, as in the subtitle of the book and in the title of this chapter, it is used in its broadest sense; elsewhere, the context should make clear its more limited meaning.

Devices for Coordination: In Washington

As the need for coordination began to be felt by planners and administrators within the federal government—and as external criticism mounted—the government responded by moving to create an elaborate structure of coordination, both in Washington and at the community level (with some innovation, too, at the regional and state levels). In doing so, the government chose to rely almost wholly upon systems of mutual adjustment rather than of central direction, upon what could be attained through negotiation among equals rather than through the exercise of hierarchical authority.

At the Washington level the government designated coordinators—not one but several, each with responsibility for coordination in a particular field but without power to enforce coordination. Two of the coordinators were assigned on a geographical basis; the Secretary of Housing and Urban Development was made responsible for coordinating urban development programs and the Secretary of Agriculture for coordinating rural development programs. The Appalachian Regional Commission and the five other regional commissions subsequently established had responsibility, however, for coordinating development programs in their designated regions, and the Secretary of Commerce was charged with coordinating their work and regional development in general. Beyond that were functional coordinators in a series of fields—the director of the Office of Economic Opportunity for antipoverty programs, the Secretary of Labor for manpower programs, the Secretary of Health, Education, and Welfare for programs in those fields insofar as other departments or agencies were involved. In 1965, coordinators were being designated with such frequency and regularity that one of them referred to the group irreverently as "the coordinator-of-the-month club."

The coordinating authority was assigned to the department and agency heads by statute or executive order, usually in restrained language—but language broad enough, and indefinite enough, to cover all of the aspects of coordination discussed above. Recognizing that Cabinet members cannot exert power over one another, the documents proceeded in two ways: they authorized the coordinator to "assist" or "advise" the President in the exercise of the presidential coordinating power; and they established mechanisms for lateral coordination and negotiation of agreements—Cabinet-level interdepartmental committees with fixed membership, initially, and later a "convener" procedure by which the coordinator was empowered to call meetings and representatives of the other agencies were directed to attend. The first of the coordinators—the director of OEO—was established by law in the Executive Office of the President in order that he might partake of the President's coordinating authority, and the President initially announced that the director would be the presidential "chief of staff" for the war on poverty. If he had so functioned, there might conceivably have been no need for other coordinators; in fact, however, he did not develop his chief of staff role, nor is there evidence that the President really tried to use him in that capacity. OEO became absorbed instead in organizing and operating the Job Corps and setting up community action agencies and became, in effect, one more operating agency of the government. On matters of coordination the director of OEO negotiated with Cabinet members as their equal, not as their superior.

Excerpts from the official charters of some of the coordinators follow (italics added).

Director of OEO:

It is the purpose of this Act to strengthen, supplement, and coordinate efforts in furtherance of that policy [elimination of poverty].

In order to insure that all Federal programs related to the purposes of this Act are carried out in a coordinated manner—(1) the Director is authorized . . . to assist the President in coordinating the antipoverty efforts of all Federal agencies. . . .

. . . There is hereby established an Economic Opportunity Council, which shall consult with and advise the Director in carrying out his functions, including the coordination of antipoverty efforts by all segments of the Federal Government.

The Council shall include the Director, who shall be Chairman [and eight Cabinet members and several agency heads]. [Economic Opportunity Act of 1964, Sections 2, 611, 604(a)(b).]

Secretary of HUD:

. . . the Congress finds that establishment of an executive department is desirable . . . to assist the President in achieving maximum coordination of the various Federal activities which have a major effect upon urban community, suburban, or metropolitan development. . . .

The Secretary shall . . . exercise leadership at the direction of the President in coordinating Federal activities affecting housing and urban development. [Department of Housing and Urban Development Act (1965), Sections 2, 3(b).]

To assist the Secretary in carrying out his responsibilities . . . he shall convene, or authorize his representatives to convene, meetings . . . of the heads, or representatives designated by them, of such Federal departments and agencies with programs affecting urban areas as he deems necessary or desirable [for a series of specified purposes] . . . for the exchange of current information needed to achieve coordination. . . . To promote cooperation among Federal departments and agencies in achieving consistent policies, practices, and procedures for administration of their programs affecting urban areas. . . . To identify urban development problems of particular States, metropolitan areas, or communities which require interagency or intergovernmental coordination. ["Coordination of Federal Urban Programs," Executive Order 11297, August 11, 1966, Section 1.]

Secretary of Agriculture:

The Secretary of Agriculture shall take the initiative in identifying programs of agricultural and rural area development which require the cooperation of various Federal departments and agencies for their effective solution, and pursuant thereto *shall convene*, or authorize his representatives to convene *meetings* . . . to which he shall invite the heads of such departments and agencies as may be responsible for interrelated programs or activities, or representatives designated by them [for a series of specified purposes] . . . for the exchange of information needed *to achieve coordination*. . . . To promote cooperation among Federal departments and agencies in achieving consistent policies, practices, and procedures for administration of their programs affecting agricultural and rural area development. . . . To identify agricultural and rural area development problems of particular States, regions, or localities *which require interagency or intergovernmental coordination*. ["Coordination of Federal Programs Affecting Agricultural and Rural Area Development," Executive Order 11307, September 30, 1966, Section 1.]

Secretaries of Labor and HEW (and Director of OEO):

It shall be the responsibility of the Director, the Secretary of Labor, the Secretary of Health, Education, and Welfare, and the heads of all other departments and agencies concerned, acting through such procedures or mechanisms as the President may prescribe, *to provide for*, and take such steps as may be necessary and appropriate to implement, the *effective coordination* of all programs and activities within the executive branch of the Government relating to the training of individuals for the purpose of improving or restoring employability. [Economic Opportunity Act of 1964 (as amended in 1967), Section 637(a).]

Secretary of Labor:

Cooperative planning and execution of manpower training and supporting service programs is hereby established as the policy of the Federal Government. . . .

. . . Each Department and agency included in CAMPS [cooperative area manpower planning system] shall participate in *manpower coordinating committees* at the national and regional levels. The Secretary of Labor shall designate the chairmen of such committees. ["Cooperative Area Manpower Planning System," Executive Order 11422, August 15, 1968, Sections 1(a), 2(c).]

Appalachian Regional Commission:

. . . the [Appalachian Regional] Commission shall . . . serve as a focal point and *coordinating unit* for Appalachian programs. [Appalachian Regional Development Act of 1965, Section 102.]

Secretary of Commerce:

The Secretary of Commerce shall ... Promote the *effective coordination* of the activities of the Federal Government relating to regional economic development. ["Regional Economic Development," Executive Order 11386, December 28, 1967.]

In addition to all these, President Johnson designated Vice President Humphrey as his liaison officer with the nation's mayors, and the director of the Office of Emergency Planning (later the Office of Emergency Preparedness) as a central point of contact for governors and other state officials.[26]

An examination of the above directives shows an unavoidable overlapping of coordinating spheres. One coordinator, for example, is responsible for coordinating antipoverty programs, another for programs affecting urban areas, another for manpower programs. Is a program for the training of poor people in an urban ghetto a *manpower* program, an *antipoverty* program, or a program *affecting urban areas*? Obviously it is all three. Which coordinator is in charge?

But jurisdictional disputes, also, were left to be settled by the negotiation and voluntary acceptance of agreements among Cabinet officers. The agencies entered into bargaining and negotiation as independent equals, and their agreements—appropriately called "treaties" in Washington parlance—were as slowly and painfully arrived at as those reached among sovereign states. Sometimes the President had an observer at the bargaining sessions (in the person of a Bureau of the Budget staff member), sometimes not even that, but rarely did that representative sit at the head of the table and exercise presidential power to impose a decision—or even recommend one to the President—that would adopt one Cabinet member's position over another. Sometimes a dispute would be carried to a White House staff member for settlement, but such central decision making was occasional, impromptu, noninstitutionalized, ad hoc. The President assigned nobody the authority to construct, on his behalf or for his approval, a *system* of coordination.

Devices for Coordination: In the Communities

Essentially, of course, the Washington negotiations were not centered upon the division of power and responsibility in Washing-

26. President Nixon has given these related assignments to the same man—Vice President Agnew.

ton but their division among competing institutions in the country's thousands of communities. And this reflects the essence of the issue. As the headquarters of an army exists only to direct and support the army in the field, where the battle is, so the whole federal grant-in-aid structure exists only to influence and support what goes on in the communities. The ultimate purpose of coordination at every level of that structure is to harmonize programs and projects, and interrelate them constructively, at the point of impact—in the communities. But it is not federal programs only that must be interrelated. Federal programs must be coordinated not only with one another but also with state programs, the community's own public programs, and private endeavors of all kinds. If there were no federal grants-in-aid, coordination would need to be achieved locally in any case, and that would be the responsibility of community institutions. The addition of federal assistance programs only complicates the job of those community institutions; it in no way transfers the responsibility for the coordination process itself from the community to the federal government. Accordingly, much of the discussion that treats lack of coordination as a *Washington* problem, or a *federal field* problem, is misdirected. It is a community problem; conflict among federal agencies in Washington or in the field is important because, but only because, it affects the ability of community institutions to achieve coordination.

The proliferation and vast expansion of federal assistance programs in the 1960s soon overwhelmed the local coordinating institutions that were in existence—local governments, primarily, and area planning bodies, and such private organizations as councils of social agencies. Communities, aided in some instances by the states, had been proceeding slowly to strengthen their institutional structures for purposes of coordination. States had authorized multijurisdictional planning and development bodies, both in metropolitan and in rural areas, and these were struggling into being. A few cities were experimenting with new institutional devices (the predecessors of OEO's community action agencies) aimed at mobilizing into a concerted effort the many public and private agencies that were attacking the problems of poverty and slums. But in general, community institutions—urban and rural alike—were unequal to the demands of the new national programs for leadership, planning, and coordination at the community level. It soon became apparent to the planners of those programs that the weakness of the community institutions was itself *a national problem* that demanded a national solution, because in the absence of an adequate local institutional structure the national programs designed for the solution of substantive community problems would be bound to fail.

But, in the absence, once again, of an organizational philosophy, no one solution was devised for the problem of community-level coordination. Almost as many solutions were conceived as there were federal agencies grappling with the problems of community development. Each agency developed its own strategy of community organization, and the competing strategies were separately recommended to the Congress and enacted into law or separately established by agency authority. The "coordinator of the month" at the Washington level created his counterpart "coordinating structure of the month" at the community level—and jurisdictions overlapped in the communities as in the capital. By 1967 more than a dozen types of federally initiated, local coordinating structures could be counted. OEO had its community action agencies (CAAs); HUD, its city demonstration agencies (CDAs) under the model cities program; Agriculture, its resource conservation and development (RC&D) projects, rural renewal projects, rural areas development (RAD) committees, technical action panels (TAPs), and concerted services coordinators; Commerce, its economic development districts (EDDs) and overall economic development program (OEDP) committees; Labor, its cooperative area manpower planning system (CAMPS) and its concentrated employment program (CEP); the Appalachian Regional Commission, its local development districts (LDDs); and HEW, its comprehensive area health planning agencies. In addition, four agencies (HUD, Labor, HEW, and OEO) jointly were organizing pilot neighborhood centers. Finally, in 1968, HUD was given authority to sponsor nonmetropolitan districts (NMDs) in cooperation with Agriculture and Commerce. To complicate the situation further, several of the states had designed coordinating mechanisms of their own, which were related only imperfectly to the patterns being developed by the federal government, and local jurisdictions had formed councils of governments (COGs) and metropolitan and nonmetropolitan planning bodies.

The federally initiated community mechanisms differed not just in name, structure, and function but also in the elements of the communities' social, economic, and political structures upon which they were based. Each reflected the particular clientele of its parent agency, as well as that agency's administrative traditions and customary channels of communication. Thus, HUD relied on elected officials, particularly urban mayors, and built its mechanisms around local governments—but even so, in the case of model cities, required creation of the city demonstration agencies. The Office of Economic Opportunity, skeptical of the treatment that its clientele, the poor, would receive at the hands of local government, created in its community action agencies a new kind of institution whose control was to be shared by public officials, representatives of private organizations, and the poor themselves (although some of the agencies were, at least in name, departments of the city governments). The Department of Commerce established its relationships with business leaders and other elements of community "power structures," and the Appalachian Regional Commission—a federal-state agency—followed the same pattern. The Department of Agriculture, with its tradition of direct field operations, tended to rely upon its own employees, supported by committees of rural leaders. The Department of Health, Education, and Welfare, accustomed to dealing with local communities only through the states, followed that course in setting up its community-level planning bodies in the field of health. The Department of Labor likewise looked primarily to its principal state counterpart, the state employment service, although in the concentrated employment program it chose to bypass the states and rely upon the community action agencies as sponsors.

By 1967 the cry for coordination that was rising from governors, mayors, and other participants in the federal system at all levels was directed less toward the need for coordinating federal programs as such than to the need for bringing order to the maze of coordinating structures that federal agencies were independently propagating. That became the substance of the treaty-negotiating sessions among Cabinet departments. They negotiated the jurisdictional claims of their community counterparts—without the presence of community representatives at the bargaining table. OEO and Labor worked out, for example, the relation in each community between the concentrated employment program, the community action agency, and the state employment service. OEO and HUD entered into bilateral negotiations on relationships between the community action and city demonstration agencies (although a presidential assistant finally umpired the dispute). HUD, Agriculture, and the Economic Development Administration (Commerce) jointly considered the guidelines for establishing nonmetropolitan districts under the 1968 act (although HUD finally issued the guidelines without awaiting agreement on all particulars).

The federal agencies pressed the claims of their community counterparts as their own, for in a very real sense they were. The position of the counterpart in the community determined the status of the parent agency in Washington. OEO depended upon the community action agencies as much as the agencies depended upon OEO; if they were lost, or subordinated, then OEO would be the loser too. If Agriculture's agencies were recognized as the coordinators in the rural communities, then Agriculture would be the coordinator of rural development in Washington. And so on. Consequently, the federal agencies, in their struggle for status and authority, pressed their conflicting strategies of community organization within the communities themselves, promoting the creation or the aggrandizement of their client counterparts. Communities were being pressed and torn by the conflicting demands of federal agencies. "Our city is a battleground among federal Cabinet agencies," a local model cities director told us. And the battle went on without benefit, except intermittently on an ad hoc basis, of an umpire with the power to reconcile conflicts and enforce order among the battling agencies.

The Federal System as a Single System

This book is a study of the federal system under stress. Perhaps at no time in recent years has intergovernmental conflict, compounded by federal interdepartmental rivalry, been so severe. How much of it is inevitable, and necessary, and even desirable? Morton Grodzins concluded from his seminal study of federalism that "a little chaos" is a good thing[27]—the whole system is more responsive when jurisdictional lines are not clear and exclusive, because a citizenry thwarted at one level of government can have recourse to another. The same logic applies to interdepartmental competition

27. As interpreted by Daniel J. Elazar in his editor's introduction to Grodzins' *The American System*, p. v.

within the federal government. Certainly, if total and perfect coordination could ever be achieved—which is not conceivable—it might prove stultifying. But how much chaos is "a little chaos" and how much is too much? Is it possible to provide the citizen with recourse, to avoid the rigidity of monolithic and exclusive bureaucracies, and still minimize the waste and obstruction that arise from sheer confusion, from needless jurisdictional conflicts, and from petty bureaucratic jealousies? Is it possible to institutionalize recourse, and flexibility, and responsiveness within a system that is still *a single system* and an organizational strategy that is still *a single strategy*? How can the proper balance be attained between a little chaos and a little order?

These are the questions we set out to consider. We began at the community level, which must be the starting point of any study of the federal system. The object must be first to try to conceive the kind of structure that is needed at the community level—where, to repeat, the essential coordination must take place—and out of that to induce the kind of supporting structures that are needed at the higher levels, all the way to Washington.

Accordingly, we undertook to examine the workings of the federal system, and to observe the problem of coordination, in a cross section of American communities. For our sample we selected eight states that together are reasonably representative of the nation in terms of size, urbanization, region, and politics—California, Pennsylvania, Georgia, Minnesota, Kentucky, West Virginia, New Mexico, and New Hampshire. During the last four months of 1967 we visited from two to four communities in each of those states—typically the largest city, a smaller city, and a rural area comprising several counties. In each community we interviewed local, state, and federal officials administering federally aided programs, citizen leaders, and informed observers. In the cities we visited neighborhood as well as citywide leaders. In the rural areas we usually visited more than one community. Altogether, in the eight states, we studied patterns of operation and coordination in twenty-seven localities, if the rural areas are counted as single localities, and about forty if the individual communities are tallied separately. In addition we paid brief visits to one locality in Tennessee and one in Florida, for a total of twenty-nine. In each of the eight states we visited the state capital for a round of interviews with state officials responsible for federally aided programs, and we paid briefer calls in New Jersey, South Carolina, and Massachusetts to examine particular state governmental innovations or particular problems affecting the federal system. We talked also with federal officials at regional and state levels. During 1968 and early 1969, as we were assembling and analyzing our findings from the field survey, we met with federal officials in Washington to discuss those findings and obtain their views on the administrative problems of federalism. Toward the end of this period we participated also in three conferences that brought together practitioners from all levels of government, as well as scholars and observers, to discuss experience gained through the administration of particular programs. One of these was a Brookings Institution Round Table discussion of lessons learned from the community action program; the second, a two-day discussion of the model cities program organized by the Conference on the Public Service; the third, a three-day meeting sponsored by the Urban Coalition to consider organizational problems arising from the war on poverty in general and the community action program in particular. Finally, in February 1969 we revisited four of the states to reexamine some of the structures that were in their formative stages during our earlier visits and bring up to date our information and our impressions, and we added a visit to a fourteenth state, Missouri. In all, we talked with about seven hundred persons at all levels of government, and in a representative group of communities, about how the federal system was working in 1967–69.

We concentrated particularly upon an examination of the community-level coordinating devices in order to appraise the degree of their success and to determine the extent to which they appeared suitable as models for general applicability. In this examination we necessarily had to sacrifice intensive for extensive coverage; we cannot offer a definitive evaluation of any individual community action agency or resource conservation and development project or economic development district, but we tried to reach a judgment as to each type of institution. Some of these judgments are tempered, however, by the limited sample, in the light of the great diversity of communities in the United States. We could examine community action agencies, as an example, in almost every locality, but some of the other coordinating devices existed in only a few, or even perhaps only one, of the communities chosen. A further difficulty was the tempo of change in the fall of 1967. In the case of the newer devices, like model cities or economic development districts, officials could tell us only of their plans and intentions, and our 1969 recheck of how the plans had worked was necessarily limited. Even the community action agencies, which at the ripe age of three years were among the more mature of the federally sponsored innovations, were in a state of uncertainty because of the imminence of the 1967 amendment (known as the Green amendment) authorizing a fundamental change in their character and status.[28] Our generalizations are qualified where the data are not extensive enough, or current enough, to permit definitive judgment.

Similarly, we had to rely upon facts related and opinions expressed rather than upon verified data. We dealt to a large extent in images. But the strength and competence of institutions—as Richard Neustadt has pointed out for even so exalted an institution as the presidency—rest upon their images. If they are *considered* strong and competent by those they seek to influence, then they *are* influential by virtue of acceptance—in addition to, or more often in lieu of, power. We sought to learn, then, not only the actual scope of power possessed by the coordinating institutions but the degree of their acceptance in their communities, as reflected in their images.

As the study progressed, we narrowed our focus to the two kinds of areas where the problem of competition among strategies of organization is most acute: the concentrated areas of poverty in the urban ghettos, particularly those of the largest cities, and the underdeveloped rural (or nonmetropolitan) areas. The one is a turmoil of federal activity, administered by a profusion of federally spawned and locally grown organizations always in collision with one another; the other, in contrast, seems almost like a vacuum, and the problem is one of devising structures competent to organize effective community participation in programs administered through the federal-state-local chain of relationships.

We also became persuaded, as the study progressed, that the object in organizing for coordination must be to cover as broad a range of functional activity as possible. Coordination *within* particular fields—like manpower or housing or health—must be organized too, but each such coordinating scheme must find its place within the larger system for interfunctional coordination. We therefore concentrated upon examining those coordinating mechanisms that were

28. See pp. 38–39 below.

most comprehensive in their scope, looking at coordinating schemes in particular functional fields (like the concentrated employment and cooperative area manpower planning programs in the manpower field, or the area health planning councils) primarily for the light they might shed upon the broader coordination problem. In the cities, then, we appraised mainly the two principal broad coordinating strategies that have been developed—community action and model cities. In the nonmetropolitan areas, we examined the economic development districts, the range of coordinating devices sponsored by the Department of Agriculture, the area planning and development commissions sponsored by the state of Georgia, and the community action agencies. In addition we visited the first of the multicounty planning bodies to receive a grant from HUD as a nonmetropolitan planning district under the 1968 legislation.

The chapters that follow present, first, a historical account of the conceptions embodied in the comprehensive community-level coordinating structures; second, a summary of our findings about the workings of those structures; and, finally, a series of models that, taken together, comprise the structural features of a system of coordination for the federal structure as a whole. The history is provided in Chapters 2, 3, and 4; the findings in Chapters 2, 3, and 5; and the models in Chapters 3, 6, and 7.

If there were any remote chance that the system we have designed would be adopted as a whole, in a single stroke, we might present it with more diffidence. But it could not be. The system of federalism is so complex that it can be altered only piecemeal. Yet the piecemeal changes should be guided by some model—if not ours, then another. The federal system is an intricate web of institutional relationships among levels of government, jurisdictions, agencies, and programs—relationships that comprise a single system, whether or not it is designed as one. The time has come for the Congress and the executive branch to take that system seriously—to stop making changes in any part of that system, by law or administrative order, without considering the impact of those changes upon the system as a whole. The federal system is too important—to the national objectives and community objectives alike—for the country to continue to accept as the structure for that system whatever happens to emerge from the power struggles and treaty negotiations among mutually jealous federal agencies and the random outcome of piecemeal legislative processes. The federal system is too important to be left to chance.

CHAPTER TWO

Community Action:
Coordination versus Innovation

WHEN THE PRESIDENT and the Congress proclaimed their war on poverty in 1964, the community action agency (CAA) was their chosen instrument of leadership and coordination at the community level. Rarely has an institution departed so quickly and so drastically from the doctrine of its founders. In the communities we visited in 1967, not a single community action agency could be described as succeeding in the President's declared purpose of "bringing together these separate programs—Federal, State, and local . . . to achieve a unified . . . approach." None, indeed, was even attempting anything so difficult.

The Mission of Coordination

The coordinating role of the community action agency was stated explicitly by President Johnson in January 1964:

> Poverty stems from no one source, but reflects a multitude of causes. Correspondingly, a number of individual programs have been developed over the years to attack these individual problems of job opportunities, education, and training. Other specific programs deal with the closely related areas of health, housing, welfare, and agricultural services. I propose to establish a means of bringing together these separate programs—Federal, State, and local—in an effort to achieve a unified and intensified approach. . . .
>
> Under this proposal, locally initiated, comprehensive community action programs would be developed, to focus the various available resources on the roots of poverty in urban and rural areas.[1]

1. The Budget Message of the President, Jan. 21, 1964, *Public Papers of the Presidents, 1964*, Vol. I, p. 184.

Later the President explained:

This program asks men and women throughout the country to prepare long-range plans for the attack on poverty in their own local communities. These plans will be local plans calling upon all the resources available to the community—federal and state, local and private, human and material.[2]

An immediate question for the drafters of the President's proposed antipoverty legislation, who were assembled in February under the leadership of Sargent Shriver, was whether the communities' "comprehensive programs" and "long-range plans" had to be complete before any funds were spent to launch the action programs. That had been the rule of the President's Committee on Juvenile Delinquency and Youth Crime, whose community antidelinquency programs were one of the models upon which the community action concept was built. But it was a rule that was exceedingly unpopular among impatient legislators on Capitol Hill, especially Representative Edith Green, Democrat of Oregon.[3] Both because of congressional attitudes and because of their own conviction that the war on poverty had to show results without delay, Shriver's task force accepted what it called the "building block" approach; individual action programs that would be consistent with a community's ultimate comprehensive antipoverty plan could be initiated without awaiting the plan's completion. Accordingly, while the administration bill defined a community action program as one "which mobilizes and utilizes, in an attack on poverty, public and private resources," it provided (in section 204[c]) that assistance "may be extended for a limited period, even though a community has not completed and put into effect its community action program, if the Director determines that . . . extension of such assistance . . . will not impede the development and carrying out of a community action

2. Special Message to the Congress on War on Sources of Poverty, *ibid.*, p. 375. James L. Sundquist, *Politics and Policy: The Eisenhower, Kennedy, and Johnson Years* (Brookings Institution, 1968), Chap. 4, reviews the development of the community action concept in the years prior to 1964, its adoption by the planners of the war on poverty, and the legislative history of the Economic Opportunity Act.

3. The dispute between Mrs. Green and the staff of the President's committee on this point is the subject of John E. Moore's case study, "Juvenile Delinquency Control: A Congressional-Executive Battleground, 1961–64," in Frederick N. Cleaveland (ed.), *Congress and Urban Problems* (Brookings Institution, 1969).

program."[4] But the emphasis, on the part of the administration's planners, was on the phrase "for a limited period"; there was no intention to abandon the requirement of a comprehensive plan. Attorney General Robert F. Kennedy told the House subcommittee holding hearings on the bill that each community would be required "to face its problems, to come up with a coordinated plan, to have it coordinated within itself."[5]

Mrs. Green was a member of the subcommittee, however, and she sought to establish clearly in the law that what the Congress wanted was action, not plans. At her initiative, section 204(c) was stricken and the phrase that required the community action program to mobilize and utilize "public and private resources" was changed to read "public *or* private." The act that passed, then, was substantially watered down: the verb "mobilize" remained, but the language suggesting that the community's *total* resources were to be mobilized through a comprehensive planning process—on the pattern of the juvenile delinquency program—was eliminated.

How coordination, or mobilization, was to be achieved by the community action agencies was scarcely considered during the hearings. Coordination was discussed at length, to be sure, but almost wholly in the context of relationships in Washington. Republican committee members bore down hard upon the role of the director of the new Office of Economic Opportunity, Sargent Shriver, as coordinator—or "poverty czar," as they preferred to describe it—in a vain effort to drive a wedge between Shriver and the members of the Cabinet who, they contended, would be subordinated.[6] But little was said to clarify the concept of the community action agency.

Throughout the hearings, community action was presented as a flexible approach that would permit communities to design antipoverty programs specifically suited to their particular situations. Said Shriver:

> . . . a program useful in a rural part of the state would be different compared to what might be done in the cities of that state. A program that

4. Sections 202(a)(1) and 204(c) of the administration bill, as reprinted in *Economic Opportunity Act of 1964*, Hearings before a Subcommittee of the House Committee on Education and Labor, 88 Cong. 2 sess. (1964), p. 9.

5. *Ibid.*, p. 312.

6. See, for instance, the interrogation of HEW Secretary Anthony J. Celebrezze and Labor Secretary W. Willard Wirtz by Peter H. B. Frelinghuysen, New Jersey Republican, *ibid.*, pp. 138–41, 171, 200–02.

might be appropriate for Savannah, Georgia, would be different from one appropriate for Detroit.

We are not forcing these communities, therefore, to accept or fit themselves into some pattern that we create here in Washington or someone creates for them.[7]

Community action was repeatedly described as a device that would draw federal, state, and local programs together and meld them into an integrated assault upon the problems of poverty. The planning process would disclose needs and resources, the community action agency would "plug the service gaps" with its "versatile" money, and cooperation of all public and private agencies would be assured through their membership on the agency's governing board.

THE HANDICAPS OF COMMUNITY ACTION AGENCIES

Almost as soon as the first community action agencies were formed under the leadership of OEO, they began to evolve in directions not publicly anticipated by those who presented the legislation to the Congress or by the legislators who approved it. Although OEO continued to describe the CAAs as organizations formed "to mobilize available resources, public and private, for a coordinated attack on poverty,"[8] four major influences can be identified that shaped the agencies and their programs from the outset in ways that limited their ability to mobilize and coordinate their communities.

Participation of the Poor. What was to become the most controversial single aspect of the community action program was introduced by Sargent Shriver's task force without much discussion. Language was written into the bill requiring "maximum feasible participation of residents of the areas and members of the groups" to be served, and the phrase appeared so innocuous to the Congress that at no time was it questioned or even discussed.

When the first edition of the *Community Action Program Guide* was issued in October 1964, OEO had interpreted the language to virtually require representation of the poor on CAA governing boards, and thus in the "planning, policy making and operation of the program." Jack T. Conway, the first director of community

7. *House Supplemental Appropriations Bill of 1964*, Hearings before the House Committee on Appropriations, 88 Cong. 2 sess. (1964), p. 356.

8. Office of Economic Opportunity, *Community Action: The Neighborhood Center* (July 1966), p. ii. The identical statement is repeated in many OEO publications.

action programs (CAP) in OEO, liked to characterize community action as a three-legged stool, resting equally upon public officials of the community, representatives of social agencies and other private organizations and interest groups, and the poor. In OEO publications, statements, speeches, and testimony, "participation" became a matter of paramount importance.

John G. Wofford, then staff assistant to the director of CAP operations, says that the increased emphasis grew out of the OEO staff's attempt to deal with "the condition of powerlessness which characterized the poor."[9] But in the earliest days the provision for representation of the poor on CAA boards was not strictly enforced as mayors and the committees they had established to organize their community action programs pleaded for funds to get programs under way as quickly as possible. The inevitable consequence was organized and militant opposition to the establishment-oriented mayors' committees, and controversy began to mount in communities across the country over the meaning of the emergent doctrine of "participation of the poor." Howard W. Hallman has written of this period:

> . . . the composition of the board of the local community action agency became more and more of an issue. This was the beginning of a transitional period in the civil rights movement. The Civil Rights Act of 1964 had recently been enacted, the last major national demonstrations which produced the Voting Rights Act of 1965 were just beginning, the first significant use of the phrase "black power" was a year and a half away (in the Meredith Mississippi March of June 1966), but in many places civil rights leaders were gearing up to gain a larger role in local programs. Along came the Community Action Program tailor-made for their desires. Moreover, the key OEO staff within the Community Action Program and the Office of Inspection was more than sympathetic, for they possessed deep suspicion of municipal government and other parts of local "establishments." They were talking about power for the poor.[10]

In the South the tie between community action agencies and civil rights groups caused quick hostility. Senator John Stennis, Missis-

9. John G. Wofford, "The Politics of Local Responsibility: Administration of the Community Action Program," in James L. Sundquist (ed.), *On Fighting Poverty: Perspectives from Experience* (Basic Books, 1969), p. 79.

10. "Historical Highlights of the Poverty Program" (paper prepared for an Airlie House conference at Warrenton, Va., sponsored by the Urban Coalition, January 1969), p. 8.

sippi Democrat, roasted the fledgling agency during hearings on its second annual budget, charging maladministration. It was clear that the senator regarded the Child Development Group of Mississippi, financed by OEO, as a thinly disguised cover for civil rights activities.[11] But the southerners did not stand alone. Testimony by Mayor William G. Walsh of Syracuse, New York, before the Senate subcommittee on intergovernmental relations illustrates one type of northern mayoral reaction to OEO's experimentation:

Some of the members of the committee, I know, have heard about the part of the poverty program where Syracuse served as a horrible example of how not to handle federal-local relations. This involved a program funded directly by the OEO from Washington to Syracuse University. The funds were granted for the purpose of training community action trainees in what is known as the Community Action Training Center at Syracuse University. Lost was the original purpose of the program—to teach people how to combat poverty. In its place, they were taught how to agitate and attack city hall, and Albany and Washington. The program was developed by a staff member at Syracuse University, submitted to OEO officials in Washington, and funded directly without any member of the Syracuse administration or the principal social agencies in the community knowing anything about the program until the grant was announced.

Such programs were funded in other communities. Through the Conference of Mayors we were able to change this procedure. It gives me great satisfaction to report that the federal government in this case responded to our protest and the grant was not again funded in Syracuse.[12]

On the other side, in support of OEO, were such mayors as Richard C. Lee of New Haven, whose community action agency had been set up several years earlier under Lee's control with Ford Foundation money, and Jerome P. Cavanagh of Detroit, then president of both the National League of Cities and the U.S. Conference of Mayors. Cavanagh told the Senate subcommittee on executive reorganization that he strongly endorsed participation of the poor:

We have spent maybe some people think an inordinate amount of time in responding to the suggestions made by the residents of the so-called target areas, but I think their sense of involvement, and they

11. *Senate Supplemental Appropriations Bill of 1966*, Hearings before the Senate Committee on Appropriations, 89 Cong. 2 sess. (1966), p. 630.

12. *Creative Federalism*, Hearings before the Subcommittee on Intergovernmental Relations of the Senate Committee on Government Operations, 90 Cong. 1 sess. (1967), p. 734.

really do have a sense of involvement, has helped to make that program, and in turn other programs, a success.[13]

In 1966 the Congress, on Republican initiative, codified OEO's informal administrative requirement that at least one-third of the members of CAA governing boards be representatives of the poor, chosen by the residents of the poverty areas. But in some communities the representatives of the poor and their allies had managed to do even better—through political and parliamentary maneuvering and sometimes with the acquiescence of mayors and other leaders of the community "power structure," they had attained majority control of community action agencies.

The 1967 summer riots brought renewed charges of OEO-trained agitators. Mayor Hugh W. Addonizio of riot-battered Newark told the press:

> The cities were flat on their backs and OEO came along and instead of helping us, as Congress intended, it decided we were a bunch of bullies and it gave a club to the so-called powerless to help beat us as we lay on the ground. . . .
> It seems impossible for the federal government to stop something once it gets going, whether it is effective or not.[14]

The political reaction came in the House of Representatives in 1967. As the price of getting any extension of the Economic Opportunity Act through that body, the administration and the Senate had to accept an amendment bearing the name of Representative Edith Green that gave local governments the option of becoming the community action agency or designating the private body to be recognized. It also reserved one-third of the seats on CAA governing boards for public officials and permitted up to one-third to be assigned to representatives of "business, industry, labor, religious, welfare, education, or other major groups or interests in the community." The "power structure" could thus—assuming that its representatives attended the meetings and voted together—reassume

13. *Federal Role in Urban Affairs,* Hearings before the Subcommittee on Executive Reorganization of the Senate Committee on Government Operations, 89 Cong. 2 sess. (1966), p. 636.

14. *Evening Star* (Washington), Aug. 22, 1967. Only one month before, Addonizio had given his endorsement to the continuation of the poverty program: "I seek no scapegoats and no easy answers for the rioting which took place in our city and those who do are misguided. We are all to blame for not moving far enough, fast enough." Letter to Carl D. Perkins, chairman, House Committee on Education and Labor, printed in *The Economic Opportunity Act Amendments of 1967,* Hearings before the House Committee on Education and Labor, 90 Cong. 1 sess. (1967), p. 3710.

control of any CAAs that had come under the dominance of the poor and their representatives.[15]

Deemphasis of Planning. By June 1965, OEO had funded 415 community action agencies, exceeding even its own prediction of 300. A year later the number had grown to 1,045. After that, few new ones were created and some of those existing were consolidated, so that the total remained relatively stable.

To get the community action program under way quickly, OEO took full advantage of the House amendment that had stricken the administration proposal that local comprehensive planning be a precondition (with limited exceptions) for program grants. OEO continued to view planning as essential, but it began approving individual projects that would not be inconsistent with the comprehensive plans when and as they were developed. And it continued to do so. In 1966, nearly two years after its creation, OEO conceded that not much in the way of "community planning" had yet been undertaken by the community action agencies. In response to a Bureau of the Budget inquiry OEO wrote:

> The Community Action Program at present has no prescribed planning requirements for its local Community Action Agencies. It is, however, presently working towards the establishment of a planning capacity in every CAA. . . .
> . . . A minimum planning effort will be required of all CAA's starting soon after January 1, 1967.
> Individual CAA projects in the future, will have to be consistent with this poverty plan or show good reason why a change is required. While there is no way to "endorse" non-CAA projects to fit into the overall CAA anti-poverty plan, it is expected that the plan will increase the CAAs' influence over other program and policy decision making. The objective then, is to bring the anti-poverty efforts of the many Federal, State, local, and private agencies into a single coordinated plan both at the local and national level.[16]

To fulfill this objective, an OEO staff group developed a planning methodology designed to satisfy the Bureau of the Budget as well as the advocates of planning within OEO, but the agency discarded

15. Fewer than five percent of the local governments have availed themselves of the opportunity under the amendment to assume control of their CAAs. This is a tribute, in many cases, to the political strength of the agencies. It may also reflect a wariness on the part of mayors "not to be caught holding the bag when the federal government and its resources withdrew," as one mayor's aide put it.

16. Office of Economic Opportunity, "Survey of Federal Planning Requirements," Report to the Bureau of the Budget, July 16, 1966, pp. 4, 5, 7.

the scheme as too complex and as violative of OEO's philosophical bent against dictating programs to CAAs. As an alternative approach, it asked the local agencies how they would plan if given the capability. Selecting twelve of the more interesting responses, OEO initiated "pilot" projects in those CAAs. The lessons learned from those demonstrations were to be incorporated in a nationwide effort to strengthen comprehensive local planning that, OEO told the Congress, would enjoy "a high priority" in the fiscal year 1968.[17]

The Congress, however, sought to leave nothing to chance. In the 1967 amendments to the Economic Opportunity Act, it added a stringent planning requirement (section 221[d]) that had been initiated by the Senate Labor and Public Welfare Committee in an effort to strengthen the community action agencies:

(d) After July 1, 1968, the Director shall require as a condition of assistance, that each community action agency has adopted a systematic approach to the achievement of the purposes of this title and to the utilization of funds provided under this part. Such systematic approach shall encompass a planning and implementation process which seeks to identify the problems and causes of poverty in the community, seeks to mobilize and coordinate relevant public and private resources, establishes program priorities, links program components with one another and with other relevant programs, and provides for evaluation. The Director may, however, extend the time for such requirement to take into account the length of time a program has been in operation. He shall also take necessary steps to assure the participation of other Federal agencies in support of the development and implementation of plans under this subsection.

Thus the Congress, at least, had come full circle, back to the concepts of mobilization, coordination, and comprehensive planning with which community action had been launched in 1964. Whether the CAAs could overcome the practical difficulties that had brought about the deemphasis on planning was, of course, another matter.

The Limited War. The "unconditional war on poverty" became, very early, a highly conditional war, as budget limitations prevented the expansion of community action as rapidly as communities were prepared to proceed.

At first, congressional supporters of community action criticized the administration for not moving fast enough, but the Congress as

17. Office of Economic Opportunity, "Congressional Presentation" (April 1967; processed), p. C-11.

a whole was not dissatisfied. When the President asked $685 million for the community action program for the fiscal year 1966, Representative Daniel J. Flood, Pennsylvania Democrat, commented: "What a piddling effort we are really making at the fantastic problem of poverty. I believe—you correct me—I recall it as being one-half the profits of General Motors."[18] But Congress eventually appropriated only $628 million.

The budget request for $914 million for community action for the following year was characterized as "grossly inadequate" by Joseph S. Clark, Pennsylvania Democrat, who chaired the Senate subcommittee on employment, manpower, and poverty.[19] In the House appropriations hearing it developed that OEO had actually asked the Bureau of the Budget for $1.4 billion for community action, but the

Table 2. Allocation of Community Action Funds

Purpose	Obligations by fiscal year (in millions of dollars)			
	1967	1968	1969a	1970b
Head Start and Follow Through	349	331	353	398
Other national emphasis programs	179	217	262	301
Local initiative	278	325	332	359
Total obligations	806	873	947	1,058

Source: *The Budget of the United States*, for fiscal years 1969 and 1970.
a. Estimated.
b. Budget request as submitted by President Johnson, January 1969.

final appropriation was only $804 million. For the fiscal year 1968 the President requested $1,022 million, but the Congress appropriated $866 million.[20] These spending levels did not provide much margin for approval of new programs that might be proposed by the communities. As Table 2 shows, neither did the 1969 appropriation nor the 1970 budget request.

The National Emphasis Programs. Consistent with the principle

18. *House Supplemental Appropriations Bill of 1966*, Hearings before the House Committee on Appropriations, 89 Cong. 1 sess. (1965), p. 249.
19. *Senate Supplemental Appropriations Bill of 1967*, Hearings before the Senate Committee on Appropriations, 89 Cong. 2 sess. (1966), p. 408.
20. These appropriation figures differ from the obligation figures shown in Table 2 because of the carryover of funds between years!

that communities should study their own problems and design their own remedies, the Economic Opportunity Act did not lay out the particular programs that would be operated or coordinated by the CAAs. The director of OEO was given complete discretion in passing judgment on local proposals.

But, according to Wofford, communities were slow to take up their responsibility, and instead of establishing priorities, submitted applications indiscriminately.[21] Thus OEO—eager to get worthwhile projects under way—began to second-guess communities by setting its own priorities in the form of "national emphasis programs." Operation Head Start was the first of these, followed by legal services, comprehensive health services, foster grandparents, and Upward Bound (intensive precollege preparation of disadvantaged youth). These programs became so popular that Congress itself began to earmark funds for them, in addition to adding national emphasis programs of its own.

The first national emphasis program—Head Start—had particular appeal. Designed to prepare preschool children of poverty "to take their place beside their more fortunate classmates," it was an immediate success not only with the poor but with teachers, social workers, doctors and dentists (who examined the preschool children), and therefore with congressmen. In the first full fiscal year of the poverty war, Head Start accounted for $180 million, or 29 percent of the total community action program of $628 million. In the second fiscal year, 1967, the proportion was even more dramatic— $349 million or 43 percent of $806 million. In subsequent years the proportion leveled off at between 37 and 38 percent. Meanwhile, as Table 2 shows, the other national emphasis programs were expanding rapidly.

As more funds were earmarked within the relatively slowly rising community action appropriation, the proportion available for the innovative, locally initiated programs was limited to barely one-third and after the 1968 fiscal year actually declined. Whatever may have been the intrinsic merits of the national emphasis programs, they tended to subvert one of the central purposes of community action: local planning of programs designed for meeting specific local problems.

21. "The Politics of Local Responsibility," pp. 92–93.

This loss of program flexibility was not unnoticed. Mayor Cavanagh said in the summer of 1966:

This year less than 50 percent of the community action funds are available for some local imagination and local innovation. The rest of it is all earmarked money. I think until such time as we have [block grants] . . . , in which the local administration can come, with a comprehensive physical and social renewal plan that meets some general federal standards, that we are just going to limp along in these categorical programs in which we find ourselves today.[22]

Under these circumstances OEO was forced to devise a rigorous system of priorities. Programs were culled for "low priority" proposals—including recreation, in-school education (which had become eligible for assistance under Title I of the Elementary and Secondary Education Act), cultural enrichment, social service, counseling, homemaking and home management, and food programs. Only "high priority" projects such as multipurpose neighborhood centers and manpower projects were encouraged. The range of programs that CAAs could design and finance to meet local problems was thus sharply curtailed. Community action was still more flexible than most other grant programs, but was growing more and more to resemble the rest of the categorical grant structure (whose fragmentation it had been designed to correct) as more and more Washington judgments were made as to what kinds of programs were best for fighting poverty.

This trend, too, the Congress sought to reverse when it overhauled the Economic Opportunity Act of 1967. The 1967 amendments enumerated eight "special" programs (those formerly called national emphasis programs), but "in order to promote local responsibility and initiative" OEO was forbidden to establish "binding national priorities." Earmarking of funds was authorized only where OEO "determines that the objectives sought could not be effectively achieved through the funding of locally-initiated programs." However, Hallman, who as director of the Senate subcommittee's study of the war on poverty had initiated the attempt to restore discretion to the communities, reported in 1969 that "OEO is still earmarking on its own, to a large measure due to the vested interests which have developed around the national emphasis programs."[23]

22. *Federal Role in Urban Affairs*, Hearings, p. 624.
23. "Historical Highlights of the Poverty Program," p. 10.

CHECKPOINT PROCEDURES AND INFORMATION CENTERS

Two minor steps were taken in 1966 to strengthen the coordinating influence of the community action agencies. In order to give each CAA at least a review role in federally aided antipoverty programs within its areas, OEO negotiated "checkpoint" procedures with agencies of HUD, HEW, and Labor that administered poverty-related programs.[24] Under these procedures, CAAs were given opportunity to comment on projects of other local organizations that those agencies proposed to aid. The procedures covered all programs authorized by the Economic Opportunity Act, the leased housing program of HUD's public housing authorities, and Title I (aid for programs for educationally deprived children) of the Elementary and Secondary Education Act. Conversely, CAA projects were submitted for comment to local agencies—as, for example, Head Start proposals to local school boards.[25]

In 1966 OEO was authorized to make grants to states and communities for establishment of information service centers and was directed to establish procedures for distribution of "all current information, including administrative rules, regulations and guidelines" on "all Federal programs related to the purposes of this Act." Because of its limited community action funds, OEO made no grants, but in 1968 it was providing technical assistance to a dozen states that were interested in setting up information systems of their

24. See Office of Economic Opportunity, Community Action Memo No. 28, March 25, 1966; No. 41, June 29, 1966; No. 40, July 1, 1966; or No. 46, Aug. 29, 1966, for examples of checkpoint procedures.

25. The original Economic Opportunity Act of 1964 contained another device aimed at coordination—a preference clause (section 612) that directed the heads of federal agencies, where practicable, to give "preference to any application for assistance or benefits which is made pursuant to or in connection with a community action program approved" by OEO. Although a procedure for invoking preference was detailed in the *Community Action Program Guide*, it was rarely used, and in 1967 OEO proposed deletion of the section and the Congress agreed. In the first place, explained OEO, "overall community action programs" did not exist. But even if they did, the preference clause would direct the distribution of federal funds in a manner that would ignore relative needs as among communities—"a result very difficult to square generally with the substantive provisions and policies under which the various programs operate." "Responses of OEO to Questions Submitted by the Subcommittee on Employment, Manpower, and Poverty Re Coordination of the Poverty Program," in *Examination of the War on Poverty*, Hearings before the Senate Committee on Labor and Public Welfare, 90 Cong. 1 sess. (1967), p. 3391.

own. It also compiled and distributed a seven hundred-page *Catalog of Federal Assistance Programs*.

The Image of Community Action

Community action was one subject on which nearly everyone we interviewed at the community level had an opinion. Community leaders and officials of other community organizations were heavily critical of the CAAs. Some interviewees balanced favorable and unfavorable comment. But except for those who held positions in community action agencies, very few were wholly favorable. And even staff members of CAAs and board members and others closely associated with the program often made comments indicative of frustration and low morale.

"When the governor asked me to take charge of the state OEO technical assistance office," one state official told us, "I was reluctant to do it because of the tarnished image of community action in this state." In a middle sized city, two civic leaders—who were favorably disposed toward the war on poverty in general—summed up the status of that city's CAA: "The reason it lacks 'clout' is that the city as a whole does not have confidence in it as a responsible agency." "In our region," observed an HEW field official, "the community action programs have alienated themselves from everything that is going on. As a result, their impact is minuscule."

In our visits, which occurred during or just after the 1967 local election campaigns, we found not a single incumbent politician who was running on a platform of community action. Mayors were pointing with pride to their urban renewal authorities but not to their community action agencies—even where they had been instrumental in establishing them. "No, I have not had occasion yet to mention community action in my campaign," said one mayor running for reelection. "I may later, but I haven't yet." His campaign brochures ignored the subject. "I support the war on poverty as a matter of personal conviction," another mayor told us, "but as a politician it is not an asset to me." He went on to say that from the beginning he had never submitted any request relating to community action to the city council; he had managed to provide the local share of program costs under his own authority, usually by assigning office space. When a space shortage developed in city hall it was the CAA, rather than the local Red Cross chapter, that was moved out—a reflection of the feeling of the city council.

"Our agency has been operating quite autonomously," said the director of a community action agency that was nominally part of the city government. "That's because it has an independent board of directors and because nobody in city hall wants to get too intimate with it." A place on the board had been reserved for a member of the city council but was vacant for lack of a volunteer to fill it.

One sentence from a political science professor can perhaps summarize the scores of comments about CAAs from community influentials: "Community action doesn't stand a chance of coordinating things—not until it changes its public image."

Two fundamental reasons account for the negative image of the CAAs we found in our interviews (which were preponderantly with spokesmen for the affluent majority, it should be noted, not with the poor themselves). One was the pervasive conflict with other institutions that rose when the CAAs began vigorously to challenge the status quo, to innovate, to raise a myriad of questions about how America's communities had served their poor. The assault on the status quo came both from the CAAs directly and from the organizations of the poor that they created or supported. The second factor in the negative image of the CAAs was the frequently adverse community impressions of the agencies as administrative organizations—impressions of their competence, their leadership, their efficiency, particularly the important first impressions made upon the communities in the early months.

Based on these two factors, among the infinite variety of CAAs, three types—in terms of their public images—can be identified:

The innocuous ones, found mainly in smaller communities. They were the ones of whom it was said, "Oh, they're all right; they're not doing much." That type of CAA had found its place in the cluster of social agencies in its community, as another specialized organization quietly administering a few programs designed in Washington. Sponsored initially by the power structure, it had not challenged the institutions and leadership of that structure.

The respected ones—those that were aggressive, even militant, but with a quality of leadership and administrative competence to match. The respect was accorded not willingly but grudgingly—usually not because of their achievements but because of their political strength, which rested upon the mobilization of the poor. And they stood apart from, and in a position of confrontation with, the established institutions of their communities.

The outcasts—those that had not been able to match their militancy with a leadership and competence that compelled respect. They were effectively contained, left to administer the programs financed from Washington but otherwise ignored or even shunned.

None of these three types had potential as the community mobilizers and coordinators that were envisioned when the Economic Opportunity Act was passed. For a CAA to fill that role, it had to have either power or acceptance—either power to assert its will upon other institutions or sufficient standing in the community to prevail upon the competing institutions to accept coordination voluntarily. But the federal government could not, and did not, confer any significant coordinating power upon the CAAs. And they have failed, because of their "tarnished image," to gain acceptance.

The following sections illustrate the institutional conflicts and the administrative problems that have beset the CAAs, as gleaned from our several hundred field interviews. Though all CAAs are different, and each fits in a different way into the configuration of institutions in its community, the illustrations provide a composite portrait of the factors that bear upon the potential of the community action agencies as coordinators and mobilizers. If these sections underemphasize the successes of the CAAs, it is because coordination is the subject of this volume, and the CAAs' successes have not been as coordinators. They have been, rather, as inducers of innovation and constructive change—and those objectives, as will be seen, are at war with the objective of coordination.

THE ASSAULT ON THE STATUS QUO

Community action had a built-in opposition from the start. Public health, education, and welfare officials knew that their parent federal department, HEW, had made its bid for control of the war on poverty but had been rejected. And they knew the reason: those who conceived the antipoverty program felt that the "old line" social workers, educators, and public health agencies could not be entrusted with it. The creation of a whole new system of institutions to rival the established agencies that had been responsible for community services for the poor could only be taken as a direct affront. Moreover, CAA (and OEO) personnel often made no secret of their contempt for the ways of the local bureaucracies. The reaction was natural enough: active or passive resistance. And when the upstart CAAs made their inevitable mistakes, the established agencies seized upon those errors, made sure they were widely publicized, and no doubt in some instances magnified them. The long-standing antipathy of the agencies to the CAAs surfaced repeatedly in our interviews.

"They went about it completely wrong," said a county welfare director. "We know we have a bureaucracy and we would have welcomed their help, but OEO just came in and said to us, 'Your approach stinks,' and proceeded to split the community apart." This director went on to detail, with unconcealed bitterness, a series of illustrations of what he considered waste and malfeasance in the community action program.

A second source of built-in opposition was ideological and partisan. The bill had been enacted in the midst of the 1964 campaign, over Republican objections that it was being "rammed through" the Congress before the election without sufficient consideration and debate. President Johnson had proclaimed the war on poverty as a Democratic administration's undertaking, even a personal one, and Adam Clayton Powell, the Democratic chairman of the House Education and Labor Committee, had excluded Republican members of the committee from the sessions where the bill was marked up. The Republicans, in their 1964 platform, denounced the "so-called war on poverty" as one that "would dangerously centralize Federal controls and bypass effective state, local and private programs."

Many Republican politicians and other conservative leaders, including some newspaper publishers, were still disaffected and skeptical when community action was launched in their communities. "The community action program is not looked upon as a local program," we were told in one conservative community. "Its image is that of LBJ's program thrust upon us." So the President's political opponents were lying in wait, too, to exploit any difficulties that might befall the CAAs. The mistakes of the community action agencies were unquestionably given more detailed newspaper coverage, in many cities, than comparable mistakes of, say, the city government or the public schools.

Finally, any federal social program in 1964 would encounter built-in opposition in the South. "OEO has always been unpopular in the South," said a southern community action director. "It started at the wrong time. When it started, the feeling against integration was running quite high, and it has always been thought of as a program for Negroes. A lot of white people who would be perfectly eligible under OEO don't participate just on that basis."

Conflict between the CAAs and the established agencies arose over a variety of specific issues. They argued about who was to operate particular programs and on what terms, they wrangled over participation by the agencies in the activities of CAA neighborhood centers, and most particularly they quarreled over the activity of the CAAs in organizing the poor to make demands upon the agencies. The targets of those demands were principally the state employment services, the public welfare agencies, and the public schools, but sometimes the attack was consolidated into a kind of political warfare against the whole "establishment," including city hall itself.

CAAs versus the Employment Services. More than any other one thing, the poor who came through the doors of community action offices and neighborhood centers wanted jobs. So the CAAs found themselves at the outset in the business of job development and placement—a field already occupied in every community by the state employment service.

The United States Employment Service, which finances the state employment services and approves their operating plans, has an official policy of promoting "outreach," but when the CAAs came into being they found few local employment services with effective machinery for seeking out and finding the unemployed of the slums, getting them into training programs, and finding them jobs. "The employment service is set up to serve the employer," was the typical comment of a CAA director. "It is not in the business of finding and serving people." The CAAs, in contrast, set out to find and serve the people: they started with the jobless man or woman who came into the neighborhood center—or who was discovered by the neighborhood aides—and sought to get him into the employment service channels. If the employment services appeared slow to respond, or if their services proved unavailing, the CAAs turned toward the creation of competing machinery for contacting employers, for placement, and even for training—and, in doing so, inevitably antagonized the employment services. The following story, told by a CAA director, illustrates many aspects of the CAA-employment service relationship:

We obtained forty college students during the summer under OEO's work-study program and used them for what we called our "manpower search." We sent them into the poor neighborhoods to find the unemployed and record their qualifications, experience, training, and so on. Then we obtained from the employment service a list of their job openings. Then we wrote directly to every employer in the city who employed ten or more persons asking him what job openings he actually had—and we were able to double the number that we had gotten from the employment service.

Then our trouble began. After we had matched up the job openings with the people we had found in our manpower search, we asked the employment service to come out to the neighborhood centers, to handle the counseling, testing, and placement on a professional and official basis. But the employment service refused—said they couldn't do it. But we know the poor people won't go to the employment service downtown. It has the reputation with them of telling them either they've got to take any low-paying job that comes along or else they'll lose their unemployment compensation. So we had to intercede, through the state [OEO-financed] technical assistance office, with the employment service headquarters in the capital, and they directed the local office to station counselors in our centers on a part-time basis. Now we have one there regularly, one night a week. And we have no trouble getting our people to see him there.

If I had more money, I would like most of all to get into training. The MDTA [Manpower Development and Training Act] here is far too much like the vocational departments of the high schools, and it has been a failure in some courses. We need a new kind of training, which I think we could develop.[26]

In other cases the community action agencies were less successful in getting the employment service to station counselors in the neighborhood centers. One CAA director was refused even when he offered to pay the salaries of the counselors because, he said, he was told "only the headquarters had the proper type of facilities—such

26. In this and other quotations in this study, comments of an interviewee on a particular subject that may have been made at several points during the interview may be brought together in a single passage. Interviews have also been paraphrased, where necessary, to conceal their locale, and general terms (like "community action agency" or "neighborhood center") have been substituted for local terminology. All interviews were on a candid, "not for attribution" basis. Occasionally the interviewee's language has been altered to make his meaning clear; for example, questions simply answered "yes" or "no" have sometimes been converted to declarative statements.

as lighting, scoring machines, and so on, to perform testing." In contrast, one state employment service—California's—was given credit for aggressively seeking opportunities to "out-station" its staff, but even in that case the rigidity of state civil service regulations made it difficult to recruit Negro or Mexican-American counselors and assign them to neighborhoods made up of those minority groups.

One medium sized city CAA had a staff member working full time on the problems of the "hard-to-place"—seeking them out, counseling them, and working with employer groups to place them, all independent of the employment service. Another was financing a similar operation by a specialist assigned from the employment service, working out of a neighborhood center. "They're frank to admit that they hadn't been reaching the kind of people we are now, but they're willing to take the people we find for them," said the CAA director. He was especially proud of a short training course he had instituted for the functional illiterates—"brushing them up enough on basic literacy to enable them to take jobs."

In the large cities, private agencies had also proliferated in the manpower field, some of them financed by the CAAs, some by OEO independently, some by the Labor Department, but all engaged in recruitment, training, and placement. As viewed by the state employment services, the result was chaos. Said one employment service official:

> We have opened as many offices in the poor areas as we have money for. We ought to expand our outreach, but instead of our getting the money to do it, we see the federal dollars going instead into competitive agencies which are cluttering up the manpower field, banging upon the doors of the employers, and offering inferior training. All these new organizations get funded by criticizing us and the other existing programs. Everybody wants to get into the act.
>
> Right now there are sixty-eight organizations in this city that have the legal right, in their charters, to contact employers about jobs. Who do the employers call to straighten all this out? They call us. But there's nothing we can do about it. We learn about new training programs in this city by reading about them in the newspapers, and this even includes programs of our own Department of Labor.
>
> When it comes to counseling and placement, all these outfits have to rely on our people anyway. They do it either by contracting with us, or by pirating our personnel. Our $9,000 counselors have been taken away from us by being offered $12,000 to do the same work.

Said another:

Many of the programs initiated by these private agencies are a miserable fraud, training people for traditional jobs like kitchen helpers, janitors, and so on. One of them, after it got a direct grant from OEO, came to us saying, "We just got half a million from the feds—what do we do with it?" They all expect us to do the screening, and the paper work, and so on. They start out as demonstration programs, and what they demonstrate is that it's the employment service that should be doing the project. The federal government puts a great premium on innovation, but these agencies have not developed anything new that's valuable—they just do it differently. And they won't release young people to other training programs, because if they did they couldn't justify their own.

A Labor Department field official put it this way:

I admit the employment service resists change. It's hard for them to realize that their only justification for existence now is to help the disadvantaged. This is quite different from their former job, but now-adays qualified people don't need the employment service at all. But the employment service will change—if given a better chance. In any case, how can the federal government even try to support the employment service and then tell them that we are circumventing them to do their job?

The complaint that too many agencies were "banging upon the doors of the employers" was heard in many cities. Said a chamber of commerce president in a middle sized city: "There are just too many people in the business of trying to find jobs for the unemployed. The NAACP [National Association for the Advancement of Colored People] is involved, the churches, the youth opportunity center, the employment service people, and a lot of other groups. And not one of them is talking to any other one. But I don't blame them for try-ing to bypass the employment service. They're so cold in that office that I don't blame anyone for not wanting to go there."

In three of the cities we visited, mayors had tried to bring order out of the manpower chaos by establishing coordinating committees that represented industry, business, and organized labor as well as the agencies engaged in recruiting, training, and placement. In another city a chamber of commerce committee had organized a high-pressure campaign to persuade employers to make jobs for the hard-core unemployed. Observers generally agreed that business and industrial leaders could be more effective than anybody else in organizing job development—that is, creating jobs, or making them available, for the hard-core unemployed—because they could bring pressure upon their peers that neither the employment services nor the community action agencies could. "The CAA wasn't able to call meetings of employers and get them to come, but the mayor's committee can," said a manpower official. An employment service director conceded: "They have opened doors for us that we could never open for ourselves." In one city, employment service representatives were joining with the committee representatives in making joint calls upon employers.

The Labor Department's approach to coordination of manpower services in poverty neighborhoods—the concentrated employment program (CEP)—had been instituted in seven of the cities we visited.[27] It was serving the purpose of bringing together the community action agency, which was the prime contractor for CEP in most cities, and the employment service, the principal training agencies, and health and welfare agencies, who held subcontracts for particular services. CEP represented an intensive application of the outreach principle within the geographical areas chosen for the experiment. Within those areas, agencies reported "going door to door" to find young people to receive the concentrated and individualized counseling, health, education, and training services that the cooperating agencies provided. But the basic operating problem, a Labor Department field official told us, was still that "the CAAs don't trust the employment services and the employment services look upon the CAAs as invading their domain." Another noted that in his locality it took several months, and an appeal to Washington, before the state employment service could be gotten to participate in planning the CEP operation under the auspices of the CAA. In contrast, still another said that in his city, CAA-employment service relationships were "astoundingly good"—although they had not always been so.

In rural counties where the state employment services had no offices, the community action agencies were often filling the vacuum. "In my two counties," said a CAA staff man, "I have been making more placements than the employment service. Employers now look to us as a source of recruits." In that area the district employment service director welcomed the competition and suggested that an

27. For a description of the CEP concept and a progress report as of early 1969, see *Manpower Report of the President, January 1969*, pp. 132–34.

arrangement be formalized to permit rural CAAs to be the official representatives of the employment service in counties where the service had no offices. But in the capital the state employment service rejected the idea. "It could be done in some places," a spokesman said, "but in other places they just don't get along. The community action people in the counties tend to be young, well educated, and aggressive people who run with the ball fairly well, and in general they're saying to our staff, 'You're not on the ball; you're not taking care of our people.' There's a bureaucratic battle going on. But," he concluded, "I won't say it's not good for us. We were not the first to establish outreach."

CAAs versus the Welfare Departments. As in the case of the manpower functions, community action agencies added an outreach, or "case-finding," dimension to public welfare. Working out of neighborhood centers or directly out of CAA headquarters, neighborhood aides—many of them recruited from among welfare clients—were visiting families with problems and attempting to put them in touch with the service agencies that could help them. Often they themselves undertook what one called "amateur casework." Some CAA staff members took pride in the number of families they had added to the welfare rolls—families that had been eligible but had either been unaware of their "rights" or too intimidated by the welfare system to apply.

But welfare officials—like employment service officials—were not necessarily pleased. The deputy director of an OEO-financed state technical assistance office explained it this way:

> I'll tell you why we've run into difficulties with the welfare departments and the state employment service. Because the CAA neighborhood workers turn up a lot of people—a great percentage of whom qualify for welfare or employment programs they were not aware of. But, in some cases, welfare and [the employment service] have not been too favorably disposed. They draw the same amount of salary for sitting in the office doing nothing. When you bring in a carload of people with difficult problems they are not always welcome.

Many local welfare directors did not conceal their antipathy to the OEO-CAA approach to case finding. "There are so many people going around—neighborhood aides are going around, VISTA volunteers are going around—that they've nearly driven the staff crazy," said one. "They are turning up some new people, but others are clients we have been seeing for years. They are bringing up matters of rights, and so forth. But we try to cooperate, because we stand to take a real beating on these things."

"Sure," said a local welfare director, "we know that we have on the welfare rolls only a fraction of the people who are eligible—25 percent, maybe. But we can't go out looking for people. I could never put people on my staff to perform these types of outreach functions in a conservative county like this one." But other welfare officials defended their outreach. Said one:

The entire poverty program, not only on the local level but nationally as well, bypassed the agencies that knew the most about poverty. They said their goal was to "shake up the established institutions." So they disregarded us and talked as though we had nothing to contribute. Well, we were doing outreach in 1961—long before OEO was ever heard of. And Title V [employment and training of welfare recipients, authorized by the Economic Opportunity Act] would never have gotten off the ground if we had waited for the community action agency to act.

Public welfare agencies were particularly proud of the training and employment services they were rendering. One welfare department was experimenting with group meetings of potentially self-supporting welfare clients as a means of developing motivation. Another, in a medium sized county, claimed to have taught a thousand adults to read and write over a three-year period. A larger county, which had a full-time director for its employment functions, had initiated "job preparation" classes—designed to teach welfare recipients how to dress when applying for a job, how to present themselves to employers, how to fill out application blanks, how to read help-wanted advertisements, and so on—and had followed this with a prevocational program designed for women who had never worked and were insecure about applying for commercial employment. After the programs had been demonstrated, they were added to the regular adult education curriculum of the public schools. "The regular adult education and employment services are designed for the self-starters," the director observed. "But the people on welfare are the disadvantaged of the disadvantaged. We have had to design programs around their particular needs. If we didn't, nobody else would."

The limiting factor on such services, welfare officials often contended, was the budgets of the welfare departments. Said a welfare director:

We have undertaken some innovations as the result of the 1962 amendments, but on the whole our proposed innovations have been rejected by the county welfare board because of the additional costs involved. Most of our proposals required additional social workers. But the community is already upset over rising welfare costs, and they are not ready to accept any proposals which would increase administrative costs as well. It is the total budget that the community sees, and the welfare board reflects the community view.

I can demonstrate that the work of our employment unit has saved $650,000 in welfare costs, yet this information was not sufficient to persuade the welfare board to add some additional counselors to the employment unit. About 3,500 of our clients would be eligible for training and employment, but we can only handle about 1,000 with the number of counselors we are allowed.

Welfare departments that had unsuccessfully sought funds for innovative programs were understandably resentful when they saw federal money going to the CAAs for similar programs on the ground that the welfare departments had failed. "Our case workers are handling three times as many cases as they should, by national standards," one director complained, "yet the federal government has now set up a new agency to hire untrained people to do what amounts to a kind of case work. If the funds had been allotted to the existing agencies instead, the effect would have been much more constructive and quickly organized." Amateur case workers, she went on to say, could do more harm than good.

But others acknowledged that the "shaking up of the established institutions" had had a beneficial effect. Several welfare directors thought that the philosophy of "representation of the poor," which had been introduced by community action, should be adopted by welfare departments, too. Several directors, also, welcomed the chance to station welfare department personnel in multipurpose neighborhood centers operated by community action agencies.

A state welfare official summarized the impact of community action upon welfare in these words:

Virtually everything that OEO is doing—except maybe Head Start—could have been carried out by welfare departments under the Public Welfare Amendments of 1962. There has been enough innovation under that act to show what the range of possible programs is and to demonstrate the competence of welfare departments to run such programs. We operate the equivalent of OEO's neighborhood centers in a lot of places. All this, however, is theoretical, because we operate through a federal-state-local system which permits a veto at any one of the three levels. Any substantial innovation along the lines of OEO would require state legislation in fifty states—and even constitutional amendments in some of them.

If we in public welfare want to try something new, we first have to examine the law, then we have to examine the manuals, then we have to look at the bureaucracy, we have to see who can be pushed, then we have to see if the legislative leadership is with us, or against us, and so on. But when OEO was established, there were no state laws, no local traditions, no bureaucracy, no need for state legislatures to get involved. As the result, OEO has been the biggest damned goosing tool anybody ever created. It's pushed us into a lot of new things—home management programs, putting people in neighborhood centers, separation of money payments from social services, a better system of appeals, new eligibility regulations. Most important of all, the work programs under Title V are far better designed, with a much more significant training component, than the community work and training programs we had before. And as far as the private social agencies are concerned, it's been like a federal united fund, enabling them to expand their activities.

CAAs versus the Public Schools. When OEO put its community action agencies into the field of preschool education, through Head Start, the potential for conflict between the CAAs and the public schools arose in every community. In most localities, however, the conflict was averted. Either the program was delegated to the schools to operate with virtual autonomy, or it was administered by the CAA wholly independently of the school system—and in the latter cases the school officials seemed generally to take the view that they had enough to worry about without concerning themselves with how the CAA was handling Head Start. Occasional criticism was heard, but it was muted.

One school official, for instance, criticized the community action agency's administration of Head Start on several counts—the location of its centers, its failure to transmit information to the school system, and particularly its requirement for representation of the poor on the board of directors of the program. "On the board you need people with broad sweeping understanding of the problems," he said. "You can develop other channels of communication with the poor." The opposite point of view was expressed by a CAA director in a community where Head Start had been delegated to the schools: "If Head Start is to be truly effective, it will have to involve the parents of the poor kids. So I'm trying to get the board of education to hire some parents as teacher aides. They're resisting and I may be heading for my first big knockdown, dragout fight in this community."

Some school superintendents objected on principle to OEO's entrance into the field of education. "The public school system has never been given a chance to do what we should be doing," said one. "All of the ideas that OEO is now bringing forth are old ideas. They were either in effect in our school system or being thought about—that is, they would have been in effect here if we had had more funds. We've had an illiteracy program for years, for instance. We know what to do, and we have the talent to do it. OEO should be working through us to solve the problems they're trying to get at."

Passage of the Elementary and Secondary Education Act of 1965, with funds under Title I for special programs for poor children, answered much of the superintendent's complaint. Under that act, the antipoverty funds flowed directly from HEW through the states to the schools, and except for Head Start the CAAs were withdrawing from programs of in-school education. The result, however, was to further weaken the CAAs as coordinating agencies. A state official observed that "the coordinating reach of the CAAs extends only as far as their money extends" and went on to speculate as to the beneficial impact the agencies might have had on the public schools if Title I money had been added to community action funds instead of being channeled directly to the schools. One may speculate also, of course, about the furor that would have been aroused in community after community when the CAAs sought to bring about changes in the schools.

Under the checkpoint procedure, however, Title I projects were being submitted for review and comment to the community action agencies. Where the CAA raised an objection that could not be resolved locally, a meeting would be arranged at the state level, and if the conflict persisted it would be referred to Washington.

No dispute from any of the cities we visited had gone to Washington for settlement, but a number of controversies had reached the state level and more were brewing in the localities. Educational authorities in one state had summoned regional OEO officials to a meeting when several CAAs had, according to the educators, gone into the schools to make sure that teachers in Title I programs were qualified for their jobs; the disputes were amicably settled. One CAA director was preparing to make an issue of what he claimed was the school superintendent's plan to put Title I money into schools that were not among the poorest in the community, and another had used his checkpoint authority as leverage to induce the school system to use some Title I funds for Head Start in order to release community action money for other purposes. Some school superintendents were willing to concede that they had received good suggestions from the CAAs and their constituent organizations of the poor. In one rural county the CAA-sponsored organizations had been granted a voice initially in determining how Title I funds would be used; in two of the communities they had been instrumental in a decision to spend Title I money for community television antennae to bring the educational television network into their communities.

With exceptions such as those, the CAAs had generally taken a "live and let live" approach and given their routine approval to the Title I proposals of the school authorities. "I can't afford to alienate the board of education," said one CAA director; "they supply the buildings for too many of our activities." However, as the CAAs, and particularly the more militant organizations of the poor, became aware of the opportunity presented by the checkpoint procedure, it seemed not unlikely that they would become more assertive. As an instance of what may be in store, the board of one CAA had just dismissed its chairman at the time of our visit because, among other reasons, he had unilaterally approved a Title I program which did not include a hot lunch program that a majority of the CAA board had been insisting upon.

CAAs versus Other Institutions. As in other fields, a major contribution of the community action agencies to public health services was case finding. Some CAA directors, for example, regarded the medical care of preschool children to be a more important aspect of Head Start than the school program itself. One rural CAA official contrasted health care under the economic opportunity program with what had gone before:

> In one of our counties there are no school nurses. In the other, school nurses examine the children but there is no follow-up. All they do is refer the problem to the child's parents, but that does no good at all, because in most cases the parents already know of the child's ailment. Of the children we examined, more than half needed dental work, almost all needed immunization, more than 10 percent needed glasses

or other attention from an eye specialist, about the same number needed attention for speech impairment, and we found cases of anemia, heart trouble, rickets, hearing impairments, skin diseases, and so on. In every case, we arranged for the corrective action before the child got out of our sight.

The neighborhood centers provided convenient locations for state and local health department teams engaged in disease detection and immunization campaigns, and the neighborhood aides spread the word and brought people in for examination. But activities of CAAs in the health field were not carried on without occasional conflict. In one city the public health officials complained that the CAA—assertedly under pressure from OEO—was considering setting up its own health unit within Head Start instead of continuing its contract with the public health department. "They claim they were not getting enough community involvement when they worked through us," the health department director protested. "But they will find that it is going to be more expensive to administer their program separately, because we were providing many of the administrative services free."

Yet the OEO-CAA approach to health found its defenders within the public health "establishment." Said a state public health official:

OEO has a compulsion for innovation, and some of their innovations are successful and some are not. I think their most important success has been in setting up mechanisms whereby the people can express their views as to what is needed. The health profession has been like all professions—we have taken the view that *we* know what the public needs. But what the public wants—if, for example, they want dead dogs removed from public highways even though from a public health standpoint this is relatively unimportant—should properly be the place where public health service begins.

"This is a time of chaos, ferment, and change," said a county health director, "but out of it is coming progress. We have been pushed into a deeper involvement with poverty, and with the Negro-white problem, and that is good."

The same kinds of controversies were arising in the legal services program. Where the community action agencies had delegated the program to preexisting private legal aid societies, CAA officials were sometimes critical that effective outreach and case finding were not being carried on. "They are not dynamically looking for business," was the way one CAA director put it. But it was clear that local bar associations—already aroused at OEO policies of providing free legal services—would be further aroused if, as was reported, OEO was about to insist that all CAAs terminate their delegations to the legal aid societies.[28]

In one city a CAA-sponsored "police review board" was a continuing source of irritation. The CAA had proposed that the city establish the review board to hear complaints against the police. When the city declined, the CAA proceeded on its own initiative to establish a body that city officials called a "police review board" but CAA spokesmen identified as "just a mechanism to help establish a means of advocating with the police."

Among the "old line" organizations sometimes offended by the CAAs were those of the political parties themselves: a CAA director identified party precinct committeemen as among "the natural enemies" of community action, because neighborhood workers were making the contacts with the poor that otherwise the politicians would make.

THE MOBILIZATION OF PROTEST

"I believe in the sense of power," a community action director told us. "It builds strength, motivation. . . ."

He was speaking of the power of the poor themselves, their strength and motivation to solve their own problems and to assert themselves within their communities. The assault on the status quo, when it was carried on by the CAA directors and their professional staffs, often looked like little more than bureaucratic rivalry—over the control and direction of particular programs, over the philosophy of case finding and the techniques of outreach, over the relations between professional and nonprofessional personnel, and so on. But the CAAs also were engaged, in one way or another in most localities, in organizing the poor as a political force to carry on the assault on the status quo under their own power and in their own name. This added a new and immensely significant dimension to the conflict that community action had engendered within communities—the dimension, above all others, that has made community action "controversial." The amount of emphasis that CAAs and their neighborhood centers gave to organizing the poor for political action—as

28. No such formal order was issued.

distinct from providing services to them—is difficult to measure quantitatively. One OEO-sponsored study concluded that with few exceptions the neighborhood centers had not attempted to organize the poor.[29] However, in terms of the CAAs' image—which is the concern of this chapter—they were seen in their communities as putting great emphasis on organizing the poor. The difference between the perception and the fact (assuming the OEO-sponsored study to be correct) may lie in two factors: first, the organizing work done by groups identified with the CAA and its centers, rather than by the centers themselves; second, the fact that one or two dramatic instances of political action by groups identified with the war on poverty in a locality can go a long way in forming the community perception of what all concerned with the antipoverty program, including the CAA, are doing.

Where the community action agencies attempted to organize the poor for political action, they were not the first to do so, of course. Among the Negroes, civil rights groups were gaining political power in the mid-1960s, and Mexican-Americans had organizations for political action in some places. But OEO through the CAAs multiplied the political strength of the poor many times over by offering them the jobs, the status, the governmental sanction, and the authority over public programs that the civil rights and comparable movements alone could never provide. In many instances, moreover, the civil rights movement and community action reinforced each other through an overlapping of leadership and membership.

The activities of the CAAs provided a ready-made training ground for new leadership cadres for minority groups and for the poor in general. In almost every community, by 1967, representatives of the poor held one-third or more of the seats on the CAA governing boards. Usually they were elected by blocks or neighborhoods, and they maintained communication with their constituencies and developed and maintained political support in a manner not unlike that of a Republican or Democratic precinct politician. At the neighborhood level, also, the poor served on neighborhood center boards or advisory councils, and were sometimes chosen for those positions by election. And the neighborhood center staffs fostered the forma-

29. Cited by Sar A. Levitan, in *The Great Society's Poor Law* (Johns Hopkins Press, 1969), p. 130.

tion of citizens' groups, or the strengthening of existing groups, for purposes of civic and political action.

A CAA staff member described the political role of the poor on his agency's board:

The representation feature [of the representatives of the poor] is extremely important. They are just like other politicians: they seek the office by getting a petition signed by eligible poor persons, and after they're elected they hold meetings with the constituents who sent them here, and those meetings keep them honest in terms of trying to be truly representative.

Some CAA directors looked upon board participation explicitly as a leadership training process. Said one:

We're now going through the process of developing next year's program. It would be easy for me and my staff to put the program together and get the board's approval, as we did last year. But that defeats the purpose of having a board. This year I'm forcing the board to create committees to take a fresh look at every single thing we're doing and recommend what we continue and what we change. The committees will have representatives of the poor participating, and they will be out in the neighborhoods listening to the poor as well. Then the whole board will thresh out the committee recommendations.

As the poor were organized to discuss and make known their problems and their needs, and as they developed confidence, they inevitably extended their concern beyond the planning and operation of the local community action program. Many of their problems could not be dealt with through that program, anyway; the solution lay with city hall or some other element in the community power structure. Having been invited to express their grievances, they were bound to insist upon being heard. In the communities we visited, CAA-organized or CAA-encouraged community groups had led vocal citizen protests against particular urban renewal projects, against a rezoning for a public housing project, against school consolidation and busing plans, against plans for a neighborhood center, and against city plans for administering the model cities program. In some of these instances they succeeded either in blocking the official proposals or forcing compromises. And as they discovered that they possessed political power, they tended to mobilize it not just to react to city hall but to initiate their own demands. Often they won a favorable response. In Atlanta, for example, the residents of a poor neighborhood obtained the assignment of two members of the city planning staff to prepare, in conjunction with a committee of neighborhood residents, a comprehensive assessment of the area's development needs—a study that produced twenty general and specific recommendations.

But the groups went beyond peaceful testimony at public hearings. In more than half of the larger cities we visited, and in a substantial proportion of smaller places, we were told of at least some instances of militant direct action by groups of poor persons associated with the local CAA. In one community a neighborhood group succeeded in getting a school repaired by threatening a strike. In another the superintendent of schools complained of having been picketed by a hundred persons organized by the antipoverty agency when the school board refused to accept OEO money for additional Head Start classes. In another the CAA was accused of instigating the picketing of a speech by a subcabinet federal official. In still another the organized poor picketed the school board—successfully—for an increase in the school lunch appropriation. In West Virginia and Kentucky, volunteers paid with OEO funds,[30] and in some instances CAA staff, were organizing poor mountaineers to assert themselves on local issues, such as bad roads or strip mining, or even to seek political control. In Mingo County, West Virginia, the antipoverty groups organized a fair elections committee to challenge irregularities in election procedures and a political action league to back candidates in the Democratic primary.[31] A "people's congress" was held at Concord College, in West Virginia, in 1967 to develop what one CAA director called "platforms and strategies" for the poor, and position papers coming out of the Congress were being discussed at community action meetings in the area. In New Mexico, persons associated with community action were publicly sympathetic with the militant Spanish-American leader Tijerina, who had "arrested" forest rangers and led an assault on a county courthouse in asserting the validity of old Spanish land grants, and allegations were current that some CAA personnel had provided transportation for Tijerina while he was being sought by state police. In California a

30. These included both VISTA (Volunteers in Service to America) personnel and Appalachian Volunteers, a group financed by OEO and headquartered in Berea, Ky. While the volunteers were formally independent of the community action agencies, they were identified with them and in some instances worked out of the CAA offices.
31. *Evening Star* (Washington), May 15, 1968.

legal services group funded by OEO had brought the court test that invalidated certain administrative regulations issued under the state's medicaid law.

"Many of the OEO workers went into communities around our state that were relatively poor but relatively happy and told them that they were living in poverty because their leaders were exploiting them," a federal field official told us. "This has caused a civil war in many communities as OEO organizes local political groups that are opposed to the power structure." Even a CAA board chairman accused OEO of encouraging militants to come into his community to get the local Negroes "all riled up." And a mayor's aide commented: "OEO has concluded, apparently, that they have to set up a new representative government. The federal government is paying a bunch of guys to destroy representative government in this city. Instead of spending money on voter education and concentrating on giving the Negro some incentive to get to the ballot box, they are systematically routing him around the ballot box."

In some of these cases, CAA personnel denied any direct participation in the events described, but they could not escape public identification with militants. In other cases they not only admitted having stirred up the protest groups but took pride in having done so. "The system operated like a sponge when we just put claims on them," said one state-level community action leader, "but we found out that if we hit them hard enough they will respond to some of our demands." "It doesn't seem exactly right that the government should put dollars into a community to get people to fight one another— but we have to change the system," said a state senator. "We have people in the state legislature who tremble when representatives of industry speak. We have to have a counterbalance." One militant CAA director—who insisted he was merely reflecting the attitudes of the Negro community, not shaping them—referred repeatedly to what he called "the politics of confrontation."

But a community's "power structure" is so named for a reason— it does have power. And the force of its retaliation has been sufficient to cripple a number of community action agencies or, in at least a few rural cases, to disband them. In some cases the power structure has worked through the boards of the agencies to replace militant directors. "In this state, a CAP agency director has to decide at some point whether he wants to *do* his job—or *keep* it," mused one observer who would be classed among the militants. "In too many cases they have begun to decide that they like their jobs." In other communities, where the board as well as the director is militant, the community action agencies are set wholly apart from the rest of the community—operating their own activities but generally excluded from communitywide endeavors. In a few cities, of course, the politics of confrontation have so polarized the population that few communitywide endeavors are undertaken any longer.

The militant CAAs fall into the two general types noted earlier (with the caveat that some inevitably are in between)—those with an image of strength and competence that are respected, if not liked, in their communities; and those with the opposite image, that do not possess the community's respect. These variations depend upon how the individual agencies have weathered the administrative ordeal that, in the chaos surrounding their creation, they all went through.

THE ADMINISTRATIVE ORDEAL

All of the agencies with which the CAAs compete and to which they are compared—the school systems, the health and welfare departments, the councils of social agencies—are manned by corps of professional personnel whose missions are well defined and, by now, noncontroversial. They draw upon a settled body of doctrine. They offer their staffs a reasonable degree of job security. The community action agencies, in contrast, began life with none of these advantages; yet they were expected to mobilize the total resources of their communities and coordinate all of their programs and agencies, and begin doing so at once. "We had to race forward like a panzer platoon to get as large a share of the federal money as we could before the other cities got it," a CAA director explained. But there existed no corps of professionals who could organize a thousand community action agencies with experience and assurance. Nobody had a graduate degree in community action as such; nobody knew, indeed, precisely what it was.

The first crisis, in each community, came with the selection of the executive director. Because of the necessity for speed in organizing, the emphasis tended to be on availability. That meant local availability; there was no time for seeking outside talent. Members of a community's "establishment" were generally not available—professional men were loathe to give up secure positions to attempt an undertaking so controversial, so ill defined, so tinged with political partisanship, so insecure. Community action agencies did recruit some directors from establishment ranks who were either attracted by the cause or were politically ambitious, and some agencies were able to bid reasonably high in terms of salary. But often the CAA boards were left with a choice among candidates who were ill established in their current positions or who otherwise had little to lose by taking the gamble with community action. The appointments were from the most varied assortment of backgrounds—politicians, businessmen, ministers, salesmen, school teachers, social workers, YMCA directors, and so on. Experience in the management of large enterprises was not made a prerequisite for appointment—as it would be in the case, say, of a superintendent of schools or city manager.

In the absence of any professional criteria, the directorship—and to an even greater degree the subordinate staff positions—sometimes became the object of patronage scrambles. Some of the conflict was of the old-fashioned Democratic-Republican variety. In one Republican community, we were told, the chairman of the Democratic organization insisted upon control of the appointments "because this was Lyndon Johnson's program" and won a compromise that gave the Democrats a share of the jobs. In other places the political struggle took the form of demands by minority groups for key positions—if not the directorship, then subordinate offices. Not only the CAA boards but members of city councils, ward leaders, mayors, and even congressmen became involved in some of the appointment conflicts.

As would be the case in any new undertaking, some of the choices for top staff positions turned out to be excellent and others proved to be mistakes—but the incidence of mistakes, if resignations and dismissals may be taken as an indication, was extraordinarily high. In only three of the thirteen largest cities visited in our study was the original community action director on the job in the fall of 1967, three years or less after the agency's creation. Not all the turnover was due to failure on the job, of course: one director had died, another had become deputy director of an OEO regional office, and a third had returned to his original private welfare agency job. But one city had had four directors within a year before the fourth finally brought stability to the position. Caught in the midst of a swirl of conflict, directors found themselves unable to remain on good terms simultaneously with influential politicians and other members of the establishment, the militant poor, the rival community agencies with which they had to deal, key members of their own staffs, and the OEO that held the purse strings. Continued trouble with one or more of these groups could mean a turnover in the directorship, and the high rate of replacement in the top position was reflected in abnormally high turnover rates in subordinate positions also.

Another source of demoralization has been the year-to-year struggle for existence. The annual rumblings from Washington that OEO was to be abolished—or at least dismembered—and the annual budget struggle, which invariably was still unsettled well after the fiscal year began, gave an air of transiency to CAA employment that interfered both with recruitment and with retention of directors and other key staff people.

The unsuitability of some executive directors, the haste with which organizations were put together and programs launched, and the absence of professional standards for personnel gave rise to charges of mismanagement in many communities. "We have been investigated seventy-six times," said one CAA board member, "and that has taken up at least one-third of the time of our professional staff." One common charge related to slipshod fiscal controls; that problem appeared on its way to correction as the agencies matured, but not before examples of payroll falsification and extravagant spending had received not only local but national publicity. Another widespread complaint was of petty politics in the hiring of personnel, particularly neighborhood workers. In some instances the favoritism in hiring conformed to existing practices of local government and drew criticism, it appeared to us, primarily because the distribution of jobs was in the hands of a new political force. But in cases where old-fashioned patronage had vanished from the local scene its reintroduction could jar community sensibilities, and the circulation of anecdotes—no doubt magnified by the agencies' enemies, and often played up by a hostile press—contributed to tarnishing the image of community action. Following are some comments upon the politics of poverty at the community level.

By a CAA staff member:

The neighborhood organization consists of people who were originally invited to a meeting by Mr. J. and immediately elected J. as chairman. At the meetings, J. succeeds in talking down the rest of the committee, particularly the newer members. They have no way of doing homework before coming to the meetings and are intimidated by J. and his clique. The clique is interested in power as much as in program and are especially concerned with the patronage involved in community workers, aides, Neighborhood Youth Corps enrollees, and so on. Since all of this patronage is limited, the clique is taking care of its nieces and nephews, sons, daughters, and cousins before the community at large participates. I see no solution to this except to have enough jobs to go around.

By a university official:

You must remember that all government programs in this area are used for political gains. The politicians particularly like the OEO program because there are no restrictions on whom they can employ. Under the "new careers" program, a great many relatives of politicians have become teacher aides and other subprofessional specialists, which would have been illegal if they had been employed directly by the school system.

By an observer at a CAA board meeting:

I was impressed at a number of junctures by the fact that apparently many of the people even on the governing board of the CAA regard one of the main benefits of the program the jobs that the agency is able to provide. The question was raised a number of times: Why can't we hire more neighborhood aides? It was painfully apparent that the aides were not needed for the jobs they would perform, but rather for the jobs they would provide.

By a federal official responsible for a specific program operated through CAAs:

If we didn't have authority to approve the project directors, the CAAs would end up putting political hacks in these jobs.

By a neighborhood center director:

Mr. T. [the CAA director] came down here to attend our policy board meeting and insulted the board by telling them they were the worst board in the entire community and were showing favoritism in appointments.

By a state technical assistance officer:

Our governor has never vetoed a community action application, but sometimes we have to work things out with a community before we approve it. For instance, we have to pare down the top-heavy administrative staffs they put in their proposals.

Patronage quarrels could also react against the "establishment." In the county where the chairman of the CAA board of directors had just been ousted at the time of our visit, one of the reasons given was that he had hired a business associate—described as "a former political boss of the county"—as a program aide without clearance with the board or the staff director.

The administrative ordeal has been complicated by the size and character of the CAA boards. Many were unwieldy in size, with forty to sixty or even a hundred members or more.[32] In some rural areas where the agencies had been formed by inviting all interested citizens to a public meeting, the practice of holding such a meeting annually had continued, with an executive committee chosen to transact business between those meetings. Even in one medium sized city, any citizen who filed an application was automatically added to the board of directors. It consisted in 1967 of more than a hundred members—nearly half of them poor. "We are not advertising the fact that anybody may join, but the word has gotten around in the neighborhoods where the poor live," the executive director explained. "How can you have confidence in that kind of board as a responsible agency?" asked a civic leader. After the poor were admitted to the policy-making boards, members representing the "establishment" complained that meetings had come to be unduly prolonged and that petty administrative (including patronage) problems occupied most of the time.

Representation of the poor on policy-making boards had severely impaired the confidence in the CAAs of a large segment of community leadership. While they did not speak out publicly, business and civic leaders were incredulous in private: "How can people who have never worked, who are on relief, be entrusted with running a multi-million-dollar enterprise?" was a typical question.[33] Those close to the operation of the CAAs might be tolerant of the idea, or even agree with it in principle, but they complained of the practical difficulties encountered in applying it and these complaints also became part of the CAAs' image.

32. The 1967 amendments to the Economic Opportunity Act of 1964 limited the boards to 51 members.
33. To which a defender of the principle of representation of the poor responded: "How can people who have failed to develop programs either to get people off relief or to provide adequately for them on relief be entrusted indefinitely with running programs in aid of the poor?"

A former judge who had founded the CAA in his community commented:

The poor ought to have a voice in the programs that affect them. And, after all, one of the objectives of the program is to develop leadership. But really effective leadership obviously is not yet in that segment of the community. Our board has been hampered by a lack of ability to shoulder responsibility.

A CAA board chairman thought the doctrine "verged on unreality":

Participation of the poor is sensible, as long as people are sensible about it. We've worked things out; the president of the bank is willing to sit down with the welfare recipient, but we have had problems. There is a certain kind of naivete or mysticism which surrounds this doctrine with some people. There is the notion that poor people are more objective about their own predicament, that they are able to make simple, naive pronouncements which are far closer to the truth than their more sophisticated but affluent neighbors. There is the feeling that only the poor people know what's wrong with the poor. But I think this is a perversion of the doctrine. It's verging on unreality to expect neighborhood people, without experience with a large bureaucracy, whether government or private, to decide how a sizeable staff should operate. Besides, there is a considerable amount of anti-intellectualism.

Observed a private social agency director:

Participation of the poor without professional advocates is like Vietnam—thrusting democracy on people who are not ready for it.

A private social agency official noted that the poor, too, were frustrated:

The elected representatives of the poor were supposed to be a source of ideas for projects in the community and the staff was supposed to write their projects in acceptable form. This relationship made sense. But in practice none of the ideas of the poor got accepted because, first, the CAA staff always put their own ideas in the applications which somehow changed the whole idea, either because they had personal biases or were influenced by what Washington would accept. Or, second, the ideas were rejected by Washington.

A university faculty member had a similar complaint:

The poor can make good decisions, if the alternatives are presented to them by the professional staff. But here the staff doesn't do that, either at the neighborhood centers or in the central board meetings. Our board meetings are almost exclusively concerned with administrative details.

A CAA director talked of the limitations of the poor:

The poor are not necessarily able to decide what kinds of projects will do most to alleviate their situation. A local neighborhood group may feel that top priority should go to obtaining a swimming pool and not even mention health or education or jobs. They need somebody to guide them. The poor are not virtuous simply because they are poor, and often they have a difficult time evaluating their own needs.

A CAA staff member offered a more positive appraisal:

They [representatives of the poor] may be slow in developing the capacity to initiate ideas, but they're very useful to test ideas against. They are able to hit the raw nerve. They have a way of pinpointing the problems of their areas.

There was hope that some of the difficulties could be classed as growing pains. Most community action officials testified that as the representatives of the poor overcame their initial diffidence, they were taking a more significant part in the meetings and the other members were gaining respect for them. One difficulty, however, was a high turnover rate as the representatives of the poor accepted paid jobs as neighborhood aides or in other subprofessional capacities on the CAA staffs.

A final source of demoralization was what the CAAs considered to be excessively tight control by Washington over local community action programs. Said a CAA board chairman:

Things would be better if federal officials set performance standards and then held us to them instead of getting into every little pecking decision that we get into every day of the week—but I'm sure there is a Parkinson's law.

A state technical assistance official complained particularly of the absence of local discretion over program content:

First they tell people, "You're going to do something unique and develop a program tailored to local needs; you're going to sit down and face up to how to solve your own problems," but then Congress says "so much for Head Start, so much for Foster Grandparents," and so on. There is an unfortunate uniformity in the program. I can't believe that every community can have exactly the same set of problems. The federal government seems unwilling to experiment with new, unique, or different programs. It's a most thwarting experience. The people in the communities end up with a rubber stamp and they know what it is, having wanted to do something else, and they get very mad.

Another CAA director concurred:

> The OEO regional office told me, "Don't keep sending up these canned proposals; come up with something more innovative, because anything is fundable with OEO." So I complied. We developed a number of top priority innovative projects. They included putting employment counselors in neighborhood centers, setting up a small business development corporation, a nurses' aide program which would have provided not only services but training, and a teen-age girls' project we called "special services for homebound women." They were all turned down by OEO.

Still another CAA director told us:

> I've stopped scheduling regular board meetings because there's nothing for our board to decide—all the decisions are made in Washington. They make us go through all the motions to get the community involved. But once the community is involved we find out that what the community wants is out. Recreation, for example, is out. Head Start is in. But Head Start is not what we need in this county. This is an area with a disproportionate number of senior citizens. In particular, we would like some programs for them. If Washington would give us a block grant, that would bring back to life the old idea of the people having something to say about this program.

And the result was to discredit the concept of representation of the poor, too. Said a former CAA director:

> The poor have lost faith in creditability of participation in the program. There simply is nothing left to decide after budget cuts, analyst comments, and rules are satisfied. If the community group takes the time to develop a proposal to eliminate the causes of poverty in that particular area, the chances of having the proposal funded are extremely limited. Thus the question of whether participation is worth it for anybody becomes real.

Budget restrictions, which virtually eliminated the possibility of program expansion, meant that innovative programs could be introduced only at the expense of going activities like Head Start. But the established programs had developed their own momentum and citizen support, and few CAA directors appeared ready to face the opposition of both their local constituencies and OEO in order to try to move funds from one program to another—even though the Congress in the 1967 amendments to the Economic Opportunity Act sought to encourage them to do so. Moreover, the CAA directors observed, if they volunteered to relinquish funds from an established program in order to launch a new one, there was no assurance that

OEO would not accept the relinquished funds but then disapprove the proposed new program and assign the funds to another community. For all these reasons, few community action agencies in 1967 (except, perhaps, those of the largest cities) were even talking seriously of innovating; they had reconciled themselves to the routine of operating a program that at best, in view of the budget pressures, would be a stable one. The stronger and more aggressive agencies might be turning their energies to neighborhood organization and perhaps to participation in developing a model cities program; the weaker ones were simply trying to do their assigned job while staying out of trouble and defending themselves against attack. In any case, the morale seemed to have been drained out of community action in 1967. The creative—if frenetic—vitality of the earlier years, when OEO's war on poverty was seen as the nation's highest priority and the President's foremost personal concern, was difficult to detect in the CAAs we visited.

Community Action Agencies as Coordinators

With their multiple disabilities, none of the community action agencies that we observed were anywhere near the center of the power structures of their communities. A few appeared to be at the edge, awaiting acceptance, and doing their best to conduct themselves inoffensively in the meantime. But most of them either had no evident desire to join the club, or they had been black-balled already. Inevitably, then, in their communitywide planning, mobilizing, and coordination functions—which depended on acceptance, in lieu of power—they were defeated.

"One of the reasons why community action is failing in our county," said a county official, "is that the power structure has dismissed it as being ill conceived as well as mismanaged. As long as they ignore it, it hasn't a chance of success. You have to have the power structure."

"The captains of industry have got to be involved in solving social problems," said a Negro official of a human relations commission. "The government can't do it, and even the government and the poor together can't do it."

Even where the CAA board was initially composed of representatives of major public and private institutions in an effort to design it as an arm of the power structure—on the New Haven model[34]— the board did not usually serve a coordinating function. "The local agencies weren't on the boards to coordinate but to protect their vested interests," a former CAA director said at the Brookings Round Table discussion of community action in late 1968. "They banded together in a mutual defense alliance." In its survey of thirty-five community action agencies in the summer of 1967, the staff of the Senate's poverty study found only "a few CAA's so situated within the governing coalition that they are able to accomplish significant coordination: Jacksonville, New Orleans, and Detroit, for example" but observed that "the attempt to coordinate in cities is perpetually bumping into resisting agencies" and "competition has made it difficult to achieve broader planning and fuller coordination."[35]

Most of the examples of coordination by the CAAs cited in the Senate study, like those in our survey, were of coordinating influence exerted on *less* than a communitywide, comprehensive basis. As the prime contractor in most cities for the Labor Department's concentrated employment program, for example, community action agencies have operated a coordinating mechanism covering the range of manpower functions in limited geographical areas. Neighborhood centers operated by the CAAs directly or through neighborhood corporations have asserted a significant coordinating influence upon agencies and programs in those neighborhoods. In their supervision of programs that they delegate to other community institutions, too, the CAAs act as coordinators—although their influence waned as soon as it became clear that they were not likely either to withdraw

34. New Haven's Community Progress, Inc. (CPI), was the most successful and best known of the half dozen community action agencies that had been created and financed under the Ford Foundation's "gray areas" program prior to passage of the Economic Opportunity Act of 1964. Members of the CPI board initially included persons designated by the mayor, the school board, two private organizations of social agencies, a business group, the urban renewal agency, and Yale University. Representatives of the poor were added only after CPI began receiving OEO funds.

35. Howard W. Hallman (director, poverty study staff, Senate Committee on Labor and Public Welfare), "Community Action Program: An Interpretative Analysis of 35 Communities," in *Examination of the War on Poverty*, Hearings before the Senate Committee on Labor and Public Welfare, 90 Cong. 1 sess. (1967), Vol. 4, pp. 912–13.

their funds or have additional money to make available. But insofar as they operate rather than delegate their programs they were bound to be competitors with other institutions for money and manpower, and in a competitive situation one of the rival claimants for resources will not be accepted as coordinator of the other claimants.

After reviewing the limited success of community action agencies as coordinators and analyzing all the difficulties involved, the staff of the National Advisory Council on Economic Opportunity told the council in October 1967 that "it is unfair for the Congress to exhort the Community Action Agencies to coordinate other federal programs."[36] Nevertheless, earlier in the year, OEO had asked the Congress to do just that—by adding an amendment to the Economic Opportunity Act declaring that a "specific purpose" of community action was "the strengthening of community capabilities for planning and *coordinating* Federal, State, and other assistance related to the elimination of poverty" (italics added). The Congress not only accepted OEO's language (in section 201[a] [1] of the amended act) but went considerably further. In section 221(d) it prescribed that every community action agency assisted after July 1, 1968, must have adopted a "planning and implementation process" that, among other things, "seeks to *mobilize and coordinate* relevant public and private resources, establishes program priorities, links program components with one another and with other relevant programs, and provides for evaluation" (italics added).

When OEO issued its instructions to CAAs in response to the amendments, however, it deemphasized the agencies' coordinating role, specifically warning that "the CAA is not to become a substitute for the legitimate roles of other public or private organizations which have responsibility for planning, conduct, and coordination of programs at the local level."[37] By 1969, even Hallman, who was primarily responsible for drafting section 221(d) and guiding it through the Congress, was ready to concede that the planning and coordinating mandate for the community action program "should be

36. "Issues and Alternatives in the Community Action Program" (staff report transmitted by Bradley H. Patterson, Jr., executive director, to the National Advisory Council on Economic Opportunity, Oct. 27, 1967).
37. Office of Economic Opportunity, "CAP Mission and Objectives," Instruction No. 1105–1, Aug. 7, 1968.

diminished." In its place, he suggested, the mandate of the model cities program for these purposes should be strengthened.[38]

But the very factors that have disabled the community action agencies as coordinators have led them to remarkable achievements of quite another kind. Whatever becomes of the CAAs, they have already had a drastic impact upon an entire range of governmental services—they have shaken the established agencies out of a too often prevailing "let them come to us" philosophy into a case-finding and outreach approach. At the same time, a new dimension of democracy has been accepted in principle and is being established in fact in American communities: the direct and effective participation of the poor in decisions on matters that govern their lives. The assault on the status quo, for all the tension that it has created, has been useful, necessary, and constructive—as many of the leaders of the assaulted institutions have been willing to acknowledge. The words we heard over and over were, "This community will never be the same again."

Moreover, the same organizational effort and "sense of power" that went into—and grew out of—protest and confrontation were being turned to uses that did not involve confrontation of any sort. "The trouble with the Negro community in this city," a Negro leader told us, "has been its internal division, and the great contribution of community action has been to provide a means for organizing our divided people. Now we've become a united working community for all kinds of community improvement purposes." In a rural community the organized poor had set up three voluntary day care centers, operated by mothers serving in rotation, with no public funds at all. More and more effort was being devoted by the organized poor to developing economic enterprises—efforts that seem likely to be assisted through one or another of the proposed governmental programs that are being advanced in the Congress and considered within the Nixon administration. Community action had unquestionably proved effective as a training institution—occasionally for agitators, to be sure, but more significantly for political and civic leaders, administrators and subprofessional workers, and entrepreneurs, all desperately needed by slum communities whose greatest weaknesses had been disorganization and inertia.

38. Howard W. Hallman, "The Future of the Poverty Program" (paper prepared for an Airlie House conference at Warrenton, Va., sponsored by the Urban Coalition, January 1969), p. 22.

Yet the community action agency as the organizer and advocate of the poor remains—and must remain, if it is to serve its purposes—an institution of challenge and competition to the rest of the community. The question is one of finding the practical and effective limit, for too severe a challenge can only invite retaliation at both the local and the national levels. The Green amendment of 1967 is one evidence of the latter. So is the virtual freezing of community action appropriations. So is President Johnson's remark in his final address to the Congress that the war on poverty should be reorganized. Finally, if the CAAs are destined to help arouse the conflict that is latent in every community, then the need is greater, rather than less, for the kind of coordinating machinery that will bring those conflicts to constructive solution. The most promising prospect for such machinery is the model cities program discussed in Chapter 3.

CHAPTER THREE

Model Cities
as a Coordinating Structure

LESS THAN THREE YEARS after President Johnson had launched the nationwide system of community action agencies as coordinating bodies that would plan and carry out "comprehensive" antipoverty programs calling upon "all the resources available to the community—federal and state, local and private, human and material," he was describing still another program in almost the same language:

> To be effective, concerted attacks on city problems must be planned by the cities themselves. The new model cities program is *now* the *primary* incentive provided by the Federal Government to accomplish this objective. Special grants will be made to help transform entire blighted areas into attractive and useful neighborhoods. To receive these grants, cities must:
> • Develop imaginative and *comprehensive* plans of action; and
> • Enlist Federal, State, local, and private resources in a *concerted* effort to bring their plans to fruition.[1]

The President's budget message of January 1967, from which those words are taken, made clear that the new model cities program had supplanted community action, in the minds of the President and his staff advisers, as the central instrument for coordinating the Great Society's attack upon the problems of the urban slums. While introducing the model cities program as "now the primary incentive" offered by the government, the 1967 message made no mention of the war on poverty as a coordinating concept nor of the community

---

1. The Budget Message of the President, Jan. 24, 1967, in *The Budget of the United States Government for the Fiscal Year Ending June 30, 1968*, pp. 25–26. Italics added.

action agencies as coordinating bodies. Under the heading "Economic Opportunity Programs," some of the specific programs the community action agencies administered, such as Head Start, were mentioned—but that was all. The Office of Economic Opportunity (OEO) had clearly taken its place as one more operating agency of the government, and its community action agencies had found their place as one more in the array of local limited-purpose institutions. In the budget itself, covering the year ending June 30, 1968, the President asked $412 million in special model cities appropriations, plus an additional $250 million in urban renewal funds—amounting to almost two-thirds as much federal money, for an estimated 140 model cities, as was being sought for the thousand community action agencies that then existed.

The idea that became the model cities program originated in a task force on urban problems convened by President Johnson in 1965 in anticipation of the creation of the Department of Housing and Urban Development. Members of the task force—headed by Robert C. Wood of the Massachusetts Institute of Technology (who was to be appointed the first under secretary and later the secretary of HUD)—were concerned with the rising criticism of the urban renewal program. While urban renewal might remake the physical structure of a city slum, the critics observed, it did little to improve the lives of the slum's inhabitants. Indeed, it worked the other way— it added to the problems of the poor by forcing them out of their neighborhoods into other slums to make way for the "federal bulldozer."[2] Residents of black ghettos commonly referred to urban renewal as "Negro removal." The task force therefore sought a means by which urban renewal and social programs could be brought together to meet both the needs of the slum residents and the objectives of the city planners—in other words, to recreate not just the physical environment but the social environment as well. As the group began its deliberations, the eruption of violence in Watts enveloped its purpose in an atmosphere of crisis.

The community action program, then only a few months old, did not seem to be the answer. In few places had the community action agencies brought housing and renewal programs under their coordinating "umbrella." Moreover, it was already clear that most of the

2. The phrase is from the title of Martin Anderson's harsh critique of urban renewal, *The Federal Bulldozer* (M.I.T. Press, 1964).

agencies were defining their roles as those of advocacy, confrontation, and delivery of services rather than of communitywide planning and coordination. Accordingly, Wood and his colleagues came forward with their own approach to coordinated planning at the local level, which they labeled "demonstration cities."

On sending the proposal to the Congress in January 1966,[3] President Johnson declared that it would "concentrate our available resources—in planning tools, in housing construction, in job training, in health facilities, in recreation, in welfare programs, in education—to improve the conditions of life in urban areas." It would "join together all available talent and skills in a coordinated effort." It would "mobilize local leadership and private initiative." It would alter "the total environment of the area affected." "For the first time," said the President, "social and construction agencies would join in a massive common effort, responsive to a common local authority."

The new program reasserted the principle of the early community action theoreticians that had been set aside in the rush to get the war on poverty under way—namely, that comprehensive and coordinated planning must be the precedent to action. Indeed, the applicant cities were required to enter into a process of competitive planning. First, they were to submit applications for planning grants that would be judged according to fourteen guidelines stated in the President's message. HUD would appraise the potential of each application for changing "the total environment" of the demonstration area, its comprehensiveness in making use of "every available social program," the commitment of the city to utilizing its own resources, the competence of the local administration, and the adequacy of the administrative machinery it proposed for carrying out the program. From the community action concept came one of the President's guidelines: "The demonstration should foster . . . widespread citizen participation—especially from the demonstration area—in the planning and execution of the program." After the proposals were judged, the winning cities would be given another year in which to perfect five-year action plans—and federal funds to finance the planning.

3. Special Message to the Congress Recommending a Program for Cities and Metropolitan Areas, Jan. 26, 1966, *Public Papers of the Presidents, 1966*, Vol. I, pp. 82–91.

To administer the program, the President specified that each city must designate "a single authority with adequate powers to carry out and coordinate all phases of the program." The program would utilize "the complete array of all available grants and urban aids in the fields of housing, renewal, transportation, education, welfare, economic opportunity, and related programs," plus supplemental funds to be provided through HUD as a kind of block grant to the cities available for purposes not eligible under existing grant-in-aid programs. The secretary of HUD, said the President in the same message, would "assume leadership among intergovernmental agencies dealing with urban problems" and "mesh together all our social and physical efforts to improve urban living." To assist it in mobilizing federal programs, each demonstration city would be assigned a federal coordinator. There was no question as to the breadth of the coordinating concept—the message was studded with such words as "all," "every," "total," and "complete."

The year 1966 was one of waning public support for President Johnson and his Great Society (in November, three Democratic senators and forty-seven Democratic representatives were to lose their seats to Republicans), and the reception of the new proposal on Capitol Hill was chilly. Members of the Congress objected to the length and cost of the commitment they were asked to make for so experimental a program—$3 billion for a six-year effort—and they shied from the integrationist implications of the proposal, including an explicit provision that housing programs aided under the act have elimination of segregation as an objective. After accepting some amendments and by dint of intensive lobbying, the administration managed to win approval of the proposal, by a comfortable majority in the Senate, but by a margin of only twenty-six votes in the House. The authorization was reduced from six to three years and the funds scaled down accordingly. The housing integration provision was dropped, and an amendment was accepted that prohibited HUD from requiring school busing as a condition of assistance. But except for elimination of the federal coordinator for each city,[4] the organizational scheme and coordinating concepts outlined in the President's message were accepted by the Congress.

4. In lieu of the federal coordinator, Congress authorized assignment of a "metropolitan expediter" to any metropolitan area whose central city requested it (no expediters had been requested, as of early 1969).

HUD called upon the cities to submit their initial proposals by May 1, 1967. In a booklet issued as a guide to the cities, the department elaborated on the standards established in the act.[5] It suggested nine components to be considered in the development of a "comprehensive" program:

1. Physical improvements, including recreational facilities, parks and landscaping, street and sidewalk repair, street lighting and refuse collection, as well as stores, theaters, and other commercial facilities.
2. Housing, particularly for low- and moderate-income families.
3. Transportation.
4. Education, particularly for the poor and disadvantaged.
5. Manpower and economic development, including creation of job opportunities in the demonstration areas and recruitment and training of workers.
6. Recreation and culture.
7. Crime reduction.
8. Health, including mental health.
9. Social services and public assistance, involving the services of both public and private agencies.

Half a hundred federal programs, administered by seven Cabinet departments and OEO, were enumerated as candidates for inclusion in the cities' plans.

As for the administrative machinery, which the statute did not define, HUD specified that the "city demonstration agency" (CDA) must be a public agency. It could be the city itself, or a county, or an established agency, or a new one, but "it should be closely related to the governmental decision-making process in a way that permits the exercise of leadership by responsible elected officials." If the city or county designated itself as the demonstration agency, the responsibility should be assigned to a single administrative unit that could "draw upon the powers of the chief executive officer." If a new agency were created or an existing agency designated, it "should function in fact as though it were an integral part of the municipal government or the county, with clear accountability to the local elected officials." The contrast with OEO's community action agencies could hardly have been more pointed.

5. U.S. Department of Housing and Urban Development, *Improving the Quality of Urban Life: A Program Guide to Model Neighborhoods in Demonstration Cities* (December 1966). A revised edition with the same title is dated December 1967.

A total of 193 communities responded to the invitation for proposals, and in November 63 were announced as winners of the competition and awarded grants to complete their plans. A few months later, 12 more were announced. By that time, incidentally, in deference to the adverse connotation the word "demonstration" had acquired, the President and HUD had quietly changed the name of the program to "model cities" (although the city demonstration agencies, so named in the statute, were not relabeled). A deadline of April 15, 1968, was set for a second round of applications; 164 cities, including many of those that failed to win first-round approval, applied and another 75 were approved in 1968 and awarded planning grants—for a total of 150 participating cities. Plans for the first 9 cities were approved by HUD just before President Johnson left office. The final Johnson budget showed expenditures under the program—that is, expenditures from the supplemental funds appropriated to HUD for use on model cities projects—rising to $871 million in the fiscal year 1970.[6] Thus the 150 city demonstration agencies, whose responsibilities were limited to designated neighborhoods, would have at their disposal almost as much as would be expended by the community action agencies in all of the poor neighborhoods of the country.

Sixteen of the cities we visited in our initial field interviews, in the last four months of 1967, were among the first round of model cities applicants, and in November eleven of them were announced as winners. Each city, in its application, had described the structure it planned to use for purposes of coordinated planning. Most of them intended to enlist the participation of a broad array of agencies in the committees and task forces that would prepare the components of the comprehensive plan—city, county, and state agencies, school boards, community action agencies, private welfare organizations, and so on—in addition to residents of the designated neighborhoods. The structures had yet to be established, however; the first real test of model cities as a coordinating scheme would come in 1968, when the committees and task forces would be formed and the comprehensive plans prepared.

To assess the 1968 experience, we revisited in February 1969 four of the eleven cities that were included in our earlier study and added

6. President Nixon's budget revisions reduced the appropriation request by $75 million. *New York Times*, April 16, 1969.

a fifth selected from among those whose plans had been approved. In those five cities we interviewed fifty-six persons who had participated in various capacities in the planning process. We also examined the detailed chronologies and evaluations covering four other first-round cities prepared under contract to HUD;[7] talked with HUD officials in Washington and in two regional offices and with staff members of HEW and OEO, and participated in a two-day conference organized to review the first year's experience under the model cities program.[8] What follows, then, is based upon observations in sixteen cities (four visited by us in both 1967 and 1969, seven visited only in 1967, and one visited only in 1969, and four studied by the HUD contractor field teams), supplemented by information and opinions obtained from federal officials and others concerned with the operation of the program on a national scale.

The Struggle for Control

As in the case of community action, the phrase and concept of "citizen participation" became the center of a struggle for power and influence that began in some cities almost as soon as the model cities program was enacted and that developed in all of them, in varying degrees of intensity, by the time the planning process was under way.

The model cities legislation was no less ambiguous in its participation language than the Economic Opportunity Act had been. Instead of "maximum feasible" participation, the model cities act demanded only "widespread" participation but the term was similarly undefined. That left it to the administering agency, HUD, which in turn left it largely to the individual cities. "No precise formula for citizen involvement will be imposed," HUD Secretary Robert C. Weaver had told the Congress. "It will be up to the cities themselves to devise appropriate ways in which citizens will participate."[9] A demonstration program, he argued, should have flexibility, and that applied to the matter of citizen participation. "It is fraught with problems," he observed. "But I think, if you are going to succeed in doing what we hope to do, which is not only to revive and revitalize these areas

7. The contractor was Marshall Kaplan, Gans, and Kahn of San Francisco.
8. See Chap. 1, p. 29.
9. *Housing Legislation of 1966*, Hearings before a Subcommittee of the Senate Committee on Banking and Currency, 89 Cong. 2 sess. (1966), Pt. 1, p. 100.

physically, but also help the people psychologically and socially and humanly, you have to do it, and you have to learn to do it, and you learn to do it by having many patterns and finding out which patterns are the best patterns."[10]

When it issued its call for applications, HUD added little in the way of specific guidance. Its instructions contained nothing as specific as OEO's policy that one-third of the members of community action agency boards should be representatives of the poor. In model cities, the instructions said, neighborhood residents should have "a meaningful role" and "active involvement." Planning "should be carried out *with* as well as *for* the people living in the affected area." Mechanisms should be established for "communication and meaningful dialogue" between the city demonstration agency and the citizens of the area. Existing neighborhood organizations, "as well as new organizations developed by grass-roots organizational efforts," should be utilized.[11] But it was up to each city to design its own structure for applying those principles.

BICAMERAL AND UNICAMERAL STRUCTURES

The schemes for organizing resident participation that were presented in the first round of applications in the spring of 1967 were varied and often vague, but they could be classified into two broad categories that came to be known as "bicameral" and "unicameral." A city's choice between the two forms appeared to reflect its experience under the Economic Opportunity Act. In a city where the poor had been organized under auspices of the community action agency into a political force with a "confrontation" philosophy, an analogous confrontation structure would be incorporated into the model cities plan—a bicameral scheme in which the neighborhood residents through an independent organization would participate in developing and reviewing program proposals in more or less equal partnership with the city's public and private agencies. In a city where the poor had been unorganized or less assertive, the model cities plan would embody a unicameral structure within which the neighborhood residents and the agency representatives were to join

10. *Demonstration Cities, Housing and Urban Development, and Urban Mass Transit,* Hearings before a Subcommittee of the Committee on Banking and Currency, 89 Cong. 2 sess. (1966), p. 136.
11. HUD, *Improving the Quality of Urban Life,* p. 14.

in a single planning process. In either case, of course, the plan as drawn up by the agency and neighborhood residents was subject to approval by the city's governing body.

Of the eleven successful applicant cities that we visited in late 1967, four had proposed unicameral and seven bicameral plans. Six of the bicameral schemes called for new organizations to represent the neighborhoods; the seventh planned to use the already formed groups of the community action agency. Two of the bicameral cities—Philadelphia and Oakland—proposed to provide their resident organizations with professional staff, or "advocate planners," as they were often called.

As an illustration of a bicameral plan of organization, Philadelphia's original proposal is reproduced as Figure 1. The plan was the product of negotiations between the city and the neighborhood that were undertaken after neighborhood spokesmen angrily protested the city's failure to consult them and admit them to partnership at the outset; as finally agreed it establishes an almost equal partnership between the city and the neighborhood. On the two sides of the chart, in neat balance, are two councils—one made up of citizens of the model cities area chosen by their fellow residents, the other representing city, county, and state agencies participating in the program. In the statements of functions accompanying the chart, the areawide council (the residents' organization) had the special duty to "foster and encourage participation," but beyond that the two councils were assigned identical responsibilities: each was to "coordinate and consolidate efforts, analyze requirements, establish goals, develop projects, and review plans and proposals of the Model City Agency [the administrative body for the program]." Each, moreover, was to have its own staff. The proposed staff of the areawide council (AWC) would number thirteen, including a specialist in each of the four fields into which the model cities planning process was divided—physical environment, employment and manpower, human resources, and education. The staff "will work for, and be responsible to, only the AWC," the proposal specified.

Potential conflicts between the residents and the government agencies could be reconciled, in the first instance, by the task forces responsible for preparing the plan under the direction of the model cities administrator. The task forces would be made up of public and private agency representatives but would have available to them

Figure 1. Proposed Structure for Model Cities Planning Machinery in Philadelphia

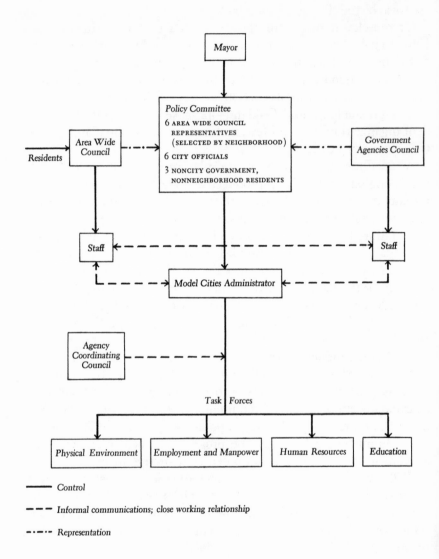

Control

Informal communications; close working relationship

Representation

Source: A diagram in "Application for a Grant to Plan a Comprehensive City Demonstration Program" (Philadelphia, Pa., March 3, 1967), p. 5-A-7 (processed).

the views of the residents as expressed through the areawide council. If the conflicts persisted, they could be negotiated by the two councils through their respective staffs. If that failed, recourse was to the policy committee, in which the residents had six votes out of fifteen.[12] The structure as a whole provided means for organizing the initiative of the residents and blending their views with those of the public officials.

The most elaborate example of a unicameral plan was that presented by Duluth, Minnesota. There, thirty-two "community foremen" selected from the neighborhood and thirty-two volunteers from business and industry would be given an intensive training course and then divided into eight panels for consideration of particular problems, each panel to consist of four foremen and four volunteers, plus one specialist from a participating agency. After they had drafted their respective segments of the plan, the panels would disband and the sixty-four foremen and volunteers would become the program's policy committee, with authority to approve each element of the proposed program.[13]

Of the first round of applicants, however, few stated with as much precision as Philadelphia and Duluth how their resident participation structures would be organized. The applications themselves had been prepared with little citizen participation; typically, a city's proposal had been written within a narrow circle—a small group of staff planners attached to the mayor's office, assisted perhaps by consultants— and so the issue had not been publicly joined. Once the approval of the application was announced, however, the organization had to be decided upon—and rapidly—so that planning could get under way. Many questions arose: If the city demonstration agency (CDA) were to be governed by a policy-making board, as many cities intended, how many seats would be allocated to representatives of the neighborhood—a majority, a substantial minority, a small minority, or none at all? How would the neighborhood representatives be chosen—by the mayor or the CDA, by existing neighborhood orga-

12. As it happened, this committee was not activated, and the model cities administrator occupied the mediating position, aided by a joint planning group made up of top staff members from each side.

13. Duluth, Minn., *Identity Through Involvement*, Model Neighborhood Application (April 1967), pp. I-6–I-7.

nizations, or through an election process? In a unicameral system, what would be the relationship of the residents to the professional staff of the CDA and other agencies in the planning process? In a bicameral pattern, how would the neighborhood organization be formed? Would it have its own staff of advocate planners? What would be its role in development of proposals for inclusion in the city's plan? Would it have a veto over the proposals of the professionals? If not, how would disputes be settled? Beyond those questions lay others: Who would control the patronage to be created under the model cities program—the professional positions, the nonprofessional jobs in neighborhood centers and other service activities, the ghetto enterprises to be created, and so on?

THE GROWTH OF NEIGHBORHOOD INFLUENCE

As the demands of neighborhood residents for greater influence, power, and control rose in the participating cities—reminiscent of the early months of community action—the response was much the same: the cities yielded to the neighborhood leadership an increasingly strong role. HUD, like OEO, encouraged the cities to move in that direction, but the extent to which a city moved reflected primarily the speed and effectiveness with which the neighborhood organized to formulate its demands and the militancy of its leaders. These factors varied greatly, and so some cities yielded authority to the neighborhoods in large measure, and at the outset, while others responded to neighborhood—and HUD—pressures at a slower pace.

Where the neighborhood was strongly organized under militant leadership—perhaps 20 to 30 percent of the cities might be put in that class—the struggle for control of model cities took on many of the attributes of labor-management negotiations, but with more attendant animosity. The contending parties struck bargaining positions: the neighborhood organizations threatened to strike (that is, boycott the program and thus bring it to an end); the city officials threatened lockouts (that is, withdrawal from the program); sometimes negotiations broke down and the program did come to a halt (in Oakland and Newark the stalemate was so prolonged that HUD removed them for a time from the list of participating cities); but, ultimately, each side made concessions and contract terms were agreed upon. Like labor and management, the city and the neighborhood were under economic compulsion to come to terms: neither side was willing to forego the cash flow to the community that an agreement would assure. And, as in the case of labor-management negotiations, the federal government sometimes assumed a mediating role but did not dictate any settlements.

Within HUD itself, there was, as would be expected, more than one point of view on the degree of neighborhood influence or control to be desired. Some officials put more stress on the values of city hall responsibility and political leadership by mayors, others on the values of citizen participation. But HUD's official position was determined on pragmatic rather than ideological grounds. The program would not work without the support of both the neighborhood and city hall, the administrators reasoned. It would fail if the city unilaterally established a unicameral structure, or a bicameral structure dominated by city hall, when residents were demanding an equal and independent voice. Therefore a citizen participation scheme acceptable to the residents as well as to the city had to be negotiated between them. If a locality failed to reconcile the conflicting views and interests, there simply "would be no program," HUD advised the cities.[14]

HUD's instructions could be interpreted as virtually prohibiting the unicameral design—and this much, at least, appeared to reflect principle rather than pragmatism. In November 1967—while repeating that it would not "determine the ideal organization pattern"—HUD laid down performance standards that seemed to require a bicameral structure, with independent staff (or other technical assistance) for the neighborhood organization.

There must be "some form of organization structure," the statement said, "which embodies neighborhood residents in the process of policy and program planning and program implementation and operation." The residents must be "fully" involved in those processes. "The leadership of that structure must consist of persons whom neighborhood residents accept as representing their interests," and

14. Remarks of Walter G. Farr, Jr., model cities administrator, at a community meeting in Richmond, Calif., Dec. 9, 1967.

the "structure must have clear and direct access to the decision-making process of the City Demonstration Agency," advance information on matters to be decided, and "some form of technical assistance" to help the neighborhood residents achieve the capacity to make knowledgeable decisions.[15] Those sentences make little sense except in terms of bicameralism; a regulation writer would hardly specify that a unicameral CDA have access to its own decision-making processes and advance information from itself. Under HUD's decentralized administration, however, regions could pursue different policies. Referring to a unicameral plan approved in one region, a HUD official in another region said flatly that "we would not approve such a plan," and in his region no unicameral structures existed.

By early 1969 the unicameral structure was rapidly disappearing. Of the nine model cities whose organization schemes we examined at that time,[16] none was of the unicameral type. Cities that earlier had not contemplated establishing independent neighborhood organizations were doing so, and those organizations everywhere were becoming stronger and more assertive—particularly as they became increasingly aware of their "rights" under HUD guidelines. And they were being provided funds to hire staffs, including advocacy planning staffs, or employ their own consultants.

City leaders forced into bicameral systems against their better judgment were often dubious about the consequences. "What it means," said a mayor, "is that all my good ideas can be shot down by one loudmouth who can carry people with him just because he says I represent the establishment." And city officials particularly resisted the idea of advocacy planning. "We're trying to bring people together, not separate them," a city planner contended. "When you get a neighborhood organization with its own staff, the attitudes of all the city agencies harden. They're not going to be pushed around by a group of citizens organizing a separate government." A CDA director agreed: "We're professionals. We have no axe to grind. I'm for partnership in planning—for getting away from 'we' and 'they.' "

15. U.S. Department of Housing and Urban Development, "Citizen Participation—CDA Letter No. 3," MGCR 3100.3 (Nov. 30, 1967).

16. Five directly, four through the HUD-contracted case studies. The nine cities ranged in size from two of over a million population to two under a hundred thousand. Five were in the Northeast, two in the Midwest, one in the Far West, and one in the South.

Neighborhood leaders, of course, took the opposite view. The chairman of a model neighborhood resident organization defended bicameralism in these words:

Poor people are afraid to talk in these mixed [unicameral] groups, because they feel they'll get cut up. The citizens should stand with some autonomy and come up with answers free and clear of what the political side thinks.

Another leader defended the advocacy planning concept:

When you go out to the airport and get in an airplane, you can't depend on one pilot—you need a copilot. In the same way, we need planners who will plan our community as the people wish without being tied to city hall. It's true the city has assigned to these projects people who identify with the community. But we feel more comfortable with people who we can terminate whenever we get ready.

The chairman of the model neighborhood resident organization in Oakland, Ralph Williams, speaking publicly at a neighborhood meeting attended by federal officials, was even more graphic:

Thirty million dollars of federal money has been spent in Oakland with no results. The city and county agencies are responsible for the diabolical way we live—why should we trust them to plan for us? We long ago got tired of people doing the planning for us. They come down from the hills for eight hours and tell us what to do, and after they are gone we are still fighting rats and mosquitoes and mice twenty-four hours a day. No longer can anybody plan for us to satisfy us. This is the new turnabout. We're trying to go down the road together. We plan what we want and then expect them to help us get it.

Advocacy planning had its defenders too, within the planning profession. These are two comments from directors of planning agencies:

The separate staff will prevent the citizens from being co-opted. It will give them a competence for either confrontation or cooperation, depending on what they want. And it will blunt the militants by letting them into the technical ball game.

We're introducing a brand new planning process. We no longer draft a blueprint and put it before an advisory board. Now we are synthesizers of what comes up from below. We have to condition the higher levels to accept what comes up from below, but we also have to create the kind of mechanisms that can come up with ideas of the kind you have to have.[17]

17. See also, Paul Davidoff, "Advocacy and Pluralism in Planning," *Journal of the American Institute of Planners*, Vol. 31 (November 1965), and Lisa R. Peattie, "Reflections on Advocacy Planning," *ibid.*, Vol. 34 (March 1968).

As the year 1968 progressed, HUD became bolder in the interpretation of its guidelines. In September, HUD Assistant Secretary Taylor was emphasizing the need for technical assistance to be *independent:*

The neighborhood structure must have the assistance it needs to bargain and negotiate effectively. This does not mean that it must do the planning, or that it must have a duplicate planning and staff capability.

It does mean making available technical assistance and expertise that the neighborhood can trust. With this assistance they can analyze, criticize, and suggest alternatives to be explored and developed, and judge whether the exploration of those alternatives has been honest and thorough.

The objective of the Model Cities program is to help develop the capacity to function in and use the system. Technical assistance is an indispensable tool. And if it is to be accepted, it must be trusted. In many places, to be trusted it must be under the direction and control of the community.

That is why we are moving to encourage the concept of Independent Technical Assistance—making available to the residents, under their control, resources to provide technical assistance and expertise they trust.[18]

HUD did not go so far as to make independent technical assistance a formal requirement, but the "encouragement" of the concept had its effect. Cities might resist the inclusion in their model cities plans of funds for advocacy planning staffs, but a protest from the neighborhood organization direct to HUD—and channels between such organizations and HUD's regional offices were open, and utilized—could bring questions if the plan, when presented for review, did not satisfy the demands of the neighborhood for the "technical assistance" required by HUD's performance standards. Accordingly, the advocacy planning function—so well developed in Philadelphia's plan, shown in Figure 1, for professional support for its areawide council—was growing, or appeared destined to grow, in other cities also.

THE CDA: COORDINATOR OR ADVOCATE?

Under the pressure for citizen participation, not only was unicameralism giving way to bicameralism but the city demonstration

18. Remarks by H. Ralph Taylor, HUD assistant secretary, before the National Association of Housing and Redevelopment Officials, at Minneapolis, Minn., Sept. 27, 1968.

agency itself, in an increasing number of cases, was coming under formal or de facto control by the resident organizations. Only a few cities, so far, have officially yielded control of the program to the residents—creating a third type of structure, a kind of unicameralism under neighborhood rather than city hall dominance—but one (Cambridge, Massachusetts) was among the nine cities covered in our analysis. There, at the very outset of the program, the residents had appeared in strength at a city council meeting and forcefully demanded the right not only to approve the city's application but to be assured a controlling majority on the governing board of the city demonstration agency; a complaisant council submitted, and the neighborhood organization actually drafted the city ordinance that granted the powers sought.

However, of the cities that have a balanced bicameral structure on paper, at least some have de facto resident control. There the resident organization has won the right, openly or tacitly acknowledged, to nominate or approve selection of the CDA director and his key staff.

Figure 2 illustrates diagrammatically the unicameral, bicameral, and resident-control patterns of resident participation. However, it breaks the dominant bicameral type into three subtypes based upon the relationships among the city's governing authorities, the CDA, and the neighborhood resident organization (NRO).

The unified bicameral organization illustrates the structure in a community where relationships between the city hall and the neighborhood leadership are reasonably harmonious and the city demonstration agency has been able, so far at least, to maintain the confidence of both. CDA staff is assigned to work with neighborhood committees (or joint committees representing both the neighborhood and public and private agencies) and is acceptable to them.

The unified structure illustrates the pattern of relationships that most city authorities appear to have had in mind in submitting their original applications. However, where anti-city hall feeling turned out to be strong in the neighborhoods, and as the neighborhood organizations have become more aggressive in seeking control of the planning process, CDA directors inevitably have found themselves unable to maintain the confidence of both the city's governing authorities and the neighborhood leadership and to bridge the gap between them. Thus caught in the middle between antagonistic

Figure 2. Model City Organization Schemes

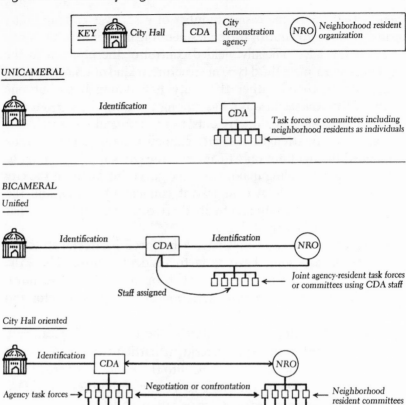

UNICAMERAL

BICAMERAL

Unified

City Hall oriented

Neighborhood oriented

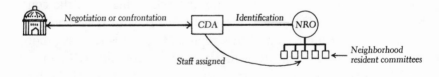

RESIDENT CONTROL

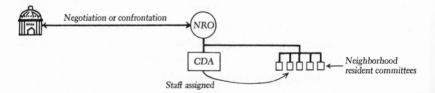

forces, the CDAs have had to concentrate upon maintaining the confidence and the political support of one or the other. As illustrated in the diagram of the city hall oriented structure, some of those CDAs have chosen to maintain their identification with their city halls and negotiate at arm's length with the neighborhood organizations. The latter, under the circumstances, have become the neighborhood groups most vigorously demanding, and placing most reliance upon, their own advocacy planning staffs; and the essential negotiations—or confrontations—take place between the advocate planners and the staffs of the CDA and its associated official agencies as the model cities plan is developed. In other cases, as shown in the neighborhood oriented diagram, the CDA directors have looked for their political support to the neighborhoods rather than to city hall, have located their offices in the neighborhoods rather than downtown, and have attempted themselves to assume the role of advocate planners serving the neighborhood organizations. In this subtype, the arm's length relationship—or confrontation—comes to be between the CDA itself and city hall, and the essential negotiations between the neighborhood and the governing authorities tend to take place after the neighborhood and the city demonstration agency have agreed upon the model cities plan they will present.

As the model cities program progresses, it seems unlikely that the unified structure will prove to be durable. City authorities and slum residents *do* have different interests, objectives, and outlooks, and antagonism and conflict are inevitable. They are most pronounced, of course, where the model neighborhood is a black community, but even in all-white model neighborhoods the planning process has revealed an unexpected social and political distance between the slum residents and their local governmental officials. "They don't represent us," said a white neighborhood organization chairman. "Our member of the city council is elected by the votes of two hundred people he can control with jobs. He just walks by without seeing us." The formation of neighborhood organizations, moreover, has brought into being new political forces with new leaders, and those leaders have found predictably that the way to strengthen their positions and to consolidate their followings is to exploit the latent distrust of city hall. Such leaders do not lack for issues around which to rally their new organizations—rezonings, urban renewal, freeway routes, school and recreation issues, and so on. Like the neighborhood community action groups before them, the model neighborhood organizations as they begin to provide a voice for a population theretofore largely unorganized and silent are bound to bring to the surface the abeyant antagonism between the slum dwellers and the "power structure." It then becomes less and less possible for the city demonstration agency to keep both sides persuaded that it can simultaneously represent their respective interests.

Of the eight bicameral structures we examined, two could be judged in early 1969 as remaining in the unified subtype. But in one of these cities the CDA had moved its headquarters into the model neighborhood and the director was seeking to achieve closer identification with the neighborhood leaders; while his approach had succeeded in cementing relationships with the neighborhood leadership, his rapport with city hall was visibly weakening. In the other case the CDA appeared destined to move in the opposite direction; the residents were beginning to demand their own staff independent of the CDA, and the distance between the neighborhood leaders and the CDA seemed generally to be widening. "He's been walking the tightrope very well," an aide to the mayor observed of that CDA director, "but eventually it will come to the point where he will have to come down on one side or the other—city hall or the neighborhood."

But when a CDA director tries to resolve his dilemma by identifying with the neighborhood leadership and seeking to become, in effect, its advocate planning staff—as in the neighborhood oriented subtype—he finds that goal difficult, and perhaps ultimately impossible, to achieve. As long as he is appointed by the city's governing authorities, he cannot entirely escape his identification as "the mayor's man." Therefore, even in those cities where the CDA directors were striving most ardently to identify with, and represent, the neighborhood organizations, leaders of those organizations were almost invariably—in the cities we examined—demanding their own independent staffs anyway, and the CDAs, still trying to be responsive to the desires of the neighborhoods, were acquiescing in varying degrees.

Moreover, since the CDA director is in fact "the mayor's man"— or at least part of the city's official family—he cannot shed his responsibility to keep the model cities program reasonably free of content that might embarrass the mayor and other elected officials

politically. On a subject where neighborhood demands are unacceptable to city hall, he may find himself in an impossible position. To
maintain the confidence of the neighborhood, he must include its
demands in the CDA's plan that goes forward for final approval,
but the burden then is upon the mayor and council to act publicly to
eliminate or modify the unacceptable provisions that—had the
CDA regarded itself as the loyal agent of city hall—could have been
throttled quietly at staff level. Beyond that, a model cities plan is a
complicated document that requires careful analysis and review from
the standpoint of a city's budget, personnel, contracting, and other
policies. Since the mayor and city council are ultimately responsible
for the model cities plan, they inevitably feel the need for the kind
of staff assistance in reviewing its components that the CDA was
designed originally to give them.

But a more basic question is what becomes of the coordination
process. The original doctrine of model cities emphasized that without strong political leadership the enormous task of coordinated
planning and action that the plan envisaged could not be accomplished. HUD's early instructions, quoted above, specified that the
CDA should be an "integral part" of the municipal government,
"clearly accountable" to the elected officials, "closely related to the
governmental decision-making process" so that those officials could
provide leadership, and drawing upon the powers of the chief executive officer. If coordination is to be achieved, those preconditions still
apply. When the community action agencies became advocates for
the residents, they lost what potential for coordination they may
originally have had. The CDAs can follow the same course. When
they come under resident control, whether in law or in fact (as in
many cases of the neighborhood oriented subtype), they will similarly sacrifice their potential as coordinators exercising the powers of
mayors, city managers, and city councils to bring about concerted
action by the many public and private agencies whose resources are
to be mobilized.

To make the model cities coordinating concept work, then, a new
mechanism would have to be established as an "integral part" of the
city government responsive to the mayor or city manager to fill the
vacuum that the CDA was originally designed to fill. Such mechanisms have not yet been developed, but the problems of inadequate
coordination have already appeared. In cities where the CDAs have

become resident-dominated, the plans sent to Washington lack something in the degree of official commitment to them; heads of city agencies that were left out of the planning process regard themselves as less than fully bound. And agencies outside the city government, that may be difficult to harness into a concerted effort even with the mayor's active leadership, have even less attachment to the process.

What seems to be in prospect for cities in the neighborhood oriented subtype, then, is a complicated, unstable structure containing two elements not shown in the diagram in Figure 2 that might be portrayed as follows:

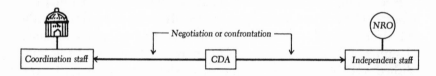

The coordination staff and the independent neighborhood organization staff might remain relatively undeveloped for a time, depending upon how well the CDA was able to satisfy the respective needs of the city's governing officials and the neighborhood leaders. But, in any case, the CDA would be back in the middle position it found untenable in the first place, trying to mediate between two contending forces but without the full confidence of either. The CDA would appear to be at a disadvantage in competition with the two staffs that do enjoy the confidence of their respective sponsors, and eventually its functions would probably be divided between the other two—with a resulting pattern comparable to the city hall oriented subtype.

In the case of the resident-control type of structure, the need for a new mechanism responsive to the mayor and city council will, presumably, prove to be even more pressing. If and as that mechanism grows, this type would become in fact bicameral, also on the pattern of the city hall oriented subtype, but with labels reversed:

Stability, therefore, would appear to lie in the city hall oriented scheme. CDAs should recognize that their allegiance must be to city hall rather than to the neighborhood—the neighborhood in the long run is not likely to trust them anyway, and if they become neighborhood advocate planners, the essential coordination function will be lost. Instead of trying to perform the advocacy function themselves, they should assist the neighborhood organizations in the development for that purpose of independent staffs.

Such a course is not wholly free of problems. Neighborhood organizations with power to hire staff may appoint neighborhood residents who are less than fully qualified or they may choose militants who, from the standpoint of the city, make irresponsible demands and add unnecessary tension and conflict to the bicameral negotiation process. "Their staff meetings are indoctrinations in black power," a city official said of the neighborhood organization in one community we visited. But where the gulf between a city's officialdom and its slum leadership is wide, an open bicameral structure that compels communication and negotiation on a sustained basis appears to offer the most promising mechanism for reconciliation. It not only forces the city to be responsive but provides a means for bringing about a better understanding in the neighborhood of the problems faced by the city as a whole.

A final compelling argument for a city hall oriented organization is that it can serve additional neighborhoods within a city. In the event of extension of the model cities process, neighborhood organizations in the added areas can be related to a single CDA in city hall, but a resident-controlled CDA can hardly serve more than one such organization. The prospects for inclusion of additional neighborhoods in the program are discussed below.

Processes of Coordination

Despite the tensions and conflicts engendered within the communities by the struggle for control of the model city ogranization, the plans that emerged at the end of the planning year 1968 represent a remarkable achievement in coordination.

They were impressive in their scope. Even the most comprehensive of the community action agencies, for all the reasons discussed earlier, had had little influence beyond the fields in which projects could be financed by OEO—community organization, education, health, welfare, rehabilitation, employment counseling and placement, and so on. But model cities planning embraced all these fields and many others as well—housing and urban renewal, municipal services, public investment of all kinds, and economic development, including transportation, industrial site preparation, and formation of development corporations. "This is the first legislation to bring together programs like urban renewal and package them with programs that deal with people," explained a city manager. A model cities planner exulted: "Model cities will concern the *total* development of the community. Our concern will be as broad as the life of the city." No such broad planning had ever been attempted before, by any city, yet the plans submitted by the first round of model cities— whatever the quality of the proposals they contained—came creditably close to achieving the boast of total coverage. There were gaps, of course: all cities could not organize successfully to cover every field, and in some of its sections a plan might simply call for further planning. Yet even in those instances the conception of the program had not narrowed; the city demonstration agency had staked its claim to complete coverage of all activities affecting the model neighborhood, and the planning machinery was either in being or in process of formation.

The range of participation was also impressive. In addition to the residents of the model neighborhood, the city demonstration agencies had been able to bring into the planning process professional staff representing city and county agencies, public schools and other educational institutions, community action agencies, and a host of social service and other private organizations. The cooperating groups may have been enticed into the effort by the prospect of obtaining supplemental federal funds for their organizations, but in any case they were there—planning jointly with other public and private agencies for often the first time.

The CDA director (and here we exclude those of resident-controlled CDAs) was thus at the hub of an intricate coordinating network that was itself "as broad as the life of the city." First, he had to look to the neighborhood, to mobilize and coordinate the participation of the residents. Second, he had to look laterally to the panoply of public and private agencies in the community, to enlist their resources and coordinate their proposals. And all the while, he had to reflect the views of the city's governing authorities and keep in touch with the various federal agencies to assure that his proposals would satisfy their requirements for funding. To maintain liaison with all these groups and cope with the conflicts within and among them, he had only a hastily built organization operating without benefit of experience and established status. At the end of the year, however, the whole process could be said, in general, to have worked—and to have worked in the manner that was intended. The goal of coordinated planning, comprehensive in scope, with widespread citizen and official participation was not fully achieved in all of its aspects in the initial year, to be sure, but it was assuredly served. And the body of experience that was accumulated should prove to have laid the basis for progressive improvement of the process as time goes on.

MOBILIZATION OF NEIGHBORHOOD RESOURCES

When the model cities program got under way, ready-made organizations of residents already existed in most model neighborhoods—the community action agency (CAA) groups chosen to represent the neighborhood in antipoverty activities. But rarely were these organizations accepted in the same role in the model cities program.

There were many reasons. The CAA and its local structures might be in ill repute in the city generally. The neighborhood organization might be, by common consent, weak and poorly led. It might have fallen under the domination of a clique: "I wanted new blood in the leadership [of model cities], and not people with a dual loyalty," said a CDA director. The CAA-sponsored organizations might have different boundaries. Sometimes the CAA groups were not effective representatives of those residents above the poverty level; whether or not a formal means test was required for participation in CAA activities, the nonpoor had not become active because they did not see the program as designed for them. But the model cities program sought to enlist the more prosperous property-owning groups as well as the poor, and with evident success. "The beauty of this program," said a neighborhood leader, "is that it does not divide the community by income." Another put it this way: "People work together in model cities that wouldn't work together in community action. The welfare family and the family next door that owns its own home are now talking to one another. Model cities has even pulled some new people into community action."

The new model cities organizations were formed in several ways. In some cases, existing neighborhood groups were allowed to designate representatives to a central body, but usually this pattern was not acceptable as sufficiently open and representative. In some cases, regular municipal election processes were used. The most common pattern, however, was a series of subneighborhood open meetings, which might choose their representatives at large or by smaller areas or blocks. The community action agency frequently took responsibility for organizing the meetings, distributing the publicity, and promoting attendance. And the leaders of CAA groups often emerged as the leaders of the new model cities organization. The community organization staff of the CAA might also be a source of technical advice to the leaders of the new model neighborhood resident organization. "The CAA ran our meetings from the sidelines for the first eight months or so," said a dissident member of a model neighborhood board. "They coached our chairman on every move he made." But often new groups of leaders emerged. In one city, said its CAA director, "the people rejected by the CAA crowd are the new force." And a former CAA official in another community commented: "All our resident leaders in model cities came out of community action— either the defeated candidates in the CAA elections, or the winners."

As the planning period began, the first problem both for the newly elected neighborhood leaders and for the professional staffs of the CDA and other participating agencies was to establish a mutually satisfactory citizen-professional relationship. Where the neighborhood residents won formal or de facto control of the planning process, the basis of the relationship, at least, was clear—the residents were in charge. In one such city, for instance, the CDA director laid down an explicit policy: "The professional staff will work only in a technical capacity. The ideas for the area will come from the citizens living in the area. They will be studied and details will be worked out with the residents by the city professionals."

But in most cities the struggle for power and influence went on throughout the planning period and the ground rules governing joint participation often remained ambiguous. Were the meetings to be scheduled on the initiative of the residents to give direction to CDA staff, or by the staff when it felt the need of consultation? Were the residents to take the lead in suggesting projects for review by the staff, or vice versa? Sometimes a relationship of equality was postulated, with residents and professionals working together as individuals on committees and task forces with designated chairmen. Sometimes the CDA director and staff openly took the initiative; in other cases, the residents were given the impression that the plan was to be theirs and the role of the professional staff was essentially to help them assemble it.

But the residents were necessarily slow in getting started.[19] The leadership was untried, the members diffident, the task overwhelming, the meetings long and tortuous and marked by parliamentary tangles. The resident organizations were troubled by what might have been an excess of democracy; they consulted elaborately in subneighborhood meetings, and in many cities membership on committees was open to all residents who wished to join. (HUD encouraged, even at times insisted upon, open committees.) Communication was difficult; one CDA director remarked that residents and professional staff often emerged from meetings with quite divergent impressions of what had happened. The professionals fretted over the delays, and the residents were resentful if the staff moved ahead independently.

Finally, as the end of the twelve-month planning period approached (and, at the same time, a possible change in national administrations that might alter the prospects for the program), the professionals frequently took matters into their own hands in order

19. While this discussion is centered upon relationships in cities with bicameral systems where the CDAs had not come under resident control (either unified or city hall oriented structures, as set forth earlier), it is clear that many of the same problems of resident-professional relationships exist in cities where the residents have formal or de facto control of the planning process. Relationships between resident groups and their advocacy planning staffs present analogous difficulties, too, as in any organization of laymen that employs professionals; questions of the balance of authority and actual power, and of effective layman participation and control, are always present.

that the mammoth product could be put on paper before the end of the year in a form satisfactory to HUD. The shift of responsibility away from the resident representatives was especially remarked upon in about half of the cities in our small sample. In two of them, indeed, volunteer consultants were called in—in one case from a university, in the other from a major industry—to add manpower and skill in the compilation stage. The processing job alone was enormous: Atlanta's plan, for example, comprised 78 specific projects for which supplementary funds were sought for the first year, in addition to many not requiring such funds, and the presentation filled 828 solidly packed pages of description and budget detail. If the plans were to reach HUD in time for action before the planning year (and the Johnson administration) expired, there was not time to review those pages, line by line, with the citizens' organization (or, for that matter, with city departments, budget officers, and other responsible officials). Resident groups that had thought of themselves as the responsible initiators of the plan found themselves reduced to a responding and legitimizing role at best—and that not always systematically.

A resident leader expressed one citizen's reaction:

What has many in the neighborhood so irritated is that you squander your valuable time in committee meetings and board meetings and neighborhood meetings night after night and get the residents' views and feed them into the staff and when the document comes out you can hardly recognize any of those ideas in it. I received my copy of the document at 1:00 p.m. on the day that the policy board met at 2:00 p.m. to give final approval to it on its way to the city council. Some of the members got their copies even later than that. We approved it without any of the members having had a chance to read it. And the executive committee of the neighborhood organization approved it only after it had already gone through the policy board.

Despite the time pressures and all the other problems of resident-professional relationships, the contribution of the residents to the model cities process was significant. CDA professionals credited the residents with originating many of the most innovative specific proposals—community education activities, resident-controlled health centers, recreation projects, youth programs, new types of training programs, new bus routes and other transportation services, ghetto entrepreneurship schemes, and many others. Residents had substantial impact upon the planning of neighborhood facilities and programs, such as neighborhood centers, that might be initiated by professionals. And they had a strong voice in determination of priorities among the approved projects. The relative contributions of the residents and the professionals could not be calculated with any accuracy (and the skill of a CDA professional, no doubt, is to make *his* contribution appear to have been the residents' own), but in the cities where the residents had been organized from the outset to participate in the planning, they themselves at least felt they had been influential—and the CDA staffs invariably agreed that they had been. And where the residents had been squeezed partially or wholly out of the planning process in its closing days, they appeared to be intent on reestablishing their prerogatives as the program entered its second year, and the CDA staffs conceded at least the principle.

Moreover, the influence of the resident organizations extended beyond the specific projects proposed for federal assistance in the model cities program. Model cities was to mobilize not just federal programs but state and local resources, both public and private, as well. Part of the struggle for control was centered upon the neighborhood's right to approve or veto regular city or state activities—urban renewal plans, freeway routes, school building plans and sites, rezoning actions, and so on. In many—perhaps most—participating cities, that right was openly or tacitly granted. In one city, for example, the residents used the model cities machinery as the means of forcing the city to reconsider a rezoning action that would have concentrated high-rise apartments in one section of the model neighborhood. In another they blocked a proposed freeway. In still another they got housing inspection suspended. Street, sidewalk, playground, and even sewer construction plans were formally submitted by the city departments for review and inclusion in the model cities plans. Urban renewal was, for the first time, subject to neighborhood review: "Under this program we're seeing to it that when they clear a block or two they put up other structures and give the people a chance to move right back in," said a neighborhood organization chairman.

Finally, the whole tone of resident-city relationships appeared often to have been changed. Said a resident leader:

They're not doing anything now without consulting us since model cities came in. That's quite a change. We used to not know what the city was doing until it was all over with. They'd just come in and tear your house down.

But now they're beginning to listen to what the people have to say and to cope with the ideas the people have. We used to not be able to get to anybody in city hall. But now we can reach anyone in city hall. We don't even need to make appointments—we just drop in.

Another leader may have given the essential reason: "We had the biggest mass meeting ever held in this part of the city. They have to respect us: There are hundreds of votes here."

COORDINATION OF PUBLIC AND PRIVATE AGENCIES

Just as patterns of resident participation vary widely from city to city, so do patterns of participation of public and private agencies— and the latter reflect the former. The early rhetoric of model cities implied a common planning effort by many agencies—"social and construction agencies would join in a massive common effort" that would "join together all available talent and skills," the President had said. But the architects of the model cities program had not foreseen the struggle for control between the residents and the city government, and where that struggle became intense the resulting tension precluded an open, harmonious communitywide planning process.

In only four of the nine cities we studied in 1969 had the mayor, or the city demonstration agency acting for him, mobilized on the mayor's own authority the planning resources of the community's official and private agencies. In the other five—where the CDA was under resident control, in law or in fact, or the CDA director was seeking to identify himself with the neighborhood rather than the official establishment—the plan was looked upon as something to be developed in the neighborhood and presented *to* the city, not something to be produced in equal partnership. That did not mean that the assistance of the community's array of agencies was not sought, but it was enlisted on a highly selective basis and at the initiative of the residents.

One CDA director who identified with his neighborhood rather than city hall explained:

We don't think the agencies can be there [in the planning process] if we want to change them. The city government is an ogre in the people's minds. We invited the school board out but they refused to talk desegregation. Some of the agencies came in-house and worked, but most of them just wanted to review what we came up with.

In contrast, the CDA director in a community that did organize a communitywide planning process described that city's approach:

Every facet of our program was worked on by some existing agency, but we insisted that everybody working on the program be assigned to this office and report here. We put everybody under one roof—not in separate cubicles but in one big cubicle. That way, we were able to organize interdisciplinary teams at the beginning and not compartmentalize the work until later. Lower-echelon personnel like the interdisciplinary approach. Thirty-seven people were detailed here, in all. The social planners gladly accepted the challenge to move into the community and work. The physical planners were more reluctant.

Still a third approach was the outright delegation of responsibility for preparation of particular segments of the plan from the CDA to other agencies, such as the school board or the community's health and welfare council. If the mayor or CDA director suggested, for example, that the board of education assign some of its planners to the city demonstration agency, the school superintendent might make a counteroffer: rather than subordinate his organization to that of a bureaucratic rival, he would take responsibility himself for the education plan. If the mayor, in order to get cooperation of the school district and other independent groups, agreed to a system of delegation of responsibility, then the planning process could be fragmented instead of integrated. And often the delegate agency did not enlist widespread cooperation of other groups; sometimes what were intended to be task force operations turned out to be "one-man shows." Delegation to consultants was another form of fragmentation, particularly in smaller cities.

"The big mistake here at the outset was that the city would not debureaucratize in order to make an actual model cities agency," a CDA staff officer commented. "It would not even insist that the planners be located physically together." However, as that CDA entered its second year of planning, the issue was to be raised again.

Differences in the planning process inevitably lead to differences in the character of the model cities plans. While generalized comparisons of those massive and complex documents are hazardous, it is apparent that where the plan was the product of agency-detailed staff, the project proposals were, in the main, for agency-operated programs; and where the residents and the CDA tightly controlled the planning process, the emphasis in the plan was upon resident-controlled or CDA-operated activities. The former looked, to some extent, like the product of "logrolling"; each of the participating agencies got "a piece of the action" in the form of supplemental funds to extend services into the model neighborhood or expand them there. The latter, on the other hand, had the appearance of "empire building"; new corporations and other organizations of many kinds were planned to undertake economic activities, provide social and educational services, and so on.

To the extent that the established agencies of the community were invited to participate, they responded willingly and often enthusiastically. Few of them opposed in principle the notion of comprehensive and coordinated planning. The mayor could instruct city departments to cooperate; the other agencies did not decline his invitation—not with the prospect of extra federal funds as the reward for a year of planning effort, and with the danger that if they did not accept responsibility some rival agency would.

However the model cities plans were drafted, they did achieve a substantial degree of coordination in the sense of interrelating projects and activities. Almost all of them proposed some form of multipurpose center or "one-stop service," often more than one, and sometimes supplemented by subneighborhood outreach centers. New forms of integrated health services were designed, and related to educational and other services. Day care centers, child care programs, and childhood education programs, including Head Start, were to be linked or combined. Schools were to be opened for community activities. Concentrated employment programs (CEPs) were to be located in or adjacent to the CDA offices or centers. So, in some cases, were "little city halls." One CDA staff member described a foster home project that involved two churches, the welfare department, and the juvenile court system, and observed: "These projects that involve four or five different agencies just don't happen by themselves. There has to be a coordinating mechanism to make them happen—a mechanism with authority. Authority comes with funding, and with the influence that comes from top federal levels."

During the first year, coordination of project proposals was hampered by the time pressure under which the CDAs worked. Functional task forces worked independently, particularly in those cities where leadership had been delegated to other agencies, and the use of consultants further complicated the integrating process. In the implementation phase, when the pressure of the initial planning period would be removed, CDA staffs were looking forward to eliminating duplication among their projects, consolidating individual programs into multipurpose centers, and otherwise integrating their total plans.

Those who find shortcomings in the coordination processes are wont, currently, to place the blame upon the mayors. The program, after all, was to be theirs. Where they abdicated and turned the program over to the neighborhood residents, where they let the city demonstration agency slip out of the city's official family and become an advocate organization, where they delegated large segments of the program to agencies independent of city hall, the fault was theirs, the critics argued.

"My problem is that there is virtually no political leadership in the program," a CDA director told us. "My stature in the community and that of my office are not sufficient. We don't carry the weight of official leadership." A HUD official concurred: "The program cannot work effectively without local executive leadership and muscle. And in many cities we are not getting it." A municipal consultant added: "There is not enough involvement of mayors and department heads with clout to achieve coordination."

A mayor's handicaps, of course, are clear. In a particular community, the city government may be only one of half a dozen independent governments—coexisting with the county, the school district, the housing authority, the redevelopment authority, and perhaps a community college district, a port authority, or a transit commission. "We must recognize," commented a federal official, "that we are asking the cities to undo fifty years of work by supporters of good government, who succeeded in isolating important areas of government from the influence of the chief executive and the 'evils' of partisan politics." Municipal governments are thus limited in outlook; they have been responsible for the city's physical planning—its streets, utilities, and parks—but have had little to do with social planning. Education, welfare, rehabilitation, correction, job training, employment—these have been state, county, or independent school district functions. And even within a city government, the mayor's powers may be strictly limited; in "weak mayor" cities, the city departments may operate under independent boards or commissions and the legislative body may play a large role in day-to-day administration.

Mayors may—and do—hail the prospect of using model cities as the means of bringing all of the independent satrapies of community government into a coordinated whole under the mayor's own control. But the other agencies are bound to look upon it with suspicion, for the same reason. And the public will not necessarily be on the mayor's side. Some of our interviewees pointed out that "city hall is not trusted either" and that whatever a mayor does is liable to be tinged with personal and partisan political considerations. The experience of community action is once again instructive: the CAAs did not encounter many difficulties while they were in the planning and organizing phase; it was only after they began to operate and to aggressively challenge other community institutions that they ran into trouble. In that sense, model cities is yet to be tested.

Yet it has begun, obviously, in a much stronger position. Not only the political and governmental wing of the city's power structure—as represented in the mayor—but its civic and business elements as well have been attracted to the model cities concept. Even though the program was, like the war on poverty, part of President Johnson's Great Society, and even though it was passed only narrowly over Republican opposition in the Congress, it did not arouse the partisan resistance in the communities that the community action agencies encountered—and perhaps this, too, could be traced to the legitimizing influence of the mayor's central role. "When I was called to a meeting in the regional office of HUD, every important person in the city went with me," the mayor of a middle sized city remarked. "This program has given us the platform we have needed to bring everybody together to solve our problems through a coordinated attack." And a planning consultant observed: "Model cities has brought people from the establishment in, and forced them to realize the fact that there are poor people in this city." The head of an industrial development corporation expressed enthusiasm about his forthcoming role in planning the business and job development elements of his city's plan.

Where the model cities planning was undertaken primarily by persons identified with urban renewal—"just an evolution of urban renewal," was one planner's phrase for model cities—the new program gained from the general popularity within the establishment (if not the neighborhood) of the older program. Said a civic leader of a middle sized community:

Urban renewal is respected here. It grew slowly and carefully. It is looked upon as a local program. It has had at least the grudging support of the local newspaper. It is bipartisan. It has been sold over the years through the structure of advisory committees and through innumerable public meetings where individual projects have been explained and hashed out. Model cities is looked on as an extension of the urban renewal approach, and it will be able to build upon the general acceptance of urban renewal in the city.

The model cities program gained acceptance, too, from its slow and cautious start. The CDAs did not, as was said of the CAAs, "rush forward like a panzer platoon" in order to show results before the next session of Congress convened; instead, they would spend a year in planning. They were able to build their administrative operations slowly, relying heavily on personnel detailed from other agencies and taking more time to recruit and screen applicants for permanent positions. And the relative security of city employment may have made recruitment easier.

"I'm a firm believer in moving slowly," said a CDA director. "We learned in urban renewal that it's impossible to plan a project of any size in less than twelve months. That's where community action got into trouble in our town; they tried to do too much too quickly. Not enough time was spent talking to people and explaining the program."

By starting out as part of city government, moreover, the model city agencies were subject to the cities' systems of internal control in their purchasing, accounting, and personnel procedures, and had access to the cities' central services. This could hinder as well as expedite, of course, but it appeared likely to protect city agencies against some of the administrative blunders that tainted community action in many places durings its early months.

Finally, model cities may have been more favorably received than community action because the program was enacted before, rather than after, the riots of 1965 and 1966. The antagonism of the black poor toward the "establishment" was not so visible when the war on poverty was declared, and the CAAs could well appear as agencies intent on stirring up trouble where none existed. By the end of 1966 the country's latent racial hostility in the cities had exploded with blinding visibility, and model cities was advanced at a time when it could appear as a possible solution—not a cause.

On the whole, however, while civic and business leaders might look favorably upon the model cities program, they were not heavily involved. In the struggle for control between the city and the neighborhood the nonpolitical elements of the power structure were generally pushed aside. Some observers feared that the support of these powerful groups depended on some degree of genuine participation, and that if left outside the process they could be alienated from model cities as they had been alienated from community action. This was, however, still a fear; as of early 1969, we saw little evidence that this had happened.

But auguries of impending difficulties in relationships with other agencies were apparent. "The board of education came into the program because they saw us as a source of federal funds," a CDA planner told us. "Now they see we're not a source of quick, easy money, and the slowdown will be coming in a year or two." In one city the CDA and the city planning office collided. The city demonstration agency had assumed that its planning was exempt from the city's master plan and proceeded freely to plan its own neighborhood. But, said the city planners, a city cannot have two official land-use plans covering the same area, and they launched a move to have the CDA charter rewritten to require that its plans be cleared through the city planning office before submission to the city council. Even of the relatively slow-moving CDAs, an observer could comment: "There's been too much speed at the expense of dialogue with agencies that have felt threatened." Community action agencies, in particular, felt threatened—or even superseded. In some cities, agencies fretted at having been bypassed when the plan went forward from the CDA to the mayor and city council. It was even reported that some agencies were deliberately steering their special projects into areas other than the model neighborhood in order to escape coordination.

The weakest link in the whole coordinating structure, however, is the state. Governors were irritated at the outset when they were given no role in the model cities program; applications from the cities did not flow through them, and they were given no voice in the selection. It was not until after the participating cities had been chosen that teams of federal officials, led by HUD, made formal calls upon the governors to explain the program.

It was up to the cities, then, to enlist the participation of the states and, once more, success varied. If the state had an office or department of urban or community affairs, communication at least was easy. But most did not.[20] "I know the state should be brought in," said a CDA official, "but our state is rurally oriented throughout the bureaucracy, and there's really nobody to talk to except in individual departments. We have brought welfare and labor in; elsewhere we have been less successful." Said a mayor, complaining about a pending action that the state was refusing to clear through the model cities planning structure: "Model cities means nothing in our state capital." Some employment service local offices were never effectively brought into participation, because they had not received instructions from their state headquarters.

But some cities had made little systematic effort to enlist the states—even in states that had strong departments of community affairs. Where the planning operations were neighborhood-centered, in particular, the selective invitation process excluded state agencies as well as local ones. "In our case, there was no open invitation to state agencies to participate," a state official said of one city's operation. "The agencies that participated were those that invited themselves in; those who waited to be invited are still waiting. And to this date the state has not been asked for official comment on the city's plan [which had been submitted to HUD six weeks earlier]." In such instances the states' views were apt to be expressed through federal agencies during the federal review—the employment service through the Labor Department, the state health, education, and welfare agencies through HEW, and so on. The state's veto, at least, could be made effective, but its opportunity to make a constructive contribution was limited.

Where the states were given an early opportunity to participate, that contribution could be significant. At the instance of the mayor of Seattle, for example, Governor Daniel Evans set up an interagency team that met monthly with the CDA during the planning period. As a result, several of the state agencies put money in their budgets for model cities projects, and the governor asked the legislature for $500,000 as a lump sum. But this was the exception rather than the rule. "The states were brought in far too late, and we missed two whole cycles of budgets and state plan amendments in most states," commented a federal official. In the 1969 fiscal year, 90 percent of

20. At the end of 1966, seven states had such offices or departments. During 1967, ten were added, and three more in 1968.

HEW's money is expended through the states—$6.4 billion in all— while the department has less than $200 million in discretionary funds that can be set aside for model cities. Any concentration of HEW money in model cities areas depends, therefore, upon tapping moneys that are expended under state control. Yet, in the absence of state participation, those who drafted model cities plans did not necessarily know how to design their projects so as to qualify for categorical grants, and the program did not "milk the categories" as intended—relying, instead, on the limited supplemental funds at HUD's disposal for programs within the general sphere of HEW.

A state official summed up the coordination problem that had been faced by community action—and would now be faced by model cities—in these words:

> The reach of the community action agencies has been a money-giving reach, and it extends only as far as their money extends. In order for the CAAs to coordinate health or welfare activities the governor would have to say to the state health or welfare department, "You are going to be coordinated by OEO." The governors have issued no such orders—and neither have the mayors.
>
> For the model city organizations to fill the coordinating role that the CAAs have not been able to fill, they will have to be sanctioned. The governors and mayors will have to give them more clout than they can get through a brokerage role alone. I am not at all sure they will be given the necessary sanction.

A Model for Urban Coordination

The experience of both community action and model cities has defined the goals to be sought in designing a structure for coordinating, at the community level, the attack on the problems of the urban slums.

The initial goal must be the simply conceived objective of program coordination that gave rise to both the community action and model cities mechanisms and that was expressed in almost identical rhetoric in launching both: the mobilization of available resources— federal, state, and local, public and private—in a comprehensively planned, concerted assault on the problems of an urban community; the combination of hitherto fragmented programs and approaches in new and creative ways. The problems that led to the demand for coordination are real ones, and the values of program integration, of comprehensive planning, and of resource mobilization are also real, and significant—recognizing that over-coordination may theoretically be detrimental but is hardly likely to be attained. But beyond the simple goal of program coordination are other objectives that were barely recognized in the Economic Opportunity Act and not much more fully acknowledged in the model cities legislation but that rose to prominence, or even dominance, as soon as the acts began to be administered. These are the objectives surrounding the concept of citizen participation.

As we were told over and over again, in our field interviews, the old ways of community decision making are dead—programs and services designed by experts and accepted by the power structure can no longer be offered unilaterally to the poor, nor decisions by the "establishment" imposed upon them. Planning must henceforth be carried on, in the words of the model cities guidelines, *with* as well as *for* the residents of low-income areas. And so must program execution. The demands of the poor—particularly the Negroes and Mexican-Americans—for status and participation in decision making have compelled acceptance of the new philosophy. But the aim is not just to satisfy minority demands. It is also to get better plans, by blending more points of view, and to use the planning and coordinating processes as means for developing leadership in low-income neighborhoods and individual and collective competence for problem solving. In the process, latent conflict is brought into the open. That is inevitable, but the conflict can be made to be useful, too—if effective means are provided for ordering and resolving it. The mechanisms of coordination, then, should be designed to encourage self-expression, and self-assertion, by the poor—yet channel and contain the resultant controversy and ultimately harmonize the interests and demands of the poor with the needs and responsibilities of the larger community.

What should be the structure? The federal government has tried two models. In community action it designed a mechanism that proved adept at defining and sharpening conflicts but unsuited to resolving them, and not suited either for communitywide coordination. It then conceived another structure—model cities—that is now being tested as a coordinator and as a means both for the development and expression of conflicting views and for their mediation and reconciliation. We see no reason to devise still a third approach. As originally conceived in broad outline, the model cities structure is probably as well designed on paper as a system can be for serving the several goals that are sought—coordination, participation, and conflict resolution.

We recommend, therefore, that the federal government as a whole—and state and local governments as well—accept the model cities structure as the basic scheme for coordinating program planning and execution in urban slum areas. In making this recommendation we do not contend that the validity of the model cities concept has by any means been fully proven through experience in the first one hundred and fifty cities. We argue only that the *potential* of the program has been demonstrated, if one looks at all the hopeful portents; and national policy—in relation to a flexible program such as this one—can be made on the basis of potential.

In a sufficient number of cities to prove its potential, model cities *has* provided the means for bringing together, in a single coordinated plan, programs for physical reconstruction, economic development, and improvement of social services—a range "as broad as the life of the city." It *has* enlisted on an unprecedented scale the cooperative efforts of the public and private agencies that have talent and resources to contribute. It *has* provided a structure within which a city's elected officials can exert energetic leadership in attacking the city's ills. It *has* mobilized an extraordinary degree of resident participation in the formation and execution of plans to attack the deep-seated problems of slum neighborhoods—despite the difficulties of organizing participation in the initial year. And, at the same time that it has encouraged self-assertion by the poor—and hence confrontation with the established agencies—it *has* required the resolution of conflict as a condition to the continuance of the program; ultimately, an agreed plan must and does go forward.

While the preceding pages have pointed to many shortcomings of the program in individual cities in its first two years of operation, these do not necessarily reflect weaknesses in conception. There are many mitigating circumstances: the time pressures under which the plans were prepared; the absence of doctrine and tradition for so complex a coordinating process; the shortage of personnel trained and experienced in anything like the activities that had to be quickly organized; and all of the pains that accompany the establishment of radically new institutional and interpersonal relationships. Given such circumstances, the plans that were produced were creditably imaginative and innovative. If the model cities program is judged by comparison with the coordinating processes that were previously employed, rather than by a standard of perfection, it can be appraised as reasonably successful in its initial shakedown year and as demonstrating great promise as the central coordinating mechanism for urban programs.

If the model cities structure did not exist, something very much like it would have to be invented. The objectives sought to be achieved through model cities—coordination, participation, conflict resolution—must be achieved somehow. Facing these needs in 1965, a presidential task force followed a chain of reasoning that led to the model cities concept, which the President and the Congress reviewed and accepted. Had they not done so—in 1965 or subsequently—then some task force in 1969, facing the same needs, would in all likelihood follow the same chain of reasoning and come out with the same coordination model. On paper, the model cities scheme is difficult to improve upon. And no one has presumed to do so; no alternative general model that serves the same purposes of coordination has been advanced.

If one accepts those purposes, then the question of whether the model cities program as a whole has worked as intended—or the extent to which it has worked—is, to a large degree, irrelevant. The model cities scheme is a highly flexible one, as the preceding pages have surely shown. Within the basic concept several types and subtypes of structures have evolved—with as many variations as there are participating cities. To recommend that the model cities structure be accepted is not much more than to stress the need for a coordinating device of some kind—and one that will assure a mutually agreed upon relationship between the city and the neighborhood residents in the planning and coordination processes. The exact form of that relationship, and the exact nature of the planning and coordination processes, are left to be worked out in each participating city. The basic structure leaves plenty of room for the modification of those relationships and processes, and their improvement, as experience is gained. The object should be to get on with the experience.

What can be said, so far, about what experience has shown? We conclude that, if model cities is to serve all of its purposes in a community, three conditions are essential:

First, the model cities mechanism must be a reasonably balanced bicameral structure. This principle rules out, on the one hand (as HUD has virtually done in its guidelines), the unicameral schemes in which individual residents are co-opted into a city-organized planning structure without direct accountability to the neighborhood citizenry at large. Such arrangements defeat the objective of widespread participation by the neighborhood residents. On the other hand, the principle also rules out those structures that are overbalanced in the opposite direction—those where the neighborhood dominates the process to the exclusion of effective leadership and coordination by city hall. That type of structure defeats the purpose of mobilizing the participation of the community's public and private agencies. To define these two types of unbalanced structures as unsatisfactory is not to deny the merit of flexibility. There is still room for great variation in individual patterns—so long as the dual purposes of resident participation and central coordination are achieved. To restore the balance in the case of the unicameral structures, it is necessary only for a city to foster the formation of a representative neighborhood organization, or recognize an existing one, and admit it into partnership—as most unicameral cities are now doing under HUD pressure. To rectify the imbalance in the case of the resident-dominated structures, it is not necessary even to bring the CDA back to city hall; it is enough to create there a compensating mechanism that will perform the coordination and review functions that the city demonstration agency abandoned when it cast its lot with the residents.

Second, the city demonstration agencies and the neighborhood resident organizations must be nonoperating. The experience of the community action agencies, and that of many other bodies at all levels of government, confirms that the functions of planning and coordination of a wide range of activities are incompatible with operating responsibility for a segment of those activities. Some model cities plans now contemplate that city demonstration agencies and neighborhood resident organizations shall undertake program operations on an extensive scale. To do so would surely impair their effectiveness as coordinators. In the first place, major responsibility for operating innovative programs would bring pressing day-to-day demands upon the CDA and neighborhood organization leadership that would absorb their energies and divert their attention from planning and coordination. In the second place, coordination, to be effective, must be undertaken by a *neutral* agency: a central responsibility of the CDA and the neighborhood organization is the allocation of resources among competing operating agencies, and the authority of the allocator will be undermined if he is also one of the competitors for responsibility and funds—the umpire in a ball game does not wear the uniform of one of the competing teams. Some of the projects proposed in model cities plans may be, of course, outside the jurisdiction or competence of any of the existing agencies in the community—but in those cases new organizations should be formed independent of the CDA and the neighborhood representation structure.

Third, the representative character of the neighborhood resident organizations must be rigorously protected. A common criticism of neighborhood community action groups, during our survey, was that they were no longer representative—interest and participation had dropped off and small cliques had obtained control, and the cliquishness had further discouraged participation, in a vicious circle. This tendency is inherent in voluntary associations; it is observed in local political party organizations and private civic groups of many kinds. The neighborhood resident organizations set up in the model cities program have sometimes had phenomenal participation in their initial elections (Cambridge, Massachusetts, claimed a turnout of 40 percent of the eligible residents; Winston-Salem, 29 percent), but the leaders of such organizations, also, have considerable incentive to reduce participation. A spreading of participation, after all, means the spreading of power and influence—including such patronage as the neighborhood organization may command. The CDA and the city's political leadership must recognize that they cannot afford to entrust to the neighborhood leaders the sole responsibility for maintaining widespread resident participation.

WIDENING THE APPLICATION OF THE MODEL

If the model cities mechanism is to be accepted and developed as the solution to the coordination problem in the designated neighborhoods in the one hundred fifty cities so far participating, then logic suggests that the same approach is needed just as strongly and would be equally useful in other neighborhoods of similar character.

While cities generally chose their worst slum areas for the benefits of the program, they by no means covered all of their poor and deteriorating neighborhoods. Originally, many cities drew far more inclusive boundaries for their model neighborhoods than those that were finally fixed; when HUD set the limits at 10 percent of a city's population or 15,000 persons, whichever was larger, the cities were forced to exclude areas that needed, and had anticipated getting, model cities assistance. In some communities, considerable political jockeying went into the selection of the model neighborhood and the drawing of its boundaries. Ever since, mayors and other elected officials have been highly sensitive to the danger of charges of favoritism in the treatment of the chosen neighborhoods.[21]

As the benefits of the program begin to be visible—not only the physical refurbishing of neighborhoods but the new patterns of citizen participation in policy making—other areas can be expected to press their demands for equal treatment, and local political groups can be expected to stir up such demands and to exploit them. The task force that proposed model cities as a "demonstration" program may have seen its purpose as the testing of a theory, but the people in the cities have not embraced it because they are intrigued by theory—they hope, and expect, to get substantial tangible benefits. And for a city to discriminate among neighborhoods indefinitely in the distribution of benefits is untenable. The implication in any demonstration program is that once its merit has been shown, it will be extended generally to the eligible population—if not, why was it being "demonstrated" in the first place? And the same considerations that suggest the extension of the program's coverage within cities suggest also, of course, its extension to other cities—and to nonurban areas as well, a subject that is discussed in later chapters. The demand is already being heard for a third round of model cities to bring the benefits to more communities.

The most telling obstacle to extension of the program's coverage, of course, is that of cost. To some extent, what kind of coordinating structure should be created and how much federal assistance should

21. On April 28, 1969, HUD Secretary Romney announced that in order to give local officials "greater latitude in drawing program boundaries that conform to local conditions" the 10 percent limitation on the neighborhood would be dropped. He explained that the action did not mean the program would be expanded citywide within each city.

be channeled through it are separable questions. A city could extend the comprehensive planning and neighborhood participation processes to all its low-income neighborhoods (or, for that matter, the entire city) and expand correspondingly the jurisdiction of the city demonstration agency with no increase in federal aid. The planning could cover all projects and programs to be financed from existing sources, including all of the categorical programs of federal and state aid. But the problem of discrimination in the distribution of benefits would be only more apparent, as supplemental model cities funds would be available to finance one area's plan but not those of the other areas. It is hardly likely that cities and states would themselves be able to make up the differences. Extension of the model cities process to additional neighborhoods—and, by the same token, to other cities—is not probable on any significant scale, then, without a corresponding expansion of federal assistance.

In their initial plans the participating cities have been required to submit five-year programs, specifying their costs. If HUD has totaled the fifth-year expenditure levels for the plans it has so far received, analyzed them for reasonableness, and then estimated from that sample the needs of all participating cities—and then additional neighborhoods and cities—the figures have not been released. When such computations are made, they will show, no doubt, that the government severely overcommitted itself on the very day that it enacted into law a measure inviting the nation's cities to begin planning seriously and concretely to transform their slums into "model neighborhoods." But the commitment was made, the cities accepted it in good faith, the planning is underway, and hope has been engendered. No doubt, ambitious plans will have to be cut back (what budget aspiration is ever honored in the full?) but in any case it is urgent that some realistic estimate be made of the scale of the government's present implied commitment to neighborhoods now in the model cities program and what the cost will be of providing equal treatment to additional neighborhoods and cities.

Once the estimates are made, the rate at which the model cities program can be extended geographically will depend in large part upon a central policy decision concerning the place of model cities in the whole structure of federal aid. The federal government is certain to make additional funds available year by year to help cities cope with the problems of their slum areas (as distinct from general aid that might be provided through some form of revenue sharing). The issue concerns the channels through which the funds will flow: Will they be offered to the cities through categorical programs of aid for narrowly defined purposes or through a kind of block grant—the model cities supplemental fund—that gives the cities wide latitude in its expenditure? We believe that the disadvantages of the narrow categorical grant approach have been amply demonstrated. As one CDA director put it: "The moneys available to a city under the categorical grant system are the amounts that happen to have been lobbied through Congress by people interested in the particular categories; the amounts that come out at the end of this lobbying process bear no necessary relation to the balance of money that the city needs." The model cities system allows the city—with the participation of the neighborhood and subject to ultimate federal review and approval—to distribute the supplemental funds according to what the community conceives to be the proper balance. But the model cities supplemental fund is, so far, relatively limited; the whole system is still heavily overweighted on the side of categorical assistance.

We recommend, therefore, that a basic decision be made by the President and the Congress to channel largely through the model cities supplemental appropriation the additional moneys made available to help cities cope with the problems of slum areas. With the additional funds the model cities program should be steadily expanded to cover additional neighborhoods and cities.

When the model cities structure is extended to additional neighborhoods, where should it stop? In theoretical model-building, a strong case can be made for eventual universal coverage. Comprehensive planning is needed for all neighborhoods, and the problem of coordination is a universal one. Several mayors, during our field interviews, told us that they saw in the model cities process the basis for developing a citywide system of planning and coordination that would ultimately encompass all federal, state, and local activities within the city limits.

The practical pressures for such a system of citywide coordination, however, are not great. The problems of program coordination that gave rise to the model cities experiment—like the community action experiment before it—arose primarily from the multiplicity of special programs that have been designed (or were being advocated) for slum areas. Urban renewal, low-income and moderate-income housing programs, community action programs, public welfare, the concentrated employment program, job training and adult basic education programs, the special programs for disadvantaged children under Title I of the Elementary and Secondary Education Act—these programs are virtually limited to poverty areas. It is in the communities of the poor, too, that the population is alienated from city hall and the demand is voiced for participation in the planning and execution of programs. Spokesmen for the affluent majority may advocate city-wide decentralization of particular functions—notably education—but they are not generally advocating the creation in their own areas of neighborhood organizations to undertake comprehensive planning on the model cities pattern. The majority, presumably, already has access to city hall—indeed control of it—and effective participation in the planning and administration of governmental programs.

It is the poor who have particular need for the model cities mechanism as their means to gain the same access and participation. Model cities coverage should extend, then, as far as the programs for the poor and the disadvantaged—which are the programs that need coordination—extend, and into as many neighborhoods beyond that (and identifying the best pattern of neighborhood boundaries will be difficult) as may demand participation in the comprehensive planning process. Once the model cities planning process is operative in those areas, the city government may find it advantageous to encompass the rest of the city in the comprehensive plan—perhaps with a more limited participation structure—in order to make the document all-inclusive. If such a citywide plan could then become the basis for a single block grant of federal supplemental funds, that would appear to be a highly desirable direction for the evolution of the model cities program. The implications of a broadened model cities coordinating process for the federal system as a whole are considered further in Chapter 7.

SOME IMPLICATIONS OF A MORE EXTENSIVE MODEL CITIES PROGRAM

Model cities is simultaneously both a centralizing and a decentralizing force. By bringing together into a single comprehensive process the planning that previously took place in the separate functional segments of the fragmented local structure, it opens the opportunity for a greater degree of central leadership and influence—specifically, the mayor's. But, at the same time, by creating a neighborhood-centered process, it decentralizes to the neighborhood level a portion of the decision-making responsibility previously exercised by citywide governmental institutions. As the coverage of model cities is extended to more neighborhoods, the effects of both the centralization and the decentralization will be increasingly significant.

On the former score, the consequence of the model cities program will be in the direction of reunifying local government. The mayor, in particular, will be strengthened. Looked to now as the first citizen of his community and its chosen leader, the mayor in a typical American city—assuming he chooses to try to lead—is frustrated by the independence of counties, school districts, state agencies, and various special districts and authorities, as well as by a city charter that, in all likelihood, divides executive responsibility among various elected officials and independent boards and commissions. Model cities puts the mayor in a new position of authority, as a kind of substitute for needed structural change. Plans for the schools, the county health and welfare activities, the state employment service, and all of the other governmental functions flow into his city demonstration agency for coordinated review—and plans that originate in the CDA or the neighborhood flow out to the agencies from his office. Eventually the functional plans are subject to his approval, for his is the signature on the document that goes to Washington. As the model cities process is extended, the relations between governmental units in the community will be altered in fundamental ways, all in the direction of reduced independence of the separate entities and an enhanced opportunity for central leadership by the mayor and his associates. In some cities the tradition of mayoral leadership is not developed, but even where it is most mayors do not now have the institutional mechanisms that are required. While the city demonstration agency is the key mechanism for the mayor's new coordinating and leadership role that grows out of model cities, experience may demonstrate the need for strengthening other elements in the mayor's office as well—particularly in those cases where the CDA, as noted earlier, has slipped out of the mayor's control and come under resident domination.

The implications of the decentralizing features of model cities are perhaps in the long run even more significant. The neighborhood-centered planning process gives to neighborhood organizations a degree of influence or control over the whole range of governmental functions. Where the structure is truly bicameral, something like a new level of government is created; the neighborhood organization becomes a legislative body, chosen through electoral processes (but so far without the official participation of party organizations), with power to raise money—not through taxes but through grants—and to control expenditures. The regular activities of local government are subjected to the planning process; the residents review proposals for rezoning, for urban renewal, for housing, for streets and highways, for economic development, and so on, with disagreements between the residents and the governmental agencies (and their supporting groups) reconciled through the negotiation processes of the balanced bicameral structure. And the residents initiate proposals for all kinds of innovations in the delivery of education, health, welfare, and manpower services, with assurance that their views will be heard and considered. Decentralization, at its best, can mean reinvigoration of the agencies that serve the poor, greater competition within the political system, and the development of new leadership for the poor. But it will inevitably be accompanied, at times, by the kind of ruckus that has developed over school decentralization in New York City.

The extent to which the city can defer to neighborhood opinion varies by function. It may be able to accept neighborhood control on local rezoning issues, for example, while to defer at all on the enforcement of an open housing ordinance would be to nullify the law. Each neighborhood cannot have its own freeway plan. Each cannot be the hospital center of the community. Salaries paid to the employees of neighborhood organizations need to be standardized in the interests of equity. The quality of public services among neighborhoods has to be equalized. For all these reasons, the various neighborhood plans under an extended model cities approach would have to be subjected to a central review process, involving negotiations and balancing of neighborhood and citywide interests, that would be incredibly complex in the case of the largest cities. The city demonstration agency itself as the central coordinator would find its role, presumably, as a kind of advocate—a defender of the neighborhood planning process against the centralizing tendencies of the rest of the city government. But its relations to the city budget office, the city planning office, and the other central staff agencies with whom it shared coordinating responsibilities would have to be carefully defined.

The role of the community action agency, when the model cities approach is extended to all of a city's poverty areas, would also have to be redefined. So far, the relations between CAAs and CDAs have often been strained and sometimes downright hostile. The conflict was inevitable—both have an advocacy function, both have program interests in the same fields, both have affiliate neighborhood organizations and compete for the allegiance of the same citizens. When model cities was instituted, the community action agencies felt threatened and downgraded. Their funds were being cut back and their support from Washington eroded at the very time that the CDAs were brought into being with far more money—in relation to the area to be served—and far more official backing. Small wonder that a CAA director, when he learned during our visit that his city's model cities application had been rejected, displayed open satisfaction.

Within the present model neighborhoods, some CAAs have been ignored by the CDAs, and some are cooperating fraternally. But the community action agency still has an unchanged role in the rest of the city. When the model cities process is extended to cover all the CAA "target areas," however, how would community action be affected? The answer—if the CDA and the neighborhood resident organizations remain nonoperational, as they should—is that the CAA would be affected very little. It would be one of the agencies that would participate in the model cities planning, and it or its neighborhood organizations (or corporations) would be among the operating organizations for projects contained in the plan. Beyond that, the CAA and its affiliates would have, as might be necessary, an independent role in community organization and advocacy. Pluralism in these functions, or at least the potential of pluralism, is desirable. The possibility is always present that a model cities neighborhood organization will be co-opted by the city government—which supplies its funds—or that it will become clique-ridden and lose its representative character. For that reason we question the wisdom of the HUD-OEO agreement that looks to eventual consolidation everywhere of CDA and CAA resident participation organizations.[22] A strong CAA with its own lines into each low-income neighborhood provides an additional safeguard of the resident participation element of the model cities concept. "There's got to be someone there to keep us honest," were the words of one CDA director, "and it has to be an agency with some trappings of status and staff. Remember that CDA directors came from agencies that have regarded the citizen as their enemy."

The extensive application of the model cities mechanism to urban neighborhoods would profoundly alter the character of the governmental process in American cities. The difficulties that would be introduced by the concept of city-neighborhood partnership would be considerable. Yet the demand for resident participation in the processes of government is not likely to subside—nor should it. The alienation of the urban poor, particularly the black poor, can be traced in large measure to feelings of powerlessness, of remoteness from government, of inability to influence the forces that control events. The model cities structure provides the most systematic means that has yet been conceived to bring the views of the individual urban citizen to bear upon the programs of his government and to coordinate his contribution with those of the administrators, the planners, and the other professionals who man the city's public and private agencies.

22. "Processes for Assuring That Model Cities Can Coordinate All OEO Assisted Programs That Affect Model Neighborhoods," HUD-OEO agreement transmitted to the President, Sept. 27, 1968.

CHAPTER FOUR

The Revival
of Rural America

RURAL AMERICA has been declining for many decades. In the 1950s, more than half the counties in the nation lost population, and the losers were predominantly rural. Most of the counties in the rural areas we visited had suffered a population loss in the 1940s as well, and many had been dwindling for a much longer period. Carroll County, New Hampshire, for example, had more residents when its first census was take in 1850 than it had in 1960. Susquehanna County, Pennsylvania, and Dawson County, Georgia, have shown net declines since 1860, and Butler and Hart counties, Kentucky, since 1880. Even in the more recently settled state of Minnesota, counties like Otter Tail, Pope, Swift, and Todd have populations smaller than they had in 1910 or 1920. As the mechanization of agriculture freed a large part of the rural labor force, the nonagricultural industries that were growing in employment were located for the most part in cities, large and small. So people moved out of rural America. During the 1950s, some 6.7 million moved from nonmetropolitan to metropolitan areas, and the movement has continued at a slower pace throughout the current decade.

Yet the heavy migration did not solve the rural areas' economic problems. Rural America, particularly the South and Appalachia and the Indian reservations, has the highest proportion of unemployed and underemployed people—as measured by the poverty statistics—in the nation. Data for 1967 show 23 percent of all households in rural areas outside metropolitan counties living in poverty, and 19 percent in smaller cities and towns outside major metropolitan areas.

130

The corresponding figures are 16 percent for the metropolitan central cities and 9 percent for their suburbs.[1] The economic stagnation of rural America is visible in the shabbiness of small towns and trading centers and reflected in the demoralization and pessimism of much of the rural leadership.[2]

Responding to the appeal of the declining areas for help, the national government for the last dozen years has been groping toward a policy of intervention to stimulate the economic growth of rural areas. This effort—like the corresponding effort to cope with the problems of the cities—has involved a multiplicity of programs and agencies. In the rural areas as in the urban slums, the objective of community development has been seen to require a coordinated, multifunctional approach—the preparation and adoption of comprehensive plans for attacking simultaneously a wide range of community shortcomings; the mobilization of the resources of many agencies, public and private, federal, state, and local; new leadership and more extensive citizen participation; and for all these reasons, new devices for governmental organization at the community level. In short, the problems of organizing for development are as strikingly similar in deteriorating rural and urban areas as the settings are different.

Perhaps to an even greater degree than in the urban slums, however, rival federal agencies in the rural areas have presented separate and conflicting schemes for community organization and even less presidential-level attention has been paid to resolving the conflicts. The Department of Agriculture has promoted several kinds of organizational structures at the community level; the Department of Commerce and the Appalachian Regional Commission have other approaches, and so, most recently, has the Department of Housing and Urban Development (HUD). The Office of Economic Opportunity (OEO) has sponsored its community action agencies (discussed in Chapter 2). In addition, the states, most notably Georgia, have developed schemes of organization that may or may not be consistent with one or more of the varied federal schemes.

1. "The Annual Report of the Council of Economic Advisers," in *Economic Report of the President, January 1969*, p. 153.
2. Joseph P. Lyford has captured the dispirited mood of a small town and its rural hinterland in *The Talk in Vandalia* (Center for the Study of Democratic Institutions, 1962). See also, Arthur J. Vidich and Joseph Bensman, *Small Town in Mass Society: Class, Power, and Religion in a Rural Community* (Princeton University Press, 1968).

This chapter traces the history of the federal schemes, and that of the state of Georgia, for the creation of planning and coordinating bodies for rural (or, more accurately, nonmetropolitan) development. Chapter 5 summarizes our findings during our visits to the nonmetropolitan areas, and Chapter 6 proposes a model for coordination of developmental activities and intergovernmental relations in those areas.

The Agriculture Approach: Rural Areas Development

The efforts of the Department of Agriculture (USDA) to foster the formation of local planning and development bodies to prepare and carry out comprehensive programs aimed at economic growth can be dated from 1955, when President Eisenhower authorized establishment of a rural development program.

The new program was based upon the recommendations contained in an Agriculture Department study of the problems of low-income farm families. That study reported that a majority of all farm families were in the low-income category—3.3 million of a total of 5.4 million in 1950 had net cash income from all sources of less than $2,000 a year. These were the farmers the technological revolution in agriculture had passed by. Their holdings were small. Their farms were not mechanized. Their soil might be unproductive. They lacked credit resources and management skill. In short, they were a remnant of nineteenth century subsistence farming in the mid-twentieth century. Geographically, they were heavily concentrated in the old South—in a vast quadrangle stretching from the coastal plains of Virginia and the Carolinas westward through the Appalachians, the Mississippi Delta, and the Ozarks into Oklahoma and Texas—with outlying pockets in the upper Great Lakes states, northern New Mexico, and the mountain valleys of the Pacific Northwest.

Some of these low-income farmers, the report concluded, might be helped toward ultimate success as farmers. For others, off-farm employment was the only answer. In particular, young people growing up on farms should be educated and trained for nonfarm occupations.

For these several purposes the report proposed improvement of a number of programs and services in rural areas—credit programs, state employment services, vocational training, and health programs. It also suggested that pilot counties be selected to determine what might be accomplished through a concentrated effort by local leaders supported by intensified programs of technical assistance from the cooperative federal-state extension service and other agencies. In these localities, "county and community program development committees should be set up to consider the total problem of the area and what can be done about it."[3]

In the initial year, rural development committees were established in 51 counties and 3 multicounty areas in 24 states. By 1958 the number had grown to 100 counties in 30 states and by the time President Eisenhower left office some 350 counties in 39 states had either initiated rural development programs or were preparing to do so. "The initial pilot and demonstration phase of the Rural Development Program has been successful," the President said in his final statement on the subject. "The program can now be expanded and intensified."[4]

The rural development program "was envisioned as essentially a local program, organized and carried out by local leaders and resources."[5] Additional extension agents were assigned to act as advisers to local committees of farm, business, and civic leaders who analyzed the problems and resources of their communities, developed plans for improved use of those resources, identified specific developmental projects, and promoted the acceptance and execution of those projects.

The rural development programs generally centered upon agriculture and land use—improvement of agricultural productivity, introduction of new crops, establishment of processing facilities, improvement of marketing, improvement of timber management, and so on—but went beyond those areas. Industrial development "held a central place in the thinking of rural communities,"[6] and some of the committees moved actively into promotion of industrial develop-

3. U.S. Department of Agriculture, *Development of Agriculture's Human Resources: A Report on Problems of Low-Income Farmers* (April 1955), p. 17. General recommendations are listed on pp. 5–6.

4. Statement Upon Receiving Fifth Annual Report on Rural Development Program, Oct. 13, 1960, *Public Papers of the Presidents, 1960*, pp. 759–60.

5. Joseph C. Doherty, "A New Program for Better Living," *Land*, the 1958 yearbook of the Department of Agriculture, p. 377.

6. *Ibid.*, p. 379.

ment, or recreation and tourism, in cooperation with existing promotional groups where such had been organized.

It was anomalous that while President Eisenhower each year lauded the rural development program, he was adamant in insisting that rural areas be barred from sharing in the financial assistance contained in the then-pending area redevelopment bill, a measure specifically designed for fostering economic growth in areas that were lagging behind the rest of the country. When Senator Paul H. Douglas of Illinois and his Democratic colleagues extended their version of the "depressed areas" legislation in 1956 to include the poorest rural counties along with the distressed industrial areas for which the bill had been designed originally, the President found in that action only an additional reason for vetoing the bill. "The Rural Development Program and the Small Business Administration are already contributing greatly to the economic improvement of low-income rural areas," Eisenhower said in explaining one of his two vetoes of the bill. "Increasing the impact of these two activities, particularly the Rural Development Program, is a preferable course."[7]

FROM RD TO RAD

The Kennedy administration took both courses. Within a few weeks after taking office in 1961, the new secretary of agriculture, Orville L. Freeman, elevated rural development from an experimental innovation to a central objective of the department. When Freeman presented the administration's first comprehensive legislative program to the Congress, in February 1962, it was bound in a package labeled "ABCD"—the initials standing for abundance, balance, conservation, and *development*. The development objective Freeman defined as follows:

> We seek the maximum development of human resources and the renewal of rural communities, programs aimed at ending rural poverty, and at opportunities for education and employment that will extend

7. Veto of the Area Redevelopment Bill, May 13, 1960, *Public Papers of the Presidents, 1960*, p. 419. For an account of the political struggle over the area redevelopment issue, including the question of extending its benefits to rural areas, see James L. Sundquist, *Politics and Policy: The Eisenhower, Kennedy, and Johnson Years* (Brookings Institution, 1968), pp. 60–73, and Sar A. Levitan, *Federal Aid to Depressed Areas* (Johns Hopkins Press, 1964), pp. 1–28.

to people in every rural area in the Nation the advantage of a high, truly American standard of living.[8]

Rural development was rechristened "rural areas development," both to distinguish the Democratic program from its Republican predecessor and to make its initials—RAD—pronounceable.

To dramatize the new emphasis upon development and to provide leadership and coordination, the secretary created an office of rural areas development, a rural areas development board of department officials, and a public advisory committee.[9] The program was extended to all the rural counties of the nation, and the Federal Extension Service, working through the state extension services and their county agents, assumed the task of getting the RAD committees organized.

At the same time the administration supported making rural areas eligible to receive benefits under the Area Redevelopment Act, passed in 1961. The act earmarked half of its industrial loan funds, or $100 million, for smaller areas of "substantial and persistent unemployment or underemployment" outside the established labor market areas.[10] The smaller areas (which became known as section 5[b] areas) also were made eligible for public facility loans and grants.

As the area redevelopment bill was moving through Congress, the Department of Agriculture appealed to President Kennedy to support its claim for administrative responsibility for the program in section 5(b) areas. The Department of Commerce, which was to be the home of the new Area Redevelopment Administration, opposed such a division of responsibility. As umpire of the dispute, the Bureau of the Budget ruled in favor of Commerce but did work out an agreement whereby Commerce delegated to Agriculture responsibility for recommending designation of those section 5(b) counties "where they are essentially and fundamentally associated with agriculture and forestry." In those counties, which were termed "rural" development areas, Agriculture would provide technical assistance in the preparation of the "overall economic development programs"

8. *Food and Agriculture Act of 1962*, Hearings before the House Committee on Agriculture, 87 Cong. 2 sess. (1962), p. 34.
9. See David T. Stanley, *Changing Administrations* (Brookings Institution, 1965), pp. 91, 93.
10. The established labor market areas were those with labor forces over 15,000, of whom at least 8,000 were in nonagricultural occupations. A labor market area is usually a single county.

(OEDPs) required by the act, certify the OEDPs to Commerce, and review loan and grant proposals.[11] Most of the 657 counties initially designated under section 5(b) were classified as rural. Agriculture provided its assistance through its rural areas development structure. The RAD committee in each designated county took responsibility for preparing the OEDP, and the county extension agent, who normally served as secretary of the committee during its early months, often played the central role in assembling the document.

To the Area Redevelopment Administration, the RAD committees were known as "OEDP committees." ARA maintained a mailing list of all its OEDP committees, rural and urban alike, and on occasion communicated directly with the rural bodies. But ARA did not attempt to make the RAD committees its own. In the few instances where separate committees came into being in particular counties, the two departments succeeded in bringing about their consolidation, and the federal approach to the economic development of depressed rural areas remained a unified one under the leadership of Agriculture.

By the autumn of 1963, Secretary Freeman was able to report that rural development groups had been organized in two-thirds of the nation's counties, or 2,000 in all. "Over 65,000 people—local people—are actively working on problems of area development, creating new jobs, improved services, and developing natural resources," he said.[12] "The one essential characteristic of RAD," he said on another occasion, "is that while it provides technical and financial assistance ... the initiative for action must come from local groups."[13] Assistant Secretary John A. Baker called rural areas development a "folk movement of grass roots action," by which "the local people study their own resources and their own opportunities, take responsibility and initiative for making their own decisions as to what they want to do to develop their own future."[14] By early 1967 the depart-

---

11. U.S. Department of Agriculture, "Rural Areas Development Program Delegation of Responsibilities Under PL 87–27," Secretary's Memorandum No. 1448 (Supplement 1; Sept. 8, 1961). See also, Levitan, *Federal Aid to Depressed Areas*, pp. 42–43, 54–64.

12. Address to Land and People Conference, Duluth, Minn., Sept. 25, 1963.

13. Address to International Association of Game, Fish, and Conservation Commissioners, Sept. 10, 1963, inserted in *Congressional Record*, Vol. 109, Pt. 12, 89 Cong. 1 sess. (1963), p. 16737.

14. "Rural Renaissance" (address delivered at a series of regional rural areas development workshops, April–May 1964).

ment claimed 650 multicounty and 2,700 single-county RAD committees. The committees had reported 6,000 projects in the preceding fiscal year, resulting in 79,000 new jobs.[15]

TECHNICAL ACTION PANELS

At the time that Freeman and Baker made the RAD program nationwide, they rejected an argument advanced by some within the department that a new agency needed to be established, with an office in each county, to encourage and serve the development committees. Instead, they organized the field personnel of the three Agriculture agencies already represented in most counties—the Farmers Home Administration (FHA), the Soil Conservation Service (SCS), and the Agricultural Stabilization and Conservation Service (ASCS)—into "technical panels" charged with "coordinating the services of all Department of Agriculture agencies and making the services of these agencies available to Rural Areas Development committees." The county agent was invited—but could not be directed, since he was employed by the land grant college rather than by Agriculture—to participate as an ex-officio member. The panels were to assist the RAD committees in securing nonagricultural as well as agricultural services and assistance. Just as the Federal Extension Service had been designated to take the lead in organizing RAD committees, the Farmers Home Administration was assigned responsibility to get the panels organized and to provide the chairmen (except in counties where it did not have offices). It reported early in 1962 that 784 county panels and 77 area panels had been formed serving a total of 1,070 counties.[16]

Shortly after their creation, the panels were renamed "technical action panels." "The role of the Government employees is symbolized," explained Baker, "by the name technical action panels—the initials of which—TAP—were chosen deliberately . . . signifying that we are to be on *tap* to serve the local people—not on top of their decision-making processes."[17]

15. John A. Baker, address before Lebanon and Wilson County Chamber of Commerce, Lebanon, Tenn., March 23, 1967.
16. Testimony of Howard Bertsch (administrator, Farmers Home Administration), in *Department of Agriculture Appropriations for 1963*, Hearings before a Subcommittee of the House Appropriations Committee, 87 Cong. 2 sess. (1962), pp. 1748–49.
17. "Rural Renaissance."

RURAL RENEWAL

Even as the Area Redevelopment Act of 1961 was being passed, the Department of Agriculture had concluded that act alone would not provide strong enough measures to revive the most impoverished rural counties. About eight hundred counties—or more than one-quarter of all the counties in the nation—lay in what the department called "economically lagging rural areas," where community and private facilities had deteriorated and farmland was underutilized or even abandoned. The department saw these rural backwaters as analogous to the city slums, whose ills were being attacked through the total replanning and reconstruction of whole neighborhoods under the urban renewal program.

In the Food and Agriculture Act of 1962, therefore, the department sought and obtained authority for a program it called "rural renewal." This program, Secretary Freeman told the Congress, "would aid in developing new uses for land and water, create industrial parks, assist small farmers in farm consolidation and enlargement, and develop needed public facilities including outdoor recreation." Rural renewal authorities would be created with power—comparable to that possessed by urban renewal agencies—to plan area renewal, to acquire, develop, and resell land, and to help in the establishment of new enterprises. The Agriculture Department would be authorized to make loans for those purposes to the new public corporations.[18]

"I can visualize in my mind's eye a rural renewal authority under every board of county commissioners in counties where it is needed—a real action agency with the power to do something," Freeman testified.[19]

The states, however, did not respond with the necessary enabling legislation for rural renewal authorities as they had responded earlier in authorizing urban renewal. After five years only two states, Arkansas and North Carolina, had enacted special legislation, and North Carolina's law was limited to only a portion of the state. To overcome that obstacle, the Congress in 1967 authorized Agriculture to make rural renewal loans to private nonprofit bodies as well as to public authorities, but at that point the program was frozen by bud-

18. *Food and Agriculture Act of 1962*, Hearings, pp. 68–69.
19. *Ibid.*, p. 43.

get limitations. As of 1968, only five rural renewal areas had been designated by the secretary of agriculture, comprising twelve counties in five states, and only $6 million in rural renewal loans had been committed. Some projects in rural renewal counties had, of course, been financed through regular lending programs of Agriculture and other departments.

In each of the five areas, the Farmers Home Administration assigned a full-time program leader to assist the local renewal authorities or nonprofit groups in planning and carrying out the program. While each of the areas comprised two or three counties, the local citizen bodies were organized on a county basis.

RESOURCE CONSERVATION AND DEVELOPMENT

Under the same general language of the 1962 act that authorized rural renewal, Agriculture organized a second program along similar lines—resource conservation and development (RC&D)—for which responsibility was assigned to the Soil Conservation Service.[20]

RC&D, which had not been mentioned in the testimony, was a late starter compared to rural renewal, but it soon outstripped its rival. Whereas the Farmers Home Administration had to await the organization of rural renewal authorities, the local public agencies needed for RC&D projects were already in existence—the soil and water conservation districts that are organized in every state, usually on a county basis, to sponsor development of farm conservation plans. The SCS, which provided the technical staff for the districts, had no difficulty finding sponsors for a new program that promised an additional source of funds for local projects. By the end of 1968, 51 projects had been approved for operation or were in the planning stage, covering 293 counties in 39 states. RC&D funds to supplement

20. The statute did not mention either program by name. The language contained in Title I (sec. 102), "Land-Use Adjustment," simply authorized the department "to cooperate with Federal, State, territorial and other public agencies in developing plans for a program of land conservation and land utilization, to assist in carrying out such plans by means of loans to State and local public agencies designated by the State legislature or the Governor. . . ." The governors, or the designated state agencies, were permitted to veto any project proposed for federal assistance. In the 1962 act, Agriculture also obtained authority to lend funds for conversion of agricultural land to non-agricultural uses, primarily commercial recreation. Meanwhile, the department's credit programs for housing and community water systems in rural areas had also been expanded considerably.

the financial assistance available through regular programs were being loaned at a rate of about $500,000 a year.

The RC&D area usually comprised more than a single county and sometimes overlapped state boundaries. The county governments and the conservation districts within the area, joined sometimes by other local groups, became the sponsors of the project and designated members to serve as a steering committee. The SCS then organized a technical staff, headed by a project coordinator, to assist the steering committee in preparing the project plan. Upon approval of the plan by the Soil Conservation Service, the project sponsors then became eligible for RC&D assistance.

Since the programs for resource conservation and development and for rural renewal were organized under the same statutory language, the distinctions had to be worked out administratively. In companion memoranda issued November 2, 1962, the department offered these definitions:

Rural Renewal: A locally initiated and sponsored project designed to eliminate chronic rural underemployment, foster sound rural economy, strengthen family farming and increase farm and rural income while stabilizing, improving, conserving and developing the natural resources of the project area to assure the permanence of the economic gains achieved.[21]

Resource Conservation and Development: A locally initiated and sponsored project designed to carry out a program of land conservation and utilization in an area where acceleration of the current conservation activities plus the use of the new authorities will provide additional economic opportunities to its people.[22]

In these definitions the similarities are more apparent than the differences. Both programs sought to conserve and develop resources; both sought to provide additional economic opportunities and increase income. Two rival agencies were, in effect, given broad charters to develop programs built around their separate traditions and expertise. The Soil Conservation Service, as the department's dam-builder, selected areas with significant potential for development of water resources and built its program initially around water conservation and utilization. The Farmers Home Administration, as the depart-

21. U.S. Department of Agriculture, "Rural Renewal Program," Secretary's Memorandum No. 1517 (Nov. 2, 1962).

22. U.S. Department of Agriculture, "Resource Conservation and Development Projects," Secretary's Memorandum No. 1515 (Nov. 2, 1962).

ment's credit institution for marginal farmers and rural communities, centered its attention on the reorganization and upgrading of agriculture and the development of industrial sites, homesites, community facilities, and raw materials necessary to attract industry. Beginning with these initial points of emphasis, however, each program could be as broad as the concern and imagination of the sponsoring organizations and the professional staff. "The limitation," FHA Administrator Howard Bertsch testified regarding rural renewal, "would be the feasibility as visualized and demonstrated by the local bodies that organized and did the planning. . . . This is simply a financing device which would fund sound plans developed by such local organizations."[23]

EXPANSION OF THE AGRICULTURE MISSION

As Secretary Freeman steadily elevated rural areas development in the priorities of the Department of Agriculture, he sought and obtained from the President a ratification of the department's broadened mission and an assignment as governmentwide coordinator of programs bearing upon rural development.

In October 1963, President John F. Kennedy created a Cabinet-level rural development committee, with Freeman as its chairman, to "provide leadership and uniform policy guidance to the several Federal departments and agencies responsible for rural-development program functions and related activities."[24] While the committee met infrequently, a staff-level group met regularly and created various interagency task forces to survey systematically the problems of rural development and the effectiveness of federal programs in reaching rural areas. One outgrowth of the staff group's work was an experimental program sponsored jointly by Agriculture, Labor, and Health, Education, and Welfare called "concerted services pilot projects in training and education," under which full-time federal employees were assigned to pilot counties in five states to develop intensive programs for the utilization of available federal programs related to manpower development. In practice, the coordinators in the coun-

23. *Food and Agriculture Act of 1962*, Hearings, p. 362.
24. Executive Order No. 11122, issued Oct. 16, 1963. The order was superseded by President Johnson's Executive Order No. 11307, issued Sept. 30, 1966 (cited in Chap. 1).

ties did not limit their concern to manpower; they undertook to promote and expedite the entire range of federal programs.[25]

President Johnson in 1964 announced a goal for rural development—"parity of opportunity for rural America in every aspect of our national life"—and directed the Department of Agriculture to "assume a full leadership role within the Federal Government to help rural America, as a whole, attain its rightful place within the Great Society."[26] Secretary Freeman described the new role as effecting a historic transformation of the department. "We are broadening our concern from the field of agriculture as an industry to rural America as an element of our national society," he said. "Where we have been concerned primarily with plants, animals, and land, we must be equally concerned with people." And he directed that the research, extension, and action programs of the department be broadened accordingly.[27] A few weeks later, in his message to the Congress on agriculture, the President repeated his call for "parity of opportunity" and assigned to the Department of Agriculture what came to be called its "outreach" function: The secretary was directed "to put the facilities of his field offices at the disposal of all federal agencies to assist them in making their programs effective in rural areas."[28] To undertake that mission, the secretary converted the Office of Rural Areas Development into the Rural Community Development Service (RCDS). "Our aim," said Freeman, "is to provide 'one-stop service' to rural people who are seeking help from their federal government."[29]

The new RCDS, however, encountered an unfriendly reception on Capitol Hill. The House agriculture appropriations subcommittee denied it funds for twenty-three proposed field offices with the comment that it should operate through the established agencies of the

25. For a summary of activities under this program, see John S. McCauley, "Manpower Development in Rural Areas," *Employment Service Review*, March–April 1968, p. 10; and B. Eugene Griessman (ed.), *The Concerted Services Approach to Developmental Change in Rural Areas: An Interim Evaluation* (North Carolina State University at Raleigh, Center for Occupational Education, 1968).

26. Letter to the National Grange convention, Nov. 17, 1964.

27. Remarks at meeting of the National Advisory Committee on Rural Areas Development, Washington, D.C., Nov. 24, 1964.

28. Special Message to Congress on Agriculture, Feb. 4, 1965, *Public Papers of the Presidents, 1965*, p. 143.

29. Remarks at meeting of the National Advisory Committee on Rural Areas Development, Washington, D.C., May 26, 1965.

department.[30] The department responded by revitalizing the technical action panels early in 1967 as the operating outreach and "one-stop service" organization, with RCDS as a Washington liaison staff. The Farmers Home Administration designated a full-time person in each of its state headquarters to develop the role of the state and county technical action panels and to create new TAPs to serve multicounty districts. The heads of federal and state agencies "that conduct programs of significance to the development of non-metropolitan areas and rural parts of metropolitan areas" were invited to join the state panels, and the county panels were similarly broadened. However, at both the state and county levels the executive committees of the technical action panels were composed wholly or predominantly of Agriculture officials.[31] "Rural people now have only to call the office of any member of a technical action panel in their county to find out about government programs that deal with agriculture—housing—transportation—education and health facilities—recreation and cultural facilities—water resources—parks and forests—social rehabilitation—emergencies and disasters—loans to small business—and all the other programs which rural people can use," Freeman told rural audiences.[32] And the TAPs were equipped with a thick manual giving detailed information on how rural communities, organizations, or individuals could apply for assistance under eighty-seven programs administered by nine departments and agencies outside the Agriculture Department, accompanied by a work sheet on which TAPs were encouraged to keep a statistical record of their outreach activities.

In September 1968, the department counted 51 state, 174 district, and 2,953 county technical action panels. During the year up to that time, the county panels reported having initiated over 32,000 projects, with almost 11,000 completed, and had referred 269,123 applicants to agencies outside Agriculture.[33] By this time, little was

30. *Department of Agriculture and Related Agencies Appropriation Bill, 1967*, H. Rept. 1446, 89 Cong. 2 sess. (1966), p. 41.
31. U.S. Department of Agriculture, "Rural Areas Development Program," Secretary's Memorandum No. 1610 (Feb. 27, 1967); and Rural Areas Development Board, "Technical Action Panels," Chairman's Instruction No. 67–55 (May 10, 1967).
32. Address before the Tennessee River Valley Association, Knoxville, Tenn., Dec. 5, 1967.
33. John M. Lovorn, director, Rural Renewal Division, Farmers Home Administration, address prepared for regional TAP training meetings, September 1968.

heard about the rural areas development committees of the earlier period; in a thirty-six-page presentation to TAP training workshops in the fall of 1968 on the responsibilities of the panels, Assistant Secretary Baker did not once mention RAD committees. The department's emphasis was now on its TAPs, its RC&Ds, and the contemplated new nonmetropolitan planning districts (discussed below).

THE BOUNDARIES OF RURAL AMERICA

When the rural development program was launched in 1955, the people to be served were clearly identified: they were the "low-income farmers." The department's report proposing the program limited its statistics on rural poverty to farmers as an occupational group; if there were low-income nonfarmers in rural areas—unemployed miners, for example, or underemployed small town residents—they were not in 1955 the concern of the Department of Agriculture. The report emphasized, however, that the *solutions* to the problems of low-income farmers were not necessarily to be found in agriculture. While programs should be developed to improve farm income, they should be "an integral part of the overall development program for the community or county," which would also contain provisions for nonfarm employment and vocational training and guidance for the members of farm families.[34]

If an "overall development program" for a county were to be prepared, however, the benefits were bound to extend beyond "low-income farmers." Higher income farmers would be helped, and so would nonfarmers. Gradually the notion that rural development was a program for more than just farmers began to creep into the discourse. Upon receiving the 1959 report of the rural development program, for example, President Eisenhower commented that the report indicated progress "in aid to small and low-income farm families *and other rural people*," and went on to say that "rural families of such areas—non-farm and farm alike—need . . . more adequate incomes and greater opportunities."[35]

As the new administration promoted the rural areas development program, after 1961, it explicitly encouraged the participation of non-

34. *Development of Agriculture's Human Resources*, p. 18.
35. Statement on Receipt of the Fourth Annual Report on the Rural Development Program, Oct. 29, 1959, *Public Papers of the Presidents, 1959*, p. 759. Italics added.

farmers. But no exact boundary for "rural America"—and hence for RAD—was ever fixed. In citing statistics about rural areas, the Department of Agriculture often used the census definition of the rural population—that is, persons living in communities up to 2,500 population outside metropolitan areas. The Congress also adopted the 2,500-person limit (later raised to 5,500) in authorizing the Farmers Home Administration to make housing loans to nonfarmers and water supply loans to rural communities. Under the Area Redevelopment Act, "rural" areas were simply those counties with labor forces under 15,000 (or nonagricultural labor forces under 8,000) that were "essentially and fundamentally associated with agriculture and forestry." Many of these counties had county seats well over 2,500 in population.

As the state extension services proceeded to organize their RAD (and OEDP) committees, they found themselves working with groups of varied composition and nomenclature. Sometimes an existing organization centered upon a county-seat town was recognized and became, for reporting purposes, the "RAD committee." If, in order to obtain the participation of the small town or city leadership in a new committee, it appeared useful to drop the word "rural" from "rural areas development," that was done. In some states the committees were uniformly labeled "area development" or "resource development" bodies. In some counties, RAD committees limited their activities and participation to the farming areas outside the urban centers. In practice, then, "rural America" might exclude small urban centers, or include them, or its identity might be lost in an approach that covered both urban and rural areas without trying to distinguish between them.

The Commerce Approach: Overall Economic Development

Upon passage of the Area Redevelopment Act in 1961, each depressed area eligible for assistance was required to create an economic planning body, if it did not have one, and prepare an "overall economic development program" (OEDP) for approval by the secretary of commerce.

The planning requirement was contained in the earliest version of the area redevelopment bill sponsored by the Eisenhower administration. The bill submitted to the Congress in 1956 stipulated, in regard to loans for industrial development in "redevelopment areas":

> No such assistance shall be extended unless there shall be submitted and approved by the Secretary [of Commerce] an overall program for the economic development of the area and a finding by the state, or any agency, instrumentality, or local political subdivision thereof, that the project for which financial assistance is sought is consistent with such a program.[36]

The provision reflected the views and experience of Commerce's Office of Area Development, a tiny unit (consisting of seventeen people in 1956) which for a decade had been offering technical assistance to the approximately two thousand state and community organizations engaged in industrial development planning and promotion. In its advice to communities, the office had encouraged the formation of broadly representative community organizations—"composed of leading citizens, businessmen, labor, the press, civic officials, and other interested persons," as one of its publications put it. The organization, the publication continued, should make "a comprehensive survey of the community's assets and the industrial location advantages of the area. The survey is essentially a self-analysis of the community to determine what its strong points are and what improvements can be made."[37]

The OEDP provision remained intact through successive versions of the area redevelopment bill until its enactment in 1961. But the provision attracted little attention. Rarely did the sponsors of the bill bother to mention that a new and comprehensive economic planning process was being launched, and in none of the debates did any member of the Congress raise any question about it.

If few people had heard of an OEDP before the Area Redevelopment Act was passed, thousands learned about it within a very few weeks thereafter. Economically distressed communities found that between them and federal aid stood a complicated planning process, which some of them saw as an opportunity but others regarded—in the words of one ARA official—as an "obstruction" and a "necessary evil."

36. S. 2892, 84 Cong. 2 sess. (1956).
37. *Industrial Development Suggestions for a Vermont Community*, reprinted in *Area Redevelopment*, Hearings before a Subcommittee of the Senate Banking and Currency Committee, 85 Cong. 1 sess. (1957), p. 354.

COMMUNITY ORGANIZATION FOR ECONOMIC DEVELOPMENT PLANNING

The act was silent as to what kind of community organization should prepare the overall economic development program, and the Area Redevelopment Administration, established in the Department of Commerce by the act, was nearly so. In its initial bulletin on the subject, it said that each redevelopment area must have a "redevelopment area organization" that "would function primarily as a spokesman for the area and as a coordinator of redevelopment activities." If an organization existed "that is recognized as a spokesman for the community," a new one would not have to be established. If a new group were formed, it "should reflect various interests in the area such as business, labor, agriculture, and local government."

When the OEDP was submitted, the redevelopment area organization was required to submit a list of its members and certify that it represented "all interested groups" in the redevelopment area. Moreover, the state agency designated by the governor to exercise the state's responsibilities under the act (usually the state's economic development agency) was required to certify not only that the OEDP was substantively sound but that the organization that prepared it "appears to be representative of the Redevelopment Area and qualified to implement and/or coordinate the Program."[38]

If the state and local certificates were in proper form, ARA initially did not look behind them. But militant spokesmen for organized labor presently demanded that ARA take steps to ensure that labor was included in redevelopment area organizations, and the agency complied by assigning one staff member to review the OEDPs for labor participation and to block approval of those prepared by groups that had excluded labor. No comparable precautions were taken in regard to other groups.

Since the redevelopment area organizations were in effect self-constituted, the possibility existed that separate groups in particular areas might compete for recognition by the state and federal governments. The greatest potentiality for conflict lay in an urban-rural split, between RAD committees concerned with problems of the

38. U.S. Department of Commerce, *The Overall Economic Development Program: What It Is, How to Prepare One for Your Community* (August 1961), pp. 4, 8, 16, 17.

rural areas and industrial promotion groups formed by the business-men of the county seat or other principal town. But Commerce and Agriculture officials alike report that no serious conflicts arose. The task of preparing the OEDP was sufficiently onerous that neither the urban nor the rural groups clamored for the exclusive right to under-take it. A gentle suggestion from federal and state officials usually sufficed to bring about creation of a broader committee embracing the leadership of both groups, if only on an ad hoc basis for the single job of preparing the OEDP.

"A SURGE OF LOCAL PROGRAMMING"

The Area Redevelopment Administration's instructions to the local organizations described the OEDP as "a program of action and not merely a plan."[39] Its basic elements were these:

1. A description of the redevelopment area organization—its membership, legal authority, record of accomplishments, and finan-cial capabilities.

2. A "background picture" of the redevelopment area—a general description of its physical features, its land-use patterns, utilities and transportation, community facilities and services, followed by data on population and labor force, employment and unemployment, factors contributing to economic decline or stagnation, anticipated need for new jobs and for vocational training, and an appraisal of past efforts to solve the area's economic problems.

3. An analysis of local resources that might be developed—min-erals, forests, agriculture, recreation, industrial and commercial sites and buildings, human resources, transportation resources, and so on.

4. An analysis of the problems blocking economic progress—in-adequacies in such factors as capital, entrepreneurship, industrial sites, skilled manpower, public utility services, or community facili-ties.

5. A statement of economic goals and a program for attaining them, drafted in the light of the analyses of resources and problems. Among suggested program items were industrial site preparation, development of industries based on local resources, promotion of tourism, vocational training and retraining, comprehensive highway

39. *Ibid.*, p. 3. The discussion that follows is a summary of the "essential elements" of an OEDP as outlined in the Commerce booklet.

and land-use planning, urban and rural renewal, and research on the utilization of particular local resources. The program should include plans for utilizing state and federal assistance.

"There has been, since ARA, an unprecedented and impressive surge of local programming," ARA Administrator William L. Batt, Jr., testified at the end of the first year of the agency's operation. "We count this as a vital and unique accomplishment of the program. For the first time in a great many of these areas, people have analyzed their problems, mobilized their resources, and selected their own targets for new growth and new jobs on the basis of their intimate knowledge of their own problems."[40]

The care and attention devoted to the OEDP varied greatly, however, from community to community. In Johnson County, Tennessee, 250 volunteers participated in preparing the planning document, ARA reported,[41] but at the other extreme were counties whose citizens scarcely participated at all. In Kentucky, for example, county OEDPs were prepared in the state capitol by the state's economic development staff.[42] In Georgia many were prepared in Atlanta by the Georgia Power Company and the state association of rural electric cooperatives, and in many localities in other states the community leaders simply hired consultants to put together something that would meet the ARA requirements. Sar A. Levitan, who examined a broad sample of OEDPs, concluded that many were "superficial in content, poorly conceived, and of little potential value to the areas concerned" but that others did result in preparation of realistic plans for specific projects and in an economic education for the community that was of potential long-run benefit.[43]

Eager to begin making loans and grants, ARA decided at the outset that it could not afford to delay its action program while communities perfected their OEDPs. Accordingly, it adopted a procedure for "provisional" approval of OEDPs that would qualify the areas for assistance while ARA was reviewing the massive body of planning documents, 600 of which were submitted in the first year

40. *Departments of State, Justice, and Commerce, the Judiciary, and Related Agencies Appropriations, 1963*, Hearings before a Subcommittee of the House Appropriations Committee, 87 Cong. 2 sess. (1962), p. 555.

41. U.S. Department of Commerce, *The First Annual Report of the Area Redevelopment Administration*, 1962, p. 13.

42. Levitan, *Federal Aid to Depressed Areas*, p. 198.

43. *Ibid.*, pp. 198–99.

alone. After receiving the ARA's critique, each community was to convert the provisional plan into a "comprehensive" one. That purpose, however, was never carried out. Many of the redevelopment area organizations (which were rechristened "OEDP committees" in 1962) had disbanded or become inactive once the initial OEDPs were submitted. ARA reminded each community of its obligation to prepare a revised version of its OEDP, but no community was decertified because of failure to respond. The dominant objective of ARA was not planning but action, and within the agency itself were many who looked upon the OEDP as unnecessary busy work. The agency let the OEDP committees "die on the vine," in the words of one ARA official. By 1964, the OEDP was not mentioned by name in the 41-page body of the agency's annual report, and the entire subject of economic planning received only a 2-sentence mention reciting the bare statistics that 1,051 areas had submitted economic plans and 983 of those had been approved. More than 25,000 local leaders had served on the local economic development committees, the agency estimated.[44]

In December 1962, ARA discarded the terminology of "provisional" and "comprehensive" in favor of a "continuing" OEDP—one that would be kept continuously up to date and periodically resubmitted to, and reapproved by, ARA. This idea was incorporated in the Public Works and Economic Development Act of 1965, which superseded the Area Redevelopment Act. To be eligible for assistance, the 1965 law said, an area must maintain "a currently approved overall economic development program." The new Economic Development Administration (EDA), created by the act as the successor to ARA, placed major emphasis upon a new requirement for an annual progress report from each OEDP committee, which would summarize the activities of the organization, provide supplemental data to update the OEDP, review progress in attaining the goals set out in the planning document, and attempt to measure the economic progress of the area. In 1967, a few areas that had done nothing to bring up to date their provisionally approved OEDPs of five years earlier were finally declared ineligible for EDA assistance.

Like its predecessor, EDA emphasized that the local OEDP committees should be broadly representative, but it broadened the con-

44. U.S. Department of Commerce, *More Jobs Where Most Needed*, Annual Report of the Area Redevelopment Administration (1964), p. 6.

cept of representation to include social as well as economic groups and specifically advised that minority groups be drawn into active participation where they constituted a significant part of the population. EDA also required that the OEDPs be submitted to the local governing bodies for review, and that any dissenting opinions or comments be attached.[45]

ECONOMIC DEVELOPMENT DISTRICTS

The Area Redevelopment Act designated as the geographical base for economic development the "area"—a labor market area as defined by the Labor Department, usually comprising a single county. Some multicounty economic development organizations with considerable vitality were already in existence when the act was passed, and some of them prepared single OEDPs to cover their entire districts. But even in those cases ARA urged individual county OEDPs as well, in order to focus attention on projects, like industrial site layout and development of water supply and sewage disposal systems, that depended for their execution on local bodies.[46]

As experience grew, however, those concerned with economic development in ARA, in Agriculture, and in the states came gradually to the conclusion that multicounty planning was generally superior to single-county planning and should be encouraged for all of the country's depressed areas. Their thinking was crystallized in the deliberations during 1963 of the President's Appalachian Regional Commission (discussed below), which proposed that a network of multicounty development districts be established throughout Appalachia, and was carried over into the drafting of the Public Works and Economic Development Act of 1965. In that act the Congress authorized a new device—the economic development district, a multicounty entity usually embracing from five to ten counties.

"The experience under ARA taught us that many local development problems are more effectively dealt with on a broader geographic basis," testified Eugene P. Foley, assistant secretary of commerce. "Neighboring counties, working together, can get a better 'feel' for their common problems, and by pooling their resources they

45. U.S. Department of Commerce, *Guide for Overall Economic Development Programs* [1965], pp. 3–4, 8.
46. Levitan, *Federal Aid to Depressed Areas*, p. 205, discusses the experience of 33 southern Illinois counties with multicounty and single-county OEDPs.

can produce more effective solutions."[47] Many counties were too small, ARA had learned, "to have the variety and volume of resources to be viable or development-worthy," or "to contain a growth center, central place, or trade center in or around which economic development could be reasonably expected to take place."[48] Those counties would have to depend for their revival upon the growth of a center outside their boundaries but within commuting distance— usually a small or medium sized town or city that could offer industry a higher level of public services, better access to transportation, and other locational advantages.

As defined in the 1965 act, an economic development district had to include two or more redevelopment areas and at least one "economic development center" (or "growth center"). The center itself need not be in a redevelopment area but must be so located that its growth would contribute to the revival of the adjacent depressed counties. The growth center was made eligible for the same assistance—grants and loans for public facilities and loans and guarantees for industrial or commercial development—as that offered the redevelopment areas. To encourage formation of districts, the act also increased by 10 percentage points the federal share of the cost of public works projects in redevelopment areas located within districts. The Economic Development Administration was authorized, moreover, to pay 75 percent of the administrative expenses of the district organizations. The states were invited to draw the boundaries of the districts; if EDA disagreed with the proposed boundaries, discussion was to continue until agreement was reached.

To get a district started, EDA recommended a broadly representative committee analogous to the county OEDP committees, including representatives of "local governments, industry and labor, business and finance, agricultural interests and the professions, and the District's minority groups and unemployed."[49] The committee would develop plans for a permanent organization and draft articles of in-

47. *Departments of State, Justice, Commerce, the Judiciary, and Related Agencies Appropriations for 1967*, Hearings before a Subcommittee of the House Appropriations Committee, 89 Cong. 2 sess. (1966), p. 73.

48. Victor Roterus, former ARA official, then on the staff of the Office of Regional Economic Development, U.S. Department of Commerce, address in Toronto, Canada, Aug. 30, 1966.

49. U.S. Department of Commerce, *EDA Economic Development Districts: A Job-Creating Program* (January 1967), p. 5.

corporation and by-laws. EDA would satisfy itself that the group was properly constituted—with particular attention to its representative character—before authorizing financial assistance.

By the end of 1968, eighty-six economic development districts in thirty-two states had been organized. Three of the districts were interstate, two including parts of two states and the other parts of three. President Johnson's budget projected an increase in the number of districts to one hundred and fifteen by mid-1970. More than a thousand counties would be included.

With the passage of the 1965 act and the establishment of the Economic Development Administration came a renewed emphasis on planning. The act extended the requirement for an OEDP to the new districts as well as the established redevelopment areas and specifically enjoined the districts to include in their OEDPs "adequate land use and transportation planning" and "a specific program for district cooperation, self-help and public investment." Foley told the House Appropriations Committee that in the redevelopment areas he had visited, "I find invariably that local efforts had been made at identifying and attracting new business that might reinvigorate the community, but that almost universally such efforts have failed for lack of an essential ingredient—economic development planning."[50] A year later, his successor, Ross D. Davis, in justifying increased appropriations for planning grants, technical assistance grants, and research, observed that "EDA's most significant contribution to economic development may be stimulation of planning at appropriate levels."[51] In contrast to the two-sentence treatment of economic planning in ARA's 1964 annual report, EDA devoted most of one chapter and part of another to the subject in its annual report three years later.[52]

The planning was invariably defined as "comprehensive." President Johnson had used that adjective in his message to the Congress of March 25, 1965, transmitting the economic development legisla-

50. Departments of . . . Commerce . . . Appropriations for 1967, Hearings, p. 71.
51. Departments of State, Justice, and Commerce, the Judiciary and Related Agencies Appropriations for 1968, Hearings before a Subcommittee of the House Appropriations Committee, 90 Cong. 1 sess. (1967), p. 181.
52. U.S. Department of Commerce, Annual Report of the Economic Development Administration, 1967, pp. 15–18, 30–31.

tion.[53] EDA described development planning as "a continuous process," and "of an overall nature," encompassing not only such projects as new roads, new water lines, and new factories but "medical facilities, new schools, cultural programs, and a variety of both physical and social needs."[54]

Finally, the 1965 act authorized what may have been the most significant new departure of all—financial assistance for 75 percent of the cost of employing full-time professional planning staff to serve the citizen leadership at the district level. This assistance in 1969 exceeded $4 million a year. Davis emphasized the importance of the professional staff, as well as the comprehensiveness of the planning process, in this appraisal of the economic development districts in 1967:

> The uniqueness of this new institution springs from the marriage of wide community involvement with strong professional staff support. The objective is a comprehensive viewpoint which relates job creation with all other elements of community development. The school, the library, the hospital, the training center can be as important as the industrial park in revitalizing a community. Therefore, active involvement of the labor official, educator, and minority group spokesman is required in addition to the involvement of the banker, businessman, and public official. And a trained professional staff is also essential to play a catalytic role and to bring expert knowledge and experience to bear on a continuing full-time basis.
>
> EDA is trying to sell the concept of comprehensive planning as an active community effort and a continuous process. We are working to build viable community institutions with competent professional staffs to work with communities in the execution of their own planned development programs.[55]

"Perhaps above all," wrote EDA, "planning must involve action."[56] Davis described the mission of the economic development district as "planning, coordinating, implementing." And these functions, being comprehensive, explicitly embraced programs within the

---

53. Special Message to the Congress on Area and Regional Economic Development, March 25, 1965, *Public Papers of the Presidents, 1965*, p. 320.
54. *Annual Report of the Economic Development Administration, 1967*, p. 15.
55. *Economic Development Administration's Reply to the Subcommittee's First Interim Report and Related Matters*, Hearing before the Special Subcommittee on Economic Development Programs of the House Committee on Public Works, 90 Cong. 1 sess. (1967), p. 6.
56. *Annual Report of the Economic Development Administration, 1967*, p. 15.

jurisdiction of other federal agencies, as Davis made clear in these words:

> The idea is that at the district level . . . you will have . . . a professional group that can do planning and coordination for that multicounty area and start tapping the resources of other Federal agencies in a rational, coordinated way so that at the district level we will have in place a capability to utilize all resources as the local people would like to see it utilized to accomplish what the local people want.
>
> In due course, when that unit is operating correctly, they will be able to go to Agriculture, go to HEW, go to any agency. They will have a plan, they will have a capability of sorting out these different programs, they will have a sense of priority. . . .
>
> . . . You have to have what we call planning capability which is much more than planning. It is planning, coordinating, implementing. It is the ability to analyze what the problems are of their particular piece of real estate, develop some kinds of solutions, identify resources. That is when you get into rationalizing the Government program.[57]

He also made clear that the economic development district was to provide the same "one-stop service" for community leaders on behalf of the entire federal government that Agriculture's technical action panels had been instructed to provide. The question was raised in the House appropriations subcommittee hearing in 1967 by Representative Elford A. Cederberg, Republican of Michigan, who graphically described how his constituents were "running around in circles":

> The problem as I see it is that there needs to be some clearinghouse, and maybe this is the place to have it, I don't know, to direct these people to places where they have the best opportunity to qualify for a particular project. . . . There has to be a way of expediting this. . . . When you get down to the local community, perhaps a small community, the poor city manager doesn't know where to go. . . . A city manager with a city of 4000 or 5000 people will get bulletins from 10 different agencies, many of which have programs which may be helpful to his community. He doesn't know which one to go to. When he goes to one they say, "Go to the other one." . . . Our people are running around in circles and I cannot sort it out for them.

Replied Davis: "I think if we can get counties organized into districts in appropriate places and get the districts headed by some kind of professional capability we will begin to solve that problem."[58]

57. *Departments of . . . Commerce . . . Appropriations for 1968*, Hearings, pp. 193–94.
58. *Ibid.*, pp. 194–95.

The Appalachian Approach: Local Development

Throughout the mountainous Appalachian region—which comprises all of one state (West Virginia) and parts of twelve others—multicounty economic development bodies have been, or are being, created under provisions of the Appalachian Regional Development Act of 1965. The objectives of the Appalachian development groups, which are labeled "local development districts" (LDDs), are indistinguishable from those of EDA's economic development districts discussed in the preceding section. In structure, however, they may be somewhat different.

The local development districts were proposed initially in 1964 by the President's Appalachian Regional Commission, a temporary body appointed by President Kennedy to develop a program to revive the depressed economy of the region. The report was not specific as to how the districts would be organized and what they would do, but it was clear that the commission envisaged organizations on the pattern of the local nonprofit industrial development corporations organized by business leaders in many states—notably in New England, Pennsylvania, and the South—to lay out industrial sites and promote the development of industry. The local districts would obtain their initial capital from a regional Appalachian development corporation, and 75 percent of their administrative expenses during their first three years of operation would be paid by the federal government.[59]

The Congress rejected the proposal for the regional corporation but accepted the plan for local development districts and authorized the federal sharing of their administrative expenses. The congressional hearings and debates reveal little discussion of how the districts would be organized or what they would do. The draft bill, like the report of the President's commission, was not specific; it merely required that the districts be incorporated under state law and that their charters "include the economic development of counties, or parts of counties, or other political subdivisions...." Under Secretary of Commerce Franklin D. Roosevelt, Jr., who had chaired the President's commission, did not even mention the local development dis-

59. President's Appalachian Regional Commission, *Appalachia* (1964), pp. 55, 63–64.

tricts in his opening presentation of the Appalachian development program to the Congress but in response to a question said that a district's first objective would be to "establish the economic foundation" for industrial development, as for example through action to improve water supply and sewage disposal facilities, and that it might subsequently build plants for lease to private companies.[60]

In the absence of a clear legislative history, the Appalachian Regional Commission, the federal-state body established by the act, moved slowly. Instead of making grants to individual districts immediately, it made its initial grants to what it called a "state-level LDD" established by each state—that is, a planning unit, located usually in the governor's office, charged with preparing an "economic development plan" for that part of the state lying within Appalachia. As an element of the plan, the state would develop a scheme for its local development districts.

In June 1966 the Appalachian Regional Commission established some basic criteria for LDDs. They must be multicounty in jurisdiction—despite the statutory provision that an LDD might include "counties or parts of counties"—and each district must have a full-time staff "of sufficient professional competence to plan, coordinate, and administer an Appalachian economic development program for its area."[61] The commission also entered into a "gentlemen's agreement" with the Economic Development Administration that where one agency had recognized and made a grant to a district organization the other would designate the same organization as its development district. To satisfy the EDA requirements, the Appalachian districts—whose governing boards often represented only local governments and business and professional leadership—had to broaden their structures to admit into full participation other social and economic groups, particularly minority groups and organized labor. Like EDA, the Appalachian Regional Commission embraced the concept of growth centers, which were to be designated in each state's Appalachian plan.

Each state proceeded, then, in its own way, and the resulting patterns of LDD organization were diverse. Georgia designated as its local development districts the well-staffed area planning and de-

60. *Appalachian Regional Development Act of 1964*, Hearings before the Ad Hoc Subcommittee on Appalachian Regional Development of the House Committee on Public Works, 88 Cong. 2 sess. (1964), p. 26.

61. Appalachian Regional Commission, Resolution No. 81, June 14, 1966.

velopment councils that had been established under state law (discussed below). Kentucky similarly designated the area development councils that it had set up almost a decade earlier. Tennessee passed legislation authorizing establishment of district organizations. Several states where economic development districts were being formed designated those districts as LDDs. On the other hand, several states did not proceed at once to form locally based organizations but simply established field offices of the "state-level LDD" to serve groups of Appalachian counties. The trend, however, is strongly toward the creation of locally based planning and development groups. By mid-1968, twelve of the thirteen Appalachian states had grouped their Appalachian counties into planning districts, totaling sixty in all, and the thirteenth (Mississippi) was preparing to do so. Six of the states had LDD organizations in being or in process of formation for all of their planning districts and six other states were creating such organizations to cover at least some of their mountain territory. One state, New York, had expressed no interest in multicounty districts but instead had appointed local advisory councils to advise the state. As of June 30, 1968, a total of twenty-eight LDDs had been recognized by the Appalachian Regional Commission and were receiving federal funds for administrative expenses. Twenty more were to be organized during 1969. Of those in operation in 1968, seven were serving in a dual capacity as development districts for both the Appalachian Regional Commission and the EDA. Of these, two were receiving financial support from both agencies. The commission regards the LDDs as "the building blocks of the entire regional development program," it said in its 1968 annual report.[62]

Five other federal-state regional commissions have been established but have not yet embarked on programs for the creation of districts. The five commissions cover New England, the northern Great Lakes states, the Ozarks, the southern Coastal Plains, and the Four Corners region of Utah, Colorado, Arizona, and New Mexico.

A State Approach: Area Planning and Development

For the same reasons that the federal agencies found the nation's counties inadequate as the base for organizing planning and development activities outside the metropolitan centers, so did the states. By

62. Appalachian Regional Commission, *Annual Report 1968*, p. 90.

1969, more than half the states had plans in being, or were developing them, to group their counties into substate regions for planning and development purposes. The most elaborate of the state systems of multicounty organizations was that of Georgia, where 18 area planning and development commissions (APDCs) embraced 153 of Georgia's 159 counties.

Georgia was a logical place for multicounty organization to achieve its greatest momentum, for Georgia's counties are among the smallest, both in area and in population, in the country. As the state's leadership became increasingly concerned, in the 1950s, with the population decline and economic stagnation being experienced throughout the state except for metropolitan Atlanta and a few other urban centers, they were agreed that revival could not be organized on a county-by-county basis, with every county in competition with every other county. Beginning in 1957, representatives of the Georgia Power Company, the University of Georgia, the state government, and other statewide organizations began promoting the concept of regionalization, and two years later the first multicounty organization was born. Eleven counties in northwest Georgia, centered on Rome, formed a voluntary association to promote planning and development in the Coosa Valley region. Primarily as the result of the Coosa Valley experience, the legislature in 1960 passed an act to facilitate the formation of official multicounty planning agencies.[63]

Supported by the new legislation, the backers of regionalization assembled as a team to promote systematically the formation of additional planning and development commissions. J. W. Fanning of the University of Georgia, one of the team's organizers and leaders who spoke at innumerable meetings throughout the state, recalls the effort as a "soft sell" approach that sought to persuade local leaders that through multicounty planning they could preserve their individual county courthouses yet enjoy at the same time some of the advantages of larger units of government. The state planning agency and the university developed logical groupings of counties based upon economic, political, geographic, and other factors but these were not thrust upon the local officials. Each county was left to decide which neighboring counties it would like to be associated

63. V. R. Stuebing, Jr., "The Multi-County Region—Georgia's Experience" (address at Hot Springs, Ark., July 18, 1968).

with. Those that chose to remain separate from any area grouping retained that option.

The eighteen area commissions that have been formed generally consist of two members from each participating county, appointed for staggered terms.[64] One of the two county delegates is appointed by the county commissioners, the other by the governing body of the county seat, usually in consultation with the other municipalities of the county. The commissions also have advisory committees, established to satisfy various federal requirements. For example, in order to comply with EDA criteria for economic development districts, many commissions have set up economic development advisory councils with representation from industry, labor, and the Negro community as well as elected officials. Similarly, in 1964 and 1965 most of the commissions set up human relations committees with Negro representation in order to qualify as community action agencies. That experiment, however, was brought to an end when OEO concluded in some cases that the relation between the commission and its advisory committee was unsatisfactory, and the commissions in other cases chose to divorce themselves from OEO.

In 1961 the legislature authorized state financial assistance to each area commission. The state matches at a two-for-one ratio the first $15,000 of local funds, and at a fifty-fifty ratio thereafter up to a maximum of $50,000. In 1968 the state's contribution to the commissions exceeded $800,000. To raise the local share, the commissions assessed the participating counties at a rate of 10 to 25 cents per capita.

Most commissions have also secured support from the federal government. The Economic Development Administration assists those that qualify as EDDs; the Farmers Home Administration offers water and sewer planning grants; HUD provides help under the urban planning assistance program where the commissions plan for constituent jurisdictions; and commissions within the Appalachian region that qualify as local development districts may receive funds from that source. The federal government is now the most important source of funds for at least several of the commisions, although they still regard themselves as extensions of local government rather than as agents of the state or federal governments. A recent legislative pro-

64. The exception is metropolitan Atlanta, where the commission is composed of three members each from DeKalb and Fulton counties and the city of Atlanta, and two members each from Clayton, Cobb, and Gwinette counties.

posal to establish the commissions as state rather than local agencies was stoutly resisted by the commissions and defeated.

The objective of the commissions is officially described as the "total development of an area's resources." The state outlined their functions as follows:

(1) To provide a means whereby the towns and counties of the area can collectively consider economic development problems and needs of mutual concern.

(2) To study and analyze the human, natural and economic resources and opportunities of the area, and serve as a clearing house for all basic data on the area.

(3) To work out a program for the sound development of the area.

(4) To encourage cooperation among the local governments and groups in developing and carrying out area plans and programs. For example, the Commission's staff assists state, federal and local governments or agencies in developing coordinated regional planning in such areas as highways, recreation facilities, tourism development, economic and industrial development, and in any other areas which are regional in nature.[65]

The Georgia legislation has been widely used as a point of departure by other states in drafting plans for multicounty organization, although none has duplicated the Georgia approach exactly. A census in October 1967 conducted by the Council of State Planning Agencies, the American Institute of Planners, and the Economic Development Administration counted 171 areawide planning agencies operating in 39 states (exclusive of federally sponsored agencies like economic development districts and Department of Agriculture projects). At least 5 states, including Georgia, had assigned the district planning agencies responsibility to coordinate all federal and state aid to localities. Thirty states had delineated their states into planning regions, totaling 234 in all, the census disclosed. Seven of the 8 states of our survey had a plan for statewide regionalization either in effect (4 states), announced but not yet in effect (1 state), or in preparation by the state planning office (2 states).

Not every multicounty district has a multicounty organization, but both federal and state requirements are impelling a movement in that direction. Through section 204 of the Demonstration Cities and Metropolitan Development Act of 1966, the federal government

65. Georgia Department of Industry and Trade, *Area Planning and Development in Georgia, Progress Report* (January 1965), p. 12.

has virtually mandated the establishment of an areawide planning agency in each of the 231 standard metropolitan statistical areas by requiring that applications for certain types of federal aid to communities in the area be reviewed by a planning agency with areawide jurisdiction. And to obtain certain benefits from the Economic Development Administration, the Agriculture Department, and the Appalachian Regional Commission, as we have seen, district organizations are required.

The Council of State Governments, in its model bill for state and regional planning, proposes multicounty commissions that "could become regional planning and development commissions or service districts to provide areawide services such as water supply, sewage disposal, mass transportation, park and recreation programs, and public works" and "could apply for, administer and coordinate grants and contracts available through programs authorized by State and federal laws for physical, economic, and human resource planning and development."[66] The Advisory Commission on Intergovernmental Relations has prepared similar model bills.[67]

As an outgrowth of complaints that federal agencies were ignoring state-created districts—in particular, protests that arose from Georgia when the Office of Economic Opportunity withdrew its support from the area planning and development commissions and recognized multicounty community action agencies organized on a different territorial base (generally with fewer counties)—the Advisory Commission on Intergovernmental Relations in 1966 recommended that federal agencies be compelled to recognize the existence of state coordinating bodies and to work through them whenever possible.[68] In cases where a federal agency had valid reasons for not utilizing the state-created body for its own purposes, the ACIR recommended a checkpoint procedure whereby the district organization would at least have the opportunity to review and comment upon proposals for federal assistance. President Johnson responded by directing the Bureau of the Budget to work with the federal departments in developing a policy to coordinate federal and state

66. Council of State Governments, *Suggested State Legislation, 1969*, Vol. 28, p. E-48.
67. "Regional Planning and Development Commissions," in *1968 State Legislative Program*, pp. 422–34, and "State and Regional Planning," in *New Proposals for 1969*, subject code 405.
68. *Intergovernmental Relations and the Poverty Program* (April 1966), p. 169.

planning bodies and planning district boundaries. The result was a circular, issued in January 1967, that declared as its objective "to encourage the states to exercise leadership in delineating and establishing a system of planning and development districts. . . ."[69] Federal agencies were instructed to give governors a chance to review and comment upon proposed planning and development districts. Where possible, federally supported districts ought to conform to state-established boundaries. The survey later in 1967 showed that at least five states had acted—usually through the governor—to provide for coordination of federal and state aid to localities through a district structure.[70]

The HUD Approach: Nonmetropolitan Development

By the mid-1960s, the Department of Agriculture had concluded that its system of rural areas development committees, on which the department's entire RAD program had originally rested, had two fundamental weaknesses: the county basis on which the committees were organized was too small to permit them to mobilize leadership resources to tackle major development problems and projects, and the committees lacked full-time staff to bring sustained energy and professional expertise to the undertaking. Accordingly, taking as their model the multicounty groups that by then were showing considerable vitality in various places, including Georgia, the department proposed legislation authorizing it to provide assistance to establish a system of multicounty development districts throughout rural America.

The new districts, called "community development districts," would be governed by boards appointed by and responsible to local governments, on the Georgia pattern. Upon designation by the secretary of agriculture, the districts would be eligible for federal assistance covering up to 75 percent of the cost of their professional staffs. It was assumed that the districts, again as in Georgia, would usually be organized around one or more commuting centers and their hinterlands.

69. U.S. Bureau of the Budget, "Coordination of Development Planning for Programs Based on Multi-Jurisdictional Areas," Circular No. A-80 (Jan. 31, 1967).
70. American Institute of Planners and U.S. Department of Commerce, "Areawide Planning Activity" (Oct. 15, 1967), p. I-1.

The bill passed the Senate in 1966 but did not emerge from the House Agriculture Committee. One reason given for its failure was the opposition of the United States Chamber of Commerce on grounds that local chambers and industrial development commissions would be threatened.[71] A second factor may have been the confusion arising from the proposal for a new kind of multicounty district when the federal government was already aiding several other kinds. During the Senate debate, Hugh Scott, Pennsylvania Republican, pointed out that the Public Works and Economic Development Act and the Appalachian Regional Development Act, both passed the year before, each authorized creation of similar development districts. "The proliferation of planning bodies and their conflicting jurisdictions should be a cause for concern," he observed. Senator Peter Dominick, Colorado Republican, added that the Office of Economic Opportunity was also financing local planning bodies.

Defeated in the House, the Agriculture Department in the next Congress tried a new tactic—that routed its bill through a different and more sympathetic House committee (the Banking and Currency Committee)—and this time proved successful. By agreement with the Department of Housing and Urban Development, an amendment was drafted to HUD's planning assistance program (authorized by section 701 of the Housing Act of 1954, as amended) extending that program—which already covered individual rural counties and multicounty metropolitan planning bodies—to cover nonmetropolitan multicounty planning organizations as well. While funds under section 701 would, of necessity, be disbursed by HUD, the bill provided a statutory role for Agriculture. The secretary of HUD was required to consult with the secretary of agriculture prior to approving any planning grants for the new districts, and Agriculture was authorized to provide technical assistance both prior to and following the formal organization of the districts.[72]

Presented as a simple extension of an established program and included as a minor feature in a comprehensive housing bill that contained several highly controversial programs, the proposal attracted

71. *Congressional Quarterly Almanac 1966*, p. 127.

72. See testimony of John A. Baker, in *Housing and Urban Development Legislation and Urban Insurance*, Hearings before the Subcommittee on Housing of the House Committee on Banking and Currency, 90 Cong. 2 sess. (1968), p. 1211.

little attention during congressional consideration of the bill. The Scott-Dominick questions of two years earlier about "proliferation" and "conflicting jurisdictions" were not raised. However, the Congress wrote a third agency into the act—the Department of Commerce. Economic development districts (as well as local development districts in Appalachia) were made eligible for the HUD-administered planning grants, and the secretary of HUD was directed to consult with the secretary of commerce before approving any grant to an EDD or a nonmetropolitan district in any area that overlapped that of an EDD. Commerce was also granted technical assistance authority corresponding to that of Agriculture.

The new nonmetropolitan districts (NMDs, as they came to be called) were given a broad function. Their charter—like that of other planning bodies assisted under section 701—was to cover planning for land use, public facilities, government services, human and natural resource development; long-range fiscal planning; programming of capital improvements; and "coordination of all related plans and activities of the State and local governments and agencies concerned."

One important result, from the standpoint of Agriculture, was the broadening of that department's geographical jurisdiction. For the first time the concern of the department was explicitly extended beyond "rural" areas, which in practice had meant the open countryside and incorporated places under 5,500 population. Now the limits on Agriculture's technical assistance role and approval power would cover all of the country designated as "nonmetropolitan"—and a metropolitan area is defined as one with a central city over 50,000. What had begun in the 1950s as concern on the part of a single government department for a declining *rural* America was broadened now into a concern on the part of a complex of agencies for the development of a mixed urban-rural *nonmetropolitan* America (a shift of thinking that is reflected in the titles of this chapter and the two that follow).

In drafting its guidelines, HUD proposed to limit its aid for economic development districts to those EDDs that met the standards established for other nonmetropolitan districts. The principal controversy arose over HUD's insistence that—unless state law provided otherwise—at least two-thirds and preferably all of the voting members of an NMD board must be public officials, either elected officers of local government or "top administrative officers" appointed by the elected officials and authorized to vote in their stead. This, it may be noted, was a higher requirement than that imposed on the HUD-assisted councils of government (COGs) in metropolitan areas, which were required to have only a majority of elected officials. Faced with the prospect that many economic development districts could not qualify as nonmetropolitan districts without a basic reorganization that would displace effective citizen leaders in favor of public officials, the Economic Development Administration objected, but HUD issued its guidelines effective January 1, 1969, without either obtaining EDA's formal clearance or referring the conflict to the Executive Office of the President for resolution. On January 2, HUD and Agriculture jointly announced approval of assistance to the country's first nonmetropolitan district, an existing four-county planning and development commission in the southwest corner of Missouri.

CHAPTER FIVE

Competing Structures
for Nonmetropolitan Development

"WHAT WE HAVE HAD HERE is a process of degeneration," the farmer told us, as he stood at the edge of his hayfield. "Our population consists of the dropouts and people who barely struggled their way through high school. Those who go off to college just don't return. I took my own son to college last week. I don't expect him to come back here to live."

In the more remote sections of rural America, we heard this story many times, in one or another form. A former New York City professional man who had chosen a rural setting for his retirement and had become a civic leader put it this way: "Young people with promise have been drained out of these counties progressively, generation by generation. The greatest difficulty in the development of this area now is the shortage of leadership talent."

And this he saw as the role of the various organizations the federal government was sponsoring—to fill the vacuum of leadership and professional talent:

> What these new federal organizations are bringing us—and I'm in favor of them all, RAD, EDD, CAP, RC&D—is professional talent to compensate for the loss of what should be our home-grown leadership. And still we're understaffed. For every organization in our area, the counterpart organization in New York City would have executive talent at least twelve deep for every competent person we can get to man our organizations here.
>
> Remember, there is not a full-time elected political leader this side of the state capital, and those few of us who can call ourselves citizen leaders are spread extremely thin.

In each of nine states of our survey, we visited one or more non-metropolitan areas. Some of these areas were wholly rural, with declining populations. Others centered on small cities that had attracted some manufacturing or developed other forms of enterprise and were experiencing moderate growth. But all shared a common outlook: they were intensely preoccupied with development—with the creation of jobs and economic opportunity. Their leaders talked about opportunity for themselves; as often they talked of the need for opportunity to make it possible for their sons and daughters, after they had gone to college, to come back home.

In these areas we examined the workings of each type of non-metropolitan coordinating structure identified in Chapter 4, as well as the community action agencies discussed in Chapter 2. We talked with members of rural areas development (RAD) committees and technical action panels (TAPs) in the rural counties. And we visited with officials of twenty-four multicounty agencies and talked with community leaders about them. The twenty-four included six types of agency—seven resource conservation and development (RC&D) projects of the Department of Agriculture, seven economic development districts (EDDs) sponsored by the Department of Commerce, six area planning and development commissions organized by local governments in Georgia (outside metropolitan Atlanta), one rural renewal program, two concerted services projects, and the first of the nonmetropolitan districts.[1] Some of the Georgia commissions had been designated also as economic development districts, and those commissions within the borders of Appalachia—as well as other EDDs in the Appalachian region—were functioning as local development districts (LDDs) under the Appalachian Regional Development Act.

In the diversity of organizational forms, the principal contrast was between the older single-county structures sponsored by the Department of Agriculture and the newer multicounty devices. The difference lay not only in the size of the territory covered but in the presence or absence of full-time professional staff. The county organizations—the RAD committees (also known as OEDP committees in redevelopment areas) and the TAPs—functioned through volun-

1. One RC&D project and one concerted services project served only single counties, but for convenience in this chapter all twenty-four are referred to as multicounty agencies.

teer citizen leadership and local employees of the U.S. Agriculture Department or county extension agents in what time they could spare from their regular jobs. The multicounty agencies were manned by full-time specialists—planners, organizers, and promoters of community development.

Under these circumstances, the single-county structures were overshadowed by the multicounty bodies wherever the latter had been created. The rural areas development committees had declined, the county technical action panels had yet to be revived, and the hopes of the communities for federally aided development rested upon the well financed and well staffed multicounty organizations that were established or in process of formation. Among the latter, the similarities among the several types were more striking, and probably more significant, than the differences.

The Single-County Approach

By the time of our field visits late in 1967, little vitality remained in the rural areas development committees. They had reached the peak of their activity in 1962 and 1963 when the overall economic development programs (OEDPs) were being prepared. Since then, some of them had been instrumental in forming community action agencies under the Economic Opportunity Act and some had become sponsors of resource conservation and development projects or rural renewal programs. But by 1967, few of them were holding meetings any longer, and those that did were confining themselves to the more rural sections of their counties and to minor projects.

In each of the nine states where we visited one or more rural areas, we asked the status of the RAD committees and, if they had declined, the reasons. The following are representative answers—one from each state:

A statewide soil conservation leader, formerly active in RAD committee work:

> The RAD committees in the area are now all defunct. I would say there were three reasons: First, they had no professional staff to provide leadership and follow-through. Second, because they were organized on a county basis, they did not have enough citizen leadership. Third, they were not devoted to *total* resource development. In other words, their programs were too local and too narrow.

A multicounty agency official:

We don't even know who RAD is in this area, and no one who has come to the area recently has heard of them.

A university faculty group (a composite of comments by several participants in a joint interview):

We [the state extension service] recently circularized the county agents as to whether RAD is still a vital activity, and in general our agents said "no." . . . The RAD committees did not represent a wide enough segment of the community. In general, they represented the thrust of the Agriculture Department alone. The other segments of the community can't be subordinated to agriculture or regarded as part of agriculture. . . . It is inevitable that enthusiasm wanes on the part of citizens contributing their own time and effort. . . . The RAD approach has been successful inversely to the degree of urbanization.

Two members of a county RAD committee (a composite of their comments):

Our committee has been inactive for several months, but we plan to revive it. . . . Our big job was preparing the OEDP and the county plan [actually prepared by a consulting firm using funds provided under the federal program for urban planning assistance]. Since then, we have been publicizing the plan but we are not in a position to get anything done to actually put the plan into effect. . . . Our principal handicap is that the committee has been dominated by the rural sections of the county. We originally had urban participation but they became inactive. . . . The county agents have been irritated that this kind of work was saddled on them. And some of us feel the same way about using the county agents for RAD. If the federal government wants RAD work carried out, they should provide additional personnel for the purpose.

A state Farmers Home Administration official:

Few of the RAD committees in this state have ever gotten off the ground. In the main, the OEDPs were prepared by other groups, or by county agents who did not involve the people.

A university extension official:

Even our state RAD committee is now inactive. The chambers of commerce realized a long time ago that they would have to have a permanent staff to influence community or industrial development. Our RAD organizations failed because there was no staff nor system to implement their recommendations.

A state USDA official:

The RAD committees are dissolved in this state. The state RAD committee was officially disbanded.

Two rural civic leaders (a composite of their comments):

We were one of the pilot counties set up by the Eisenhower administration. . . . The project made a big difference in the county, but we worked generally on items like clean-up and paint-up programs—essentially self-help. No one ever got any grant money in those days. . . . Then along came the ARA program, and we tried to put together an OEDP for a seven-county area. We were also supposed to come up with an OEDP for each county, but this fizzled. You've got to have staff. The biggest problem with us is the lack of time. There are too many things going on.

The chairman of an inactive county RAD committee:

I've been chairman of our RAD committee from the first to the last, and was chairman of the rural development committee [during the Eisenhower administration] before that. The OEDP we prepared has been useful, but until we got [a multicounty organization] we never got anything with dollars attached to it, and that's what really motivates people. Now, with the [multicounty organization], we have real leadership.

Only in one state was the extension service planning a statewide effort to revive the RAD committees .The extension service director there appraised the state's RAD effort as successful in one-tenth of the counties, moderately successful in another 10 to 20 percent, and unsuccessful in the rest. He attributed the varying results to three factors: whether a county had been eligible for Area Redevelopment Administration (ARA) assistance (RAD committees flourished only in the eligible counties where they had the demanding responsibility of preparing OEDPs and thereafter the responsibility of passing upon proposed ARA loans and grants); whether a county was truly rural; and whether an individual county agent devoted time and energy to keeping the committee alive.

These generalizations appeared borne out by the experience of other states. Everywhere RAD committees made the most progress in ARA-eligible areas and in counties that were distinctly rural. Sometimes the program was confined to the agricultural areas outside incorporated places; the word "rural" in the "RAD" phrase could suggest even to persons living in county seats of 500 population that the program was not for them. For this reason, some states had renamed their committees, dropping the term "rural."

Over and over, interviewees emphasized that staff work was indispensable to keeping the RAD committees alive. "Our RAD committee could have been great if just one person had been assigned to it full time to do secretarial and leg work," one early RAD leader remarked; "I spent several weeks doing nothing else but working on the original OEDP. But I had to give that up or I couldn't keep my business."

Initially, the county extension agents, under their Agriculture Department assignment of "organizational and educational leadership," had been instrumental in setting up the RAD committees and had often served as committee secretaries. But funds were not available for expanding the county extension staff for the purpose, and the existing staffs were limited in the time they could spend on community development. The county agent and his assistants (if he had any) had full-time jobs before the RAD movement came along, and their 4-H club work and other regular duties continued. Many regarded the RAD work as an unwelcome interruption and had insisted upon returning to their regular duties as soon as the OEDPs were out of the way. The extension services—which began as "agricultural extension" services in all states and in many states are still so named—were likely to consider their first responsibility to be the agricultural community, and often the state extension directors kept their county agents under pressure to deemphasize rural development work. Indeed, the extension service was often the virtual prisoner of commercial agriculture. One state extension director told of being invited to a meeting called by farmers of two counties in order to protest the "diversion" of the county agents' time from agriculture to rural development. "The farmers think we belong to them," said another. Moreover, state and county extension personnel—who are employees of the land grant colleges, not of the Agriculture Department—are not necessarily receptive to ideas out of Washington as to how they should spend their time, whether on RAD or anything else. "Every time Washington announces a new program they expect us to stand up and salute," remarked one county agent, making clear that he, at least, did not always do so. Finally, few county agents (although there were notable exceptions) saw themselves as promoters of projects—especially projects outside the field of agriculture but even projects in that field. As faculty members of their colleges, they were trained as educators, hired as educators, and thought of themselves as educators, with a degree of academic freedom in deciding what causes they would support. "My function is formal education," said an area extension agent; "I would rather talk to twelve mayors about a problem, because that's education, than give service to one." Where the extension agents saw the service function as a job for someone else, it became the job of no one, for apart from the county agents the RAD committees had no paid staff.

The revival of the county technical action panels, to which the Agriculture Department had been devoting considerable energy throughout 1967, was getting under way at the time of our field visits.[2] The attitudes of the TAP members toward their panel duties were much like those of the county agents toward RAD. They already had full-time jobs, and now they were asked to take on new duties in unfamiliar fields—as well as to assume a status as countywide leaders that many of them felt uncertain they could sustain. In some counties the panels had identified certain agricultural projects that their members could undertake cooperatively, but in general the members seemed bewildered as to how to tackle the "outreach" function, and at times their attitudes amounted to passive resistance.

In one area, panel members had met and reached a consensus that directives out of Washington would have to be adapted by them to their area—which, one of the participants explained, meant that the instructions would be regarded as optional. He cited, as an example, a directive that the technical action panels should assist state health officers in the organization of health planning councils. "There is very little that the Department of Agriculture can do to help the public health people in doing their job," was his comment. He said he planned to give TAP functions no more than 10 percent of his time to make certain that they did not interfere with his regular responsibilities. Another chairman, a recent college graduate with a degree in farm production, said that in the past the technical action panel had drawn its assignments from the rural areas development committee but now that it was required to meet separately, it was "having trouble finding an agenda." "The TAP's are floundering all over the state," said an Agriculture official in another state. "When they meet they really don't know what to discuss."

2. Technical action panels were also being organized at the district level, but slowly, and the activity we found was being carried out by county panels. Accordingly, TAPs are discussed under this heading rather than as a multicounty approach. Many of the comments made here about their structure would appear to be applicable to district as well as county TAPs.

The panels were generally proceeding by scheduling at monthly meetings a series of presentations on individual agency programs—covering agencies inside and outside the Agriculture Department—and the members generally acknowledged that such meetings were worthwhile as a means of broadening the knowledge of the individual agency specialists. Also, in response to a directive from Washington, they were visiting rural communities to explain their programs and find out what the local people believed to be their problems. These meetings were evidently less successful; "we didn't learn about any problems except those which the members of the TAP themselves brought up," was one report.

An extension service official who had watched the rural areas development committees fail for lack of full-time staff predicted that the technical action panels would fail for the same reason. "Almost all of their time up to now has been spent on just sharing information," he said. "When they try to get into coordinating public programs or analyzing the overall problems of their counties, they will find they can't do it without full-time staff." A multicounty agency director said the panels in his area were "utterly useless" for the same reason. And the members themselves complained of the inroads on their time. "All these organizations are taking too much time to attend," said a panel chairman, referring to the technical action panel, the resource conservation and development project, and the economic development district in the same area. "I spend four to five days a month making meetings and reports that never seem to accomplish anything. Not very many people attend these meetings, and the irony is that it's the same guys who are at all the meetings." Said an Agriculture field official: "The boys in the counties feel that most of the TAP meetings are an exercise in futility because they are basically meeting with the people that they see every day."

A further weakness of the panels was their domination by the Department of Agriculture. The chairmen had been instructed to invite other federal, state, county, and local officials to participate as members, but the executive committee of each technical action panel consisted solely of Agriculture employees. Involvement of other agencies was spotty. Some county extension agents chose to participate; others did not. Some panels had invited the community action agency directors to join but others deliberately excluded them. "Our group does not want to get involved in public assistance or relief-type programs," said one chairman. A local official of a state employment service said his experience with the county TAP had been disappointing. "They concentrate on technical agriculture matters, like soil mapping and dairy husbandry," he explained. "I suggested that we put manpower programs on the agenda, and there was no objection, so I make a report each time. But when I finish my report, they go right back to agriculture."

A university faculty member told of a statewide technical action panel meeting he had attended:

> It got to be a real joke because it was very obvious that everyone was there because they had to be because of Orville Freeman's memorandum. Everyone present was a bureaucrat with a very narrow leaning. Most of the audience was made up of USDA personnel, and these agencies kept talking all day that they were the most knowledgeable group to work on the problems of our state—the only trouble was that they only talked about natural resources and never spoke about the social and economic problems which exist in the state. The Agriculture people are scared to death that the political structure will kill them if they get into such censored areas as social and economic problems.

Some technical action panels were able to report instances of effective outreach. As a nationwide activity, they had distributed information on the new medicare program among old people in rural areas. They had put prospective borrowers in touch with the Small Business Administration. They had recruited trainees for Manpower Development and Training Act (MDTA) programs. But it seemed clear that the panels had little potential as an instrument for coordinating other agencies. State and local agencies showed no disposition to subordinate themselves in any way to the leadership of the U.S. Department of Agriculture, and even if they were so disposed—or were under instructions to do so (which they were not)—the county-level representatives of Agriculture were too busy with their regular duties and too specialized by training and experience to assume a broad role of communitywide coordination and leadership.

The Multicounty Approach

In the areas where the twenty-four multicounty organizations had come into being, the organizers emphasized that only by combining their resources could rural jurisdictions obtain and support the services of competent professional staff comparable to those of metropolitan centers.

"Every big city has an industrial development staff," observed an Economic Development Administration field man. "But there is no way in the world that nine rural counties operating separately could each afford an industrial developer and compete with the cities. The economic development district is designed to help solve that problem." The head of a multicounty agency staff put it in similar terms: "The primary value of the organization is in the staff itself. There is only one city in this area that can afford this kind of staff, but by pooling their resources these smaller cities can buy continuous planning." "We need somebody from the outside to give us ideas," said a mayor. "We are too stubborn sometimes to listen to outsiders, but it is the only way we are going to learn." And a professor working with several such organizations referred to the clout that the multicounty agency gave the smaller jurisdictions. Severally they were ignored in the state capital and in Washington, but when they banded together in a single organization they were heard. "When I go to the state capital, I represent 130,000 people," said a multicounty agency director.

Though the several types of multicounty agencies evolved separately and were sponsored by groups with differing interests, they were approaching their jobs in much the same way. The mutual resemblance was particularly marked in the more mature of the agencies. Each was helping to fill the vacuum of governmental and civic leadership and of professional expertise in a nonmetropolitan area, and it was the nature of the vacuum and the size and competence of the organization's staff that made the difference. The sponsorship of the organization was secondary.

FIVE TYPES OF AGENCY: BREADTH AND ORIENTATION

As soon as the professional staff of a multicounty agency became established in a community, it became available as a resource, and citizen leaders looking for assistance in the promotion of developmental projects began to use it. "If nobody else happens to be around, they'll turn to you," an agency director explained. Even if the staff director were not aggressive, he would find himself inevitably drawn into new fields and his area of activity expanded. If he sought energetically to expand his sphere, the vacuum of leadership and expertise was there to fill, and with skill and persistence he could move steadily toward filling it. While each of the types of multicounty agency began with a particular orientation and emphasis, then, the tendency of each was to broaden its scope until the distinctions faded and the agencies became strikingly similar in the breadth and scope of their concern.

Following is an indication of the breadth of interest of one example of each of the five types of multicounty agencies we visited in the initial survey.[3] The listing shows the varied fields of governmental concern in which the agency took *some* kind of action—assisting a community, expediting a project, arranging communication, holding a conference, or performing some other kind of service. The extent of involvement of the multicounty agency varied greatly, of course, from project to project, depending upon what was being done by other organizations. The lists are not intended to be exhaustive, and each may omit a few activities that we did not discover in our interviews or in the documents made available to us. Moreover, the individual organization selected to illustrate each type of agency necessarily had a somewhat different range of concern than others of the same type—depending, again, on the extent to which particular fields of concern were being covered effectively by other organizations in the area.

A *Resource Conservation and Development Project* (Northern Rio Grande project, Taos, New Mexico)

> *Resources*: Reorganization of irrigation systems, range improvement, outdoor recreation including access roads, flood control dams and reservoirs, woodland cooperative, soil surveys
> *Agriculture*: Processing-marketing facilities, livestock water system, cropland conversion
> *Industry and commerce*: Lumber mill, clay products factory, restaurant, contracting business, furniture and native craft business
> *Community facilities*: Domestic water systems, municipal recreation, tourist information center, highway beautification
> *Transportation*: Municipal airport, road improvement
> *Health*: Hospital expansion

3. The first of the nonmetropolitan districts, in Missouri, had just been designated at the time of our 1969 visit. While the organization already existed as a four-county planning body, established under state legislation, its scope and orientation as a nonmetropolitan district had not been determined.

Education and manpower: Job training courses
Miscellaneous: Land title legislation

An Economic Development District (Southern West Virginia district, Bluefield, West Virginia)

Resources: Forest ownership study, flood control dams and reservoirs, support of RC&D project, fire prevention, reclamation of strip-mined areas, pollution abatement, soil surveys, roadbank stabilization

Agriculture: Specialty crop development

Industry and commerce: Wood products, coal satellite industries, aid to small business, resort motel

Community facilities: Sewage systems, community beautification, county planning, domestic water supply

Transportation: Road improvement, regional and local airports

Health: Comprehensive health program, hospital expansion, mental health center

Housing: Construction for all income levels

Education and manpower: Adult training, post-high school training, education conferences, graduate education center, labor force studies

Miscellaneous: Tax study

A Georgia Area Planning and Development Commission (Georgia Mountains commission, Gainesville, Georgia)

Resources: Sponsorship of RC&D project, water resource development, forest access roads

Agriculture: Horticulture development

Industry and commerce: Mountain arts corporation, industrial parks, outdoor recreation enterprises, electroplating industry, tourism publicity

Community facilities: Water and sewage systems, local planning and zoning, youth center, town and county recreation, neighborhood facilities, civil defense shelters, fire protection, libraries

Transportation: Local airports, traffic and highway study

Health: Hospital expansion, local health regulation, rat control, home nursing

Housing: Retirement housing project, survey of housing quality

Education and manpower: Vocational school, regional theater, Higher Education Act grant

Miscellaneous: Annexation studies, model cities application and studies, initiation of rural renewal project, municipal management studies and consultation

A *Rural Renewal Program* (Washington, Holmes, and Walton counties, Chipley, Florida)

Resources: Forest resources study, lime deposit study, sand and gravel study

Agriculture: Timber production

Industry and commerce: Meat packing plant, garment factory, hardware store, cooperative cold storage plant

Community facilities: Water and sewer systems, golf and country clubs, municipal recreation, courthouse

Housing: Rural homesite projects, self-help housing

Education and manpower: Assistance in education aid application, vocational school

Miscellaneous: Organization of improvement association, organization of community action agency, OEO-financed summer recreation project, recreation program development

A *Concerted Services Project* (West Central Minnesota, Wadena, Minnesota)

Resources: Ground water studies

Agriculture: Specialty crop production, irrigation, dairy products marketing, farm management and credit, pasture improvement

Industry and commerce: Organization of industrial development group, recreation development, small business loans, wood products

Community facilities: Water and sewer systems, county and municipal recreation, county planning, urban renewal

Health: Nursing home

Housing: Public housing, senior citizen housing

Education and manpower: MDTA courses, education aid applications, community work and training, unemployment and subemployment survey, aid to vocational school, junior college establishment, adult education

Miscellaneous: Coordination of programs for low-income families, programs for older citizens, organization of "Towns United," food stamp program

The most impressive feature of the above listings is their comprehensiveness and their comparability. All five types of multicounty agency were concerned, to some degree, with natural resource development, agriculture, industry and commerce, community facilities, and education and manpower. Most of the five were concerned with housing, transportation, and health. Among the categories, however, there were differences in emphasis, growing out of the original orientation of the agencies and the particular talents and interests of their professional staffs and their citizen leadership.

Resource Conservation and Development Projects. The RC&D projects tend to be the narrowest of the five in scope—at the beginning. They are sponsored initially by specialized organizations, the local soil and water conservation districts, and the original plans are drawn up with assistance from an equally specialized federal agency, the Soil Conservation Service (SCS). But nothing illustrates better the vacuum of organization and leadership in rural America than the way in which many of the RC&D projects that were originally focused quite narrowly on land and water conservation have broadened their scope. The initiative has not come primarily from the SCS staff assigned to the project but rather from citizen leaders who, having discovered that they have at their disposal a full-time project coordinator, have ignored whatever limitations he may have as a soil scientist and pushed him—sometimes against his will—into other fields.

The chairman of the steering committee of the Mountain-Dominion RC&D project in southern West Virginia and western Virginia, who happened to be a physician concerned with health services as well as resource development, described how his resource conservation and development project was broadened and reoriented:

> One of the great beauties of the project is that it is an open-end package. As fast as one problem is solved, another can be stuffed in. The Project Coordinator remains in the community to help as long as there is anything to help.
>
> From the beginning, however, I believe a weakness has been detected in the RC&D concept in that planning is usually confined to the natural and renewable resources while planning in the field of human resources is not ordinarily a part of the RC&D procedure. Therefore an RC&D plan can hardly be said to be truly comprehensive. However, to be completely candid, when the people of the Mountain-Dominion Area indicated their desire to include planning for both health and community facilities in this plan, at least we met no opposition. The worst that can be said is that some of us had the feeling that the SCS just turned its head as we continued to plan in these vital fields of human interest.
>
> That there is considerable overlapping of health and other parts of the plan is obvious to anyone who reads it carefully. That planning should take place among the other human resources, in our opinion, is also evident. As a consequence, not long after completion of our plan, the Mountain-Dominion Steering Committee discussed at length re-

gional planning for industrial development. . . . However, an interesting thing occurred as a result of these discussions. Every person on the Steering Committee came to a simultaneous conclusion—that is, that regionwide planning for education is a prerequisite to industrial planning and planning of other human resources. Therefore, the Mountain-Dominion Project is now embarking upon such educational planning on a regionwide basis.

A Mountain-Dominion Temporary Educational Advisory Council has been formed. This . . . Council will . . . consider a formal proposal for a permanent . . . Council. The Council will participate with the Mountain-Dominion RC&D Steering Committee in the development and writing of a Regional Educational Development Plan. . . . Following educational planning, it is the determination of our Steering Committee to undertake regional industrial planning. Also, it is quite possible that planning in housing, land use, and maybe even social services will follow.

I, of course, can understand the Soil Conservation Service and the Department of Agriculture's reluctance to participate actively in this type of planning. On the other hand, if the planning is to be comprehensive, then human resources must be included. Already, other RC&D projects are making moves in the same direction. I, therefore, predict that comprehensiveness in RC&D planning will increase in the future and that the Soil Conservation Service, reluctantly or not, will find itself engaged in planning for the human resources in one way or another.[4]

A chronological listing of 191 projects proposed to, and considered by, the Northern Rio Grande RC&D project showed that the first one-third were exclusively in the fields of resource development or agriculture, but the most recent one-third ranged across all of the categories shown in the listing above. "We are getting out of the Soil Conservation Service area now," observed a member of the steering committee. A committee member in another district commented with pride that "our committee has never turned down an urban project," even though most of his projects still were concerned with land use and water resources.

Nevertheless, while the project coordinators in most areas expressed no unwillingness to act as promotors of federal assistance— or "grantsmen," as they were commonly called—for airports, hospitals, small business loans, or manpower training projects, few ob-

4. Excerpts from a talk by Daniel Hale, chairman of the steering committee of the Mountain-Dominion RC&D project, at a soil conservation society meeting, Jackson's Mill, W. Va., Sept. 9, 1967.

servers credited them with a full measure of competence in these areas. "I think RC&D is doing a good job for the Department of Agriculture and particularly for the development of agricultural resources," observed an Agriculture field official, "but all RC&D will do is muddy up the water if they pretend to get into the area of social and economic development."

Economic Development Districts. The economic development districts, which were in the process of formation in 1967, began with the breadth of scope toward which the more ambitious RC&Ds were only then evolving. One reason was the district OEDP that had to be presented to the Economic Development Administration before an economic development district could be established. Since its beginnings in the early area redevelopment bills, the OEDP had been conceived as a *comprehensive* program, and the EDA instructed potential EDD organizers accordingly. Inevitably, then, the OEDP defined a broad range of concern for the new districts.

The men being hired as executive directors of the new districts came from a variety of backgrounds but, judging from the sample of districts we visited, they were characteristically "generalists." None had come from a background as specialized as the soil conservation careers of the RC&D directors. Most had had some experience with organizations engaged in economic development—a community industrial development corporation, chamber of commerce, or kindred organization. Some had held positions in federal, state, or local government, usually as political appointees. One had been a mayor, one a state department head, one secretary to a governor. They had no difficulty talking the language of comprehensive planning and development.

In discussing their role, the directors saw themselves as concerned with virtually the entire range of federal aids to local communities, as well as the whole scope of state and local public services. "Every function of government is within our scope of interest," said one director, adding after a pause: "except maybe welfare." Another defined his scope as "everything in the federal spectrum with the possible exception of the poverty program." Yet another specifically included antipoverty programs as among his major areas of concern.

Georgia Area Commissions. The scope of concern of the Georgia area planning and development commissions could be all-embracing, since the state law under which they were organized authorized them to work in whatever fields the participating communities chose. Of the six nonmetropolitan commissions we visited, the Georgia Mountains commission (whose range of activity was indicated in the above tabulation) had the largest staff—more than twenty employees—and the broadest scope. It was also the most vigorous and open in its pursuit of federal financial assistance from every agency that had aid to offer.

One of the striking aspects of that commission's program was the manner in which it had become a kind of holding company for other coordinating structures. It had been designated as the economic development district for the area, and as the local development district for the Appalachian Regional Commission. It had promoted establishment of a resource conservation and development project covering three of its counties, and by agreement with the Department of Agriculture the RC&D staff was working out of the commission headquarters as, in effect, a resource development element of the commission staff. The commission had also been seeking a rural renewal project for one or more of its counties. Like other Georgia area commissions, it was preparing the area water and sewer plans required under new legislation as prerequisites for assistance by the Farmers Home Administration to individual projects. The commission staff had consulted with the city of Gainesville in preparing its model cities application. It had served initially as the community action agency for its area, but those functions had subsequently been passed to a subsidiary body and then—at the insistence of OEO—separated altogether (as had also been done, or was being done, in the cases of the state's other commissions).

Some observers who had followed the evolution of the seventeen Georgia commissions (the eighteenth was not formed until 1969) in the decade since their authorization emphasized their diversity. In the absence of direction or guidance from any federal or state agency, they had developed distinctively individual characters, depending upon the preferences of the participating communities and the interests and competencies of the professional staff. The executive director of one commission said that the seventeen bodies could be roughly classified into two categories—those that emphasized *economic* development and those that looked more broadly toward *community* development. He believed that the choice in each case had depended upon two factors—first, the viewpoint of the particular technical adviser or advisers from whom the commission had received its guidance at the outset; second, the attitude of the pre-existing industrial development groups in the area. In some cases, the latter saw in the commission a potential ally and steered it toward industrial development; in other cases, they saw the commission as a threat and steered it in the opposite direction. Two planning and development commissions had felt constrained to remove the words "and development" from their names in order to allay the opposition of the private development groups.

Many of the commissions had turned to the city planning profession for their executive directors, and these officials had inevitably emphasized the activities in which their expertise lay—organization of city and county planning commissions; assistance in preparation of applications for federal aid for local planning under the urban planning assistance program, and participation in selection of the contractors under that program and monitoring of their work; preparation of municipal ordinances in zoning, planning, and related fields; and preparation of regional plans on matters such as transportation and public utilities that affected more than one jurisdiction. Sometimes the commissions provided planning staff services directly to constituent jurisdictions. From this beginning, some of the commissions were moving toward a full-fledged consulting service for small municipalities, including the initiation of comprehensive municipal management studies, and one had begun to provide central computerized services for billing and accounting for municipal utilities and local tax collection. Some commissions were operating training courses for local government personnel concerned with tax assessment, personnel administration, accounting, purchasing, police administration, and other specialties. All of the commissions were developing data banks and making the data available to various agencies for many purposes.

Where economic development was the focus, the commission emphasized its role in organizing studies of the area potential for developing timber, agriculture, recreation, tourism, or other resources; the selection and development of industrial sites; the preparation of data and literature used in industrial solicitation; and in some cases the organization of the promotional activity itself.

Even though the commissions had, on the initiative of the state, served for a time as community action agencies, most of them now

shunned the human resources fields. The war on poverty was regarded in rural Georgia as "a program for Negroes," federal education programs were "a hot issue" because of desegregation requirements, and health and welfare planning were state rather than local
responsibilities.

Rural Renewal. Like resource conservation and development, rural
renewal began with a relatively narrow focus—in this case the lending programs of the Farmers Home Administration (FHA)—but
broadened into many other fields to fill the vacuum of leadership and
professional expertise. The FHA lending programs are broad in
themselves, of course, covering housing, community facilities, and
recreation development as well as agricultural production. Beginning with the intensive promotion of these programs, the rural renewal project directors moved easily into related fields, acting to
assist communities and individuals in obtaining aid from the Small
Business Administration, the Economic Development Administration, HEW, OEO, and other federal agencies.

Concerted Services. The concerted services projects went through
a parallel evolution. In this case the point of departure was education
and training. But the Manpower Development and Training Act
requires that before training programs are organized, jobs that require the training must be available; the concerted services project
coordinators therefore turned to industrial development and found
themselves organizing citizen groups for that purpose. But industrial
development in turn depends upon water supply and other public
services. By 1967, the project coordinators had come to look upon
their field of interest as universal, and they were acting as initiators or
facilitators on any project that appeared to them to be related to
community development. "I may be violating the directives out of
Washington by going so far beyond the fields of education and training," one told us, "but I take a very broad approach to community
development."

THE MULTICOUNTY AGENCY AS GRANTSMAN

Response to the question of what services were rendered to the
participating communities by the multicounty agencies often centered upon one or another phase of what some called "grantsmanship." The proliferation of new federal grant programs in the 1960s

had placed a premium upon a new group of experts—those who could tell local communities what federal largesse was available to them and how to go about getting it. By the time of our survey we found staff members with the title of "federal program coordinator" or its equivalent not only in large cities but in middle sized cities, some of the larger counties, school districts, state capitals, and individual state departments (particularly education departments). These coordinators, and the officials to whom they were responsible, had a common complaint: there was no single place in Washington to which they could turn for information on grant programs, nor any way they could even keep abreast of money being received within their own jurisdictions. "Every week I learn about a new program that is operating in my own community, and there is no one on my staff who can keep up with everything that is going on," complained a mayor. "These federal programs float past the cities like clouds that they can't seem to get a handle on," was the mixed metaphor of a municipal association official.

The smaller communities, of course, could not afford the luxury of federal program coordinators on their own staffs, and it was they who had the most difficult time learning about the availability of federal assistance. The information gap between the federal government and rural America was well brought out in the following interchange between Senator Joseph M. Montoya, Democrat of New Mexico, and Jack Herrington of Fort Worth, Texas, assistant regional director of the Department of Housing and Urban Development, at a Senate Public Works subcommittee hearing in Albuquerque in 1967:

MONTOYA: How many of these programs [referring to federal aid for local street improvement] do you have in New Mexico?

HERRINGTON: I don't think we have a single one to date. These are being explored in a case or two.

MONTOYA: That is what I mean. We don't have anybody from your department telling these municipalities what they can do.

HERRINGTON: Sir, we are more than happy, in fact we encourage and are very pleased when—you know, we really believe that our programs should be made available to the people . . . and we would love to talk with them about it.

MONTOYA: How many people do you have coming into New Mexico from the Fort Worth office?

HERRINGTON: Well, now, in the renewal program, and I can't speak for the rest of the office . . . we have an area coordinator who is responsible for Texas and New Mexico, and he has, I believe, six people on his staff. These people are made available on request. . . .

MONTOYA: How many visits have they made into northern New Mexico?

HERRINGTON: Northern New Mexico, I would doubt that there have been—I would guess that there have been very few visits.

MONTOYA: Would you try to encourage them to try to visit northern New Mexico before the summer is over?

HERRINGTON: We certainly will, Senator. Here again, we work at the request of the community. . . . If we can get a request of any sort, we will have someone there.

MONTOYA: The point I am trying to make, Mr. Herrington, is that many of these municipalities do not know what HUD can do for them.[5]

Not all rural public officials expressed the need for grantsmanship service. A few expressed hostility toward the principle of federal aid and a combative disinterest in learning about the programs. Others, in the absence of any systematic flow of information about the availability of federal programs, seemed simply unaware of the possibilities of obtaining and utilizing federal aid in their communities. But those who were both interested and aware had, invariably, encountered difficulty in obtaining their federal assistance. One former city manager, who had become a planning consultant, summarized his impressions and his experience:

There are just too many federal programs. In particular, the small communities that have no staff have a difficult time sorting out the various agencies and programs and finding out just who can help them and how. As the result, the communities which need the programs the worst aren't getting them.

When I have a problem, I call the state municipal league or I know who to call in the state government. But I know my way around better than most. The ordinary municipal official would not even know who to call to find out what the possibilities were.

On one occasion, I tried to put together a project that involved both the Soil Conservation Service and urban renewal. Neither agency was equipped to deal with the composite or was even knowledgeable about the other agency's program. Consequently, the whole burden of putting it together fell upon me. On another occasion, our community and a neighboring community six miles away worked out a plan for a consolidated sewage treatment system. But we had to deal with HUD for our money while our neighbor was not big enough for HUD and had to

5. *Ozarks-Four Corners Regional Development Commissions*, Hearings before a Special Subcommittee on Economic Development of the Senate Committee on Public Works, 90 Cong. 1 sess. (1967), pp. 337–38.

deal with Agriculture. Eventually we worked it out but it required two sets of paper work with two different agencies.

A state municipal league official offered figures to show the loss to smaller communities because of their lack of ability as grantsmen. That state's largest city, with 15 percent of the state's population, had received about 50 percent of the state's share of federal grants. Beyond that, this official felt cities and towns with professional managers were receiving a greater share, proportionately, than jurisdictions without them.

"There is health and education money that is going begging in this region because people just do not know that the programs exist," a federal regional official told us. And the executive director of a new economic development district remarked: "In this area, whenever someone wants something he calls his congressman. That's the level of grantsmanship sophistication that exists here."

Various organizations were trying to fill the grantsmanship void in the rural areas. The technical action panels acknowledged that they were expected by the Agriculture Department to act as grantsmen, but they were just beginning to get organized for the purpose and it was a rare TAP member who claimed to have gathered systematic information on any programs other than those of his own agency. In several states the state extension services had appointed statewide or district specialists in rural development who kept informed on federal programs, arranged meetings of community officials to discuss their applicability, conducted training courses, and sometimes consulted with individual communities. State municipal leagues were trying to keep their members informed. Some states had established departments of community affairs with information service among their functions, and their field offices (where they existed) were serving as points of contact and arranging educational meetings. In one state the regional offices of the state department of commerce saw the flow of information about federal programs as one of their responsibilities.

And grantsmanship had become a rewarding field for private enterprise: engineering consulting firms sold not only their engineering services but their ability to identify the right federal agency to finance a water or sewer project, to help the community fill out the application forms, and to see the application through to approval. Architects were moving among local communities in some areas promoting housing projects to be financed with federal assistance. Yet these private sources were specialized; none of them served as a general source of advice on the whole range of federal programs.

By far the most effective grantsmanship service that we encountered in the nonmetropolitan areas was that provided by some of the multicounty agencies that had chosen to emphasize that phase of their work. In some cases, indeed, the need for expert grantsmanship had been the dominant purpose in the creation of the new entity, and obtaining federal aid for their communities had become their central preoccupation. The older organizations proudly showed us lists of—and, when there was time, took us on tours of—federally aided projects that, they contended, would not have been started without their help. They had provided the information to the sponsoring community or private group, arranged contact with the appropriate federal agency, advised the sponsor on how to meet federal requirements, promoted the application, assisted in filling out forms, and in general nursed the project along. One agency staff director noted that the one hundred and fifteen federal-aid projects with which he was concerned fell into ninety categories, each of which required its own approach. It is difficult to apportion credit for a particular project between its immediate sponsor and the multicounty body that may have helped the sponsor at some stage—the "catalyst," as the agency staff director often described his function. But enough corroborating testimony came from the communities themselves to attest to the value of professional grantsmen.

The director of an area vocational school described the services of a professional staff representative of that area's multicounty agency:

> At this school, we obtain federal funds through fifteen different federal programs. [He enumerated them.] Mr. Y [the representative] is constantly reminding me of all of these federal programs and their deadline dates and telling me how to maneuver among the federal agencies. A week before an application is due on one of these programs I'm sure to get a call from Mr. Y asking whether I've filled it out yet. When I had some questions on Title V of the Economic Opportunity Act, Mr. Y got me the answers. He also had a lot to do with getting Operation Head Start approved in this district, and in getting the state university to put an experimental farm here.

A small town mayor explained his need for grantsmanship assistance:

> I had a project application in to HUD, and for a while, in order to move it along, I had a standing date to telephone them every Tuesday at one o'clock. It's at great personal sacrifice that I put these things

through. I've quadrupled the city's postage and telephone bill, but there is no way to get results except to bombard them. I went to the regional office and crawled over their desks until they said, "You're hollering louder than anybody else."

All federal agencies are not the same. With the Soil Conservation Service, one letter was all I needed. The Bureau of Outdoor Recreation came in and made our application out for us. But when you get a tough one, it's a great assist to have Mr. J [the multicounty agency executive director] pick up the whole package, take it to the regional office and say, "What do we do, what are the possibilities, and what is the timetable?" and then make all those phone calls and follow through for us. And he charges us nothing for the service.

A county development authority chairman said of the director of that area's multicounty organization:

Mr. P [the director] has really provided leadership. For example, if I wanted a Small Business Administration loan, I would go to Mr. P. He got a loan of $60,000 for a pallet factory here. Small communities just don't have the leadership or direction that would enable them to apply for a water system, for instance. Frequently, it's very vague to me as to whose business on the federal level each of these programs is.

Said a community action agency director in the same area:

Our tricounty CAA came out of the area staff. Mr. P prepared the original applications when the legislation was enacted. This was the first CAA in the state, and in fact was in operation before the state office or the regional office.

In response to a question about what the staff of the multicounty coordinating body did for him, the manager of a small city pointed to a file on his desk of application forms for a federal water and sewer grant. "They take care of all this stuff. I can't fill these out. I don't know who to send them to." He explained that an urban renewal project in his community had been "put together" earlier by the multicounty staff. Two city managers gave a multicounty agency credit for the staff work on their cities' "workable programs" required as a prerequisite for certain forms of federal aid. One agency had prepared a model cities application (unsuccessful) for a small town.

We attended a community meeting called to discuss next steps in promoting a water impoundment project that was to create a small lake as a summer cottage and recreation center. The staff director of the multicounty coordinating body had arranged for drawings of the project, which he presented, and he advised on the sources of federal and state funds and on the procedural steps to be followed in applying for the assistance. While remaining in the background, it was he who guided the group at each stage of the discussion. "Without him, they'd give up," commented a local federal official afterward. "They'd become discouraged."

One of the multicounty agency directors described his own concept of his job and his method of operation:

> My job is to start things, like a community action agency or a housing project, and then find other people to operate them so I can back off and go into other projects. If I get too connected with any one particular program, I won't be able to work toward my overall goal, which is the development of this whole rural area.
>
> But I do whatever is necessary. In regard to our vocational school, I wrote up the necessary information, set up the meetings and conferences, and would have been on the board of governors if [the responsible federal agency] hadn't stepped in and stopped me.

Another director said he was not waiting for inquiries but was sending a letter to every municipality in his area listing federal aid programs and asking which ones the community might be interested in. When he received his responses, he planned to call meetings of those interested in particular programs and invite representatives of the agencies concerned to come and explain the programs. After that, he would be engaged in the follow-through on individual projects. Conversely, a multicounty agency that had resisted a general grantsmanship role was being pushed into it by a request from one of its counties for a study of the whole range of federal assistance programs for which it might be eligible.

But not all multicounty agencies emphasized grantsmanship. At least two economic development district directors expressed the hope they would not be drawn into becoming information and expediting channels on federal aid to communities—although each acknowledged that he would probably have to fill that vacuum. The Georgia commissions, which were the only multicounty agencies we visited that were not federally sponsored, ranged all the way from those putting the highest priority on grantsmanship to those that made clear they would be highly selective in pushing federal programs in their communities.

THE MULTICOUNTY AGENCY AS PLANNER

The word "planning" appeared in the jargon of all the types of multicounty agencies and recurred throughout our interviews. But, like coordination, planning has varied meanings. The plan can be a map, like a city plan, that imposes discipline on land use. Or it can be an intention to do something, like an area's plan for school improvement. A plan can be comprehensive or functional, immediate or long-range, actual or contingent. The plans that we encountered were all of these.

The most elaborate plans—in the intention-to-do-something sense—were the overall economic development programs of the economic development districts, which were in the preparation stage at the time of our field visits. While the organizers of the districts often questioned whether the OEDPs were worth the enormous amount of energy that went into their preparation, they acknowledged some value in the documents. The benefit most commonly emphasized was the motivation that the citizens gained from participation in the planning process. As one citizen leader put it, harking back to the county OEDPs prepared under the Area Redevelopment Act:

> These OEDPs took a lot of time. But they did some good in that they stimulated interest and thinking and the desire to make improvements. They started rural people to thinking about water and employment and the chance to improve themselves and started them saying, "It doesn't have to be like this."

A consultant to a newly formed district described the extraordinary lengths to which he went to obtain extensive citizen participation, through committees and subcommittees that held open meetings to obtain and discuss suggestions for particular sections of the plan. Through this process, he said, the OEDP was a means of developing both consensus and commitment. One district director, after grumbling about the work required to prepare his OEDP, explained that he found it useful as the basis for his talks outlining the EDD program to groups in the district. Preparation of a district OEDP had also compelled the cooperation of leaders of participating counties who may have cooperated but little previously. By its phrasing in regional terms, it developed regional consciousness. In its table of contents it outlined the comprehensive scope of the economic development district and, in effect, staked out the jurisdictional claim of the organization. And it served as a starting point for more detailed functional planning; in several localities, intensive studies of timber, mineral, agricultural, or recreational resources had stemmed from their identification in the initial planning process as areas of economic potential.

Nevertheless, though these values were acknowledged, it is fair to say that the OEDPs were prepared because the federal government required them—not because the citizen leaders saw the comprehensive planning process as having enough intrinsic merit to justify the effort. The attitude of the other types of federally sponsored multicounty agencies toward formal planning could be described as one of minimum compliance. Where no plan was required, none was prepared. Where a functional plan covering certain fields of activity was prescribed, as in the case of the resource conservation and development projects, that was as far as the planning went; as the RC&D organizations broadened their range of interest, they did so usually by sponsoring additional specific projects rather than by broadening—or introducing—a planning process. The Georgia commissions, before they became economic development districts, had not attempted comprehensive plans but limited themselves to various types of land-use plans along traditional city planning lines.

In expressing their impatience with planning, citizen leaders often referred to their earlier experience in preparing county OEDPs for the Area Redevelopment Administration. Those OEDPs had proved of little value, the argument went, because the communities had no professional staff to develop and promote the individual projects the plans proposed. Now that their multicounty agency had staff, the communities wanted them to push projects—not write more plans. Sometimes the professional staffs themselves agreed. These were some criticisms of planning:

An EDD director:

It took three man-years of work to compile the data and prepare that OEDP. Frankly, I don't think anybody will ever read it.

An agency chairman:

Sure, we ought to analyze our weaknesses and strengths, but we should also get some projects. We've looked at plans, relooked at plans, replanned, but what we want is action.

A federal field official:

The people in this area are tired of plans—particularly the ones that always end up sitting on the shelf and are never used. We are beyond the stage that we need a plan.

An EDD chairman:

We're going to lose a year while the district director prepares OEDPs for those counties in the district that have never had them. What we need is someone to pick up the individual ideas we already have and put the time on them necessary to dog them through.

An agency director:

We have no plan as such. The needs of the area for development are apparent. What we have to do is identify the kinds of projects that will pay off economically and that are eligible for federal or state assistance. As we design projects that qualify, then the problem is to get them carried into effect.

While planners were under pressure from their communities to stop formal planning and start "dogging" projects, there were no opposite community pressures on action-minded staffs to suspend operations and concentrate upon planning. The only criticism of them, if any, came from professional planners and academicians. One planner, for example, criticized an RC&D project as having "no plan—just a list of projects." Before developing projects to increase production of particular crops, he argued, it should prepare a total plan for the area's agriculture.

The difference between a plan and a list of projects may be an indistinct one. Most of the early county OEDPs were hardly plans in any sophisticated sense; they consisted simply of basic statistical data followed by an enumeration of projects. The RC&D project plans, while more elaborate, tend to follow the same pattern. Projects are submitted by local public or private organizations, and the plans incorporate the project lists with little ordering of regional priorities. For purposes of allocating staff time and energy, of course, priorities have to be set, but those priority decisions are made for the most part informally, on a day-to-day basis—and perhaps in response more to community pressures than to analysis. The OEDP developed by a typical economic development district, in contrast, arrives at priorities through a more systematic and refined analysis of the district's economy, its growth potential and the impediments to growth. Not limited functionally, it can focus upon the critical problems wherever they are found—whether in transportation, housing, resource development, education and training, governmental structure, or somewhere else. The interdependence of all of the various fields of developmental activity is highlighted in the comprehensive planning process, and the relation of projects to one another is more clearly perceived, leading to combination of narrow projects into broader ones and the coordination of planning of separate undertakings. The requirement of the authorizing legislation that each economic development district identify its growth center has forced the organizations, too, to think geographically in terms of priorities for public investment—a form of politically hazardous discrimination among participating communities that the other types of multicounty agencies have scrupulously avoided. Despite the tendency of paper-weary EDD officials to disparage their own OEDPs, then, the planning process does provide the means for building consensus upon a developmental strategy that will mobilize an area's resources and coordinate the efforts of all of the area's participating organizations—with resulting values closely analogous to those derived in the cities from the model cities process. Nevertheless, we admit to positive impressions of the achievements of multicounty agencies that were doing their planning piecemeal, project by project, and we cannot quarrel with the contention of the critics of "overplanning" that planning is of little value unless an action organization exists to promote the projects that the plan contains.

The tendency of those interested in action to downgrade the importance of planning has led some professional planners to contend that the two functions are incompatible in the same organization. In Massachusetts, during our visit, a proposal to convert that state's regional planning bodies to planning "and development" commissions was being hotly debated within the planning profession. Some saw the move as making planning significant; others saw it as marking the end of truly professional planning. In Georgia a few of the area planning and development commissions were steadfastly trying to confine themselves to planning—"the state law does not even permit us to get into implementation of our plans," said one commission director. But most of his counterparts in other commissions were impatient with that view—"implementation is what I get paid for," explained a staff member of another commission. In the other types of multicounty agency, the latter was the universal position.

Planning was considered most likely to be useful if the organization responsible for the planning had also the responsibility for initiating action to carry out developmental projects. The responsibility should end with the initiation and promotion of projects, however; the preponderant view was that the planning and development bodies should not themselves become administrative agencies providing governmental services.

THE MULTICOUNTY AGENCY AS COORDINATOR

All of the multicounty agencies saw themselves as coordinators, responsible for bringing together the various agencies or jurisdictions or public and private groups that might be concerned with individual projects and for bringing separate projects into relation with one another. Some defined coordination in terms of "mobilization" of community resources, both within individual jurisdictions and across jurisdictional lines.

The role of coordinator is not separable from that of planner, and some aspects of coordination were therefore touched on in the discussion of planning. In any comprehensive planning process, interrelated problems are identified and solutions can be planned in such a way as to reinforce one another. Conflicts between individual projects can be reconciled, and priorities established. Projects that need to be related geographically can be examined jointly in the land-use phase of the comprehensive plan; highway and reservoir plans can be dovetailed, for example, so that roads will be routed across dams rather than located in valleys that will be flooded later. Public facilities necessary as a base for industry can be clustered in the area's natural growth centers. Industrial development projects can be related to plans for skill training of the labor force, to development of research facilities associated with institutions of higher education, and to provision of housing for workers. Industrial development may also depend upon making the area more attractive to company executives by improving the public schools, health services, and recreational facilities. Development of timber or agricultural resources may depend upon organization of processing and marketing, and so on. Those multicounty agencies that did not undertake comprehensive planning sought the same coordination objectives by establishing committees or assigning staff to the joint consideration of related projects.

Officials of the agencies gave us many specific examples of coordination. The following suggest the types and variety of coordinating activity.

Mobilizing Several Agencies in a Single Project. A multicounty agency acted as coordinator of a municipal recreation project, bringing together the city council, which sponsored the project and donated the site; the Soil Conservation Service, which planned the reservoir and accompanying facilities; the school district, which provided equipment for clearing the site; and the Department of Housing and Urban Development, which financed the project.

Another agency took the lead in preparing a site plan for recreation development on a large reservoir, then assisted public and private sponsors in preparing twenty-four separate but coordinated applications for federal or state assistance—for boat launching ramps, golf course, access roads, water and sewer facilities, and so on.

In industrial site development, multicounty agencies mobilized many resources by serving as a communication link between local communities and development groups, on the one hand, and many sources of assistance—federal agencies, utility and railroad companies, and private planning consultants—on the other. They also provided direct services in preparation of applications, site planning, and publicity and promotion.

Obtaining Interjurisdictional Cooperation. A multicounty agency, through analysis of transportation patterns, identified what it considered a promising location for an industrial park. It then brought together officials of four counties to form a nonprofit corporation to prepare the site and made the initial contact with the Economic Development Administration to finance a three-mile water line from the nearest public water system. The agency staff felt that without their initiative the local leadership would not have developed the idea nor found means to carry it out. "It was the commission that taught people to think across county lines," said a staff member. "And in that part of the area people have been beaten down so long that if the commission had not stirred them up they never would have dared to conceive any such bold idea."

Another multicounty agency persuaded a community that was proposing to initiate a water development project to hold up its application so that three other communities in the same valley could join with it in sponsoring a single, larger project. Several agencies were drafting countywide or areawide plans for rural water and sewer systems, and one had worked on the creation of a multijurisdictional airport authority. One had brought several communities together in a sanitary landfill project. At the request of the state highway department, one had coordinated the highway plans of seven counties.

A multicounty agency used its good offices to resolve an impasse that arose when one county demanded that a community in another stop dumping its trash and garbage on unused public land across the county line. Under the agency's auspices an agreement was worked out whereby the offending community would be permitted to dump across the boundary but at a different place.

Obtaining Public Action in Support of Private Development. On behalf of a lumber mill, a multicounty agency interceded with the Forest Service to get assurance of an adequate timber supply, with the state highway department to build a direct road between the mill and a major timber source, and with state officials to get a training project for mill employees. An agency interceded with a state highway department to obtain higher priority on a road that provided access to a proposed ski resort. In one instance an agency, upon learning that an applicant for a private project was ineligible for a federal loan, persuaded a private lending institution to reconsider its initial rejection and make the loan.

THE ROLE OF NONPROFESSIONAL LEADERSHIP

Some of the examples of coordination cited above reflected primarily the activities of the multicounty agency's professional staff; others were the work of the agency board members. The agency boards were variously constituted.[6] A few were made up wholly of local public officials representing the participating counties, cities, and towns. In other cases, local officials created the agency but ap-

6. The economic development districts and Georgia commissions had governing boards with full authority over the agencies' programs and staffs; the resource conservation and development projects had steering committees that lacked power to hire staff but exercised supervision and program control over the staff assigned by the Soil Conservation Service. Rural renewal authorities, organized on a county basis, shared an area professional staff member assigned to them by the Farmers Home Administration. The concerted services projects had no boards, only a professional staff man designated as project coordinator.

pointed private citizens as well as public officials to the board. In still other cases, the board had representation from organizations other than local governments—state agencies in some instances, soil and water conservation districts and rural areas development committees in the case of the resource conservation and development projects, business and labor groups in the case of the economic development districts, and so on. Where the board members represented institutions that needed to be coordinated, then much could be accomplished in the board meetings themselves. And, where the board members were vigorous and prestigious, they could exert strong authority over organizations that might need to be coordinated. One citizen leader described how he and his colleagues exercised their authority over federal and state agencies operating in the area:

> Our agency is designed to give an action arm to the [rural areas development] committees. Until it came along, the committees had lots of project ideas, but they died for lack of someone available to carry them out.
>
> Now, when a citizen group like ours here in this county gets an idea we have a device whereby we can call a meeting of public officials and organize the action. In the old days, we had to go to the government agencies as supplicants. Now we call the meeting and they come. For instance, we called a meeting of the federal and state agencies who had money and technical assistance available for [a specific project] and the meeting didn't break up until each of the agencies had designated a staff member to serve on a technical committee to come up with a complete plan.

Another put it this way:

> All of the federal agencies respond to decisions of our committee. If we approve a project for a Farmers Home Administration loan, the FHA will go along. When we heard from a group of citizens about a crop development scheme and asked the county agent to work with the citizens, he did so automatically. We have muscle which no individual applicant could possibly have.

The role of nonprofessional board members varied greatly, however, from agency to agency. In some it appeared to be the board members rather than the professional staffs who initiated many (perhaps most) of the project ideas; they made the key telephone calls or visits to governors, state legislators, or federal political officials when their help was needed; they took the initiative to arrange the meetings where coordination of agencies and projects took place. In other areas, in contrast, the professional staff emphasized the difficulty of maintaining a high pitch of interest on the part of the citizen leaders. One agency director—whose multicounty area did not reflect a natural community—said that his citizen leaders had never developed a regional consciousness, in the absence of any regional projects, and that it was hard even to keep alive his constituent county organizations. Citizen involvement was now largely confined to community groups working on strictly local projects.

In our sample, the most dynamic leadership on the agency boards appeared to be coming from the private citizens rather than the public official members. The private citizens had been selected in the first place because of their regional standing and outlook, and they were the ones who best articulated concepts of regional planning and of comprehensive, multifunctional planning. They were most effective in promoting projects involving private investment. The public officials, by contrast, tended to be locally oriented and preoccupied with the functions of local government for which they were responsible, particularly municipal public works. They appeared to be providing relatively little leadership in such fields as education, manpower, housing, agriculture and timber resource development, and economic development in general—aspects of development for which county and small municipal governments have traditionally had no responsibility.

Professionals in the several types of agencies often saw as one of their major tasks the development of citizen leadership. "No government agency is going to develop the country," said one. "The people themselves have to do that." Accordingly, he explained, even on occasions when he could make a decision or take an action himself he utilized his executive committee and tried to act in a staff capacity to it. A few took the opposite view. "There are some fallacies in the idea of community involvement," one director remarked. "Professional staffs are paid to do a job, and our board just takes a look at the work of the staff, and approves it."

THE PROBLEM OF OVERLAP

Since the Economic Development Administration and the Department of Agriculture have proceeded independently in the creation of their multicounty organizations, it was inevitable that those organizations would overlap. The EDA is required by statute to limit its districts to depressed areas, but Agriculture tended to give those areas preference also, because they showed greater interest in, and need for, federal assistance. Consequently, in every one of the areas where we examined an Agriculture multicounty operation, an economic development district was either in being or in the planning stage. Moreover, in one of the areas, Agriculture had both a resource conservation and development project and a concerted services project, with different boundaries but with two counties in common.

The most frequent complaint against the overlapping structure was the strain it imposed upon the limited resources of rural leadership. "We are all competing for the same local leadership," said a federal field official, "and the locals just about become full-time professional meeting-attenders." Some of the citizen leaders were clearly partisans of one or another federal agency, and it seemed possible that the federal competition might tend to divide the local leadership that needed to be brought together. In the main, however, no such division was yet apparent at the time of our visits; the economic development districts were just in process of formation, and usually the leaders of the resource conservation and development or rural renewal projects were among the prime movers in bringing the EDDs into being. When asked about coordination, the citizen leaders often pointed to the interlocking directorates of the separate federally sponsored entities as an effective safeguard.

In one area that had a well developed resource conservation and development project—and one that had broadened its program significantly beyond the field of natural resources—we sought out three of the RC&D leaders who had also participated in forming the new EDD. "Why," we asked, "are you organizing an economic development district when you already have a well organized RC&D?"

The answer from each went about as follows: "Why are *we* organizing another district? It's not *our* idea. The federal government insists upon it. They tell us that if we want the Agriculture programs, we have to have an RC&D, and if we want the EDA programs we have to have an EDD. We want all the programs, so we're doing what the federal government requires. Of course we'd rather do it all through a single organization. But they won't let us."

Attitudes in other areas were similar. When asked the direct question, the citizen leaders would usually express a preference for a

Figure 3. Jurisdictions of Development Agencies in Florida

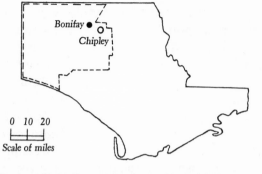

—— Northwest Florida Economic Development District (10 Florida counties)
– – – Northwest Florida Rural Renewal Area (3 Florida counties)
● EDD headquarters   O Rural renewal headquarters

Figure 4. Jurisdictions of Development Agencies in New Hampshire and Vermont

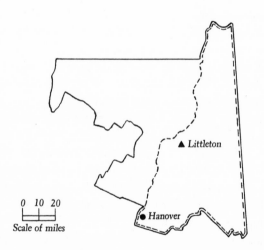

—— New Hampshire–Vermont Economic Development District
(7 Vermont and 3 New Hampshire counties)
– – – New Hampshire Resource Conservation and Development Area
(3 New Hampshire counties)
● EDD headquarters   ▲ RC&D headquarters

single, all-purpose structure, but they did not volunteer complaints about the requirement for separate organizations. They tended to equate the organizations with their respective aid programs, and in that sense welcomed each new organization as an additional source of federal money. A few saw positive advantages in dual organization. "There are a lot of parallels between the RC&D and the EDD in this area, but they are associated with separate power groups," said a state official who served on the boards of both organizations. "The RC&D is run by the more conservative, traditional agricultural interests while the EDD is allied with the more urban and progressive leadership. So there will be a difference in emphasis and in the kinds of projects undertaken. But these are not particularly competing power groups, and the EDD and RC&D enjoy the best of relationships. The EDD has used much of the RC&D planning in the preparation of its OEDP." Said an Agriculture Department field official: "Competition always keeps everybody on their toes." Said an EDD chairman: "You'd be surprised at the better service you get with two banks in town."

Good relationships between the separate professional staffs were characteristic. Asked if there were difficulties in relationships, staff directors typically answered, "None that we can't work out by getting together." The staffs of all the organizations were looking for allies, and when they found themselves in overlapping areas they appeared to develop a bond as fellow professionals. In no instance had the division of labor been formally defined, but in general the RC&D spokesmen looked to the newer EDDs to assume responsibility for development of industry and supportive public services and permit the RC&Ds to return to a more restricted concern with agriculture and natural resource development. In one instance where the EDD was the older organization, its director was expecting the new RC&D staff to develop what amounted to the agriculture and water resources section of the OEDP. He was, however, moving ahead with his own timber development program.

One obstacle to "getting together" is the divergence in boundaries and the physical separation of headquarters, which is illustrated in Figures 3–6. The Agriculture-sponsored districts are typically smaller than the economic development districts. The Florida rural renewal area, for instance, comprises three counties of a ten-county economic development district (Figure 3). The RC&D project in

Figure 5. Jurisdictions of Development Agencies in West Virginia and Virginia

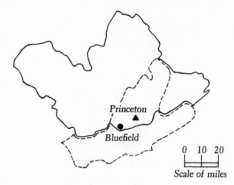

——— Southern West Virginia Economic Development District
       (9 West Virginia counties)
– – – Mountain–Dominion Resource Conservation and Development Area
       (3 Virginia and 2 West Virginia counties)
● EDD headquarters   ▲ RC&D headquarters

Figure 6. Jurisdictions of Development Agencies in Minnesota

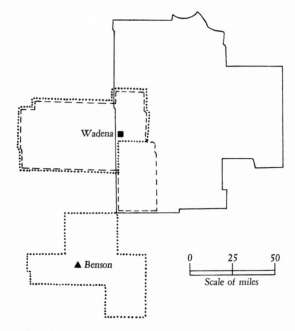

——— Central Minnesota Economic Development District (authorized)
       (7 Minnesota counties)
– – – West Central Concerted Services Project
       (3 Minnesota counties)
•••••• West Central Minnesota Resource Conservation and Development Area
       (5 Minnesota counties—not contiguous)
   ▲ RC&D headquarters   ■ Concerted services project headquarters

New Hampshire covers only that state's segment of the bistate New Hampshire-Vermont EDD (Figure 4). The Mountain-Dominion RC&D project covers two of the nine counties of the Southern West Virginia EDD, plus three counties in Virginia (Figure 5). In this instance, the EDD proposes to support the RC&D but to sponsor a comprehensive water resources study of its own to develop projects for the entire district. In west central Minnesota, the RC&D, the concerted services project, and the proposed EDD intersect and overlap in various ways (Figure 6).

In the four illustrated cases—as well as in most other instances where boundaries differed—the headquarters of the two agencies were in different cities. We asked an RC&D director whether the fact that the EDD director had his office seventy miles away interfered with coordination. "Not at all," was the answer. "I'm on the phone with him all the time." But if relations between the organizations were so intimate as to require telephone conferences "all the time," it follows that coordination would be more easily achieved if the offices were adjacent.

The one exception to the crazy-quilt pattern of multicounty organizations is that of Georgia. There the state-authorized pattern of area planning and development commissions predated the federal sponsorship of multicounty districting, and the federal districts conform to the area pattern. The commissions themselves act as the economic development districts and as the local development districts for the Appalachian Regional Commission. The two resource conservation and development projects in Georgia, while not covering the whole of their areas, were sponsored by the area commissions, and in one case the RC&D staff is housed in the commission's offices. The community action agencies were also initially organized by the area commissions on the same multicounty pattern, and while they have since been subdivided in most cases to cover smaller areas they do not overlap the commission boundaries.

In the other states, however, where state regional patterns were adopted only after the federally sponsored districts were established, adjustment of district boundaries to conform to the state pattern has been slow in coming—despite the Budget Bureau's instructions.[7] As a special handicap, the vagaries of the statute authorizing economic

7. See Chap. 4, pp. 162–63.

development districts make adjustment of their boundaries often impossible. Because each district must contain two "redevelopment areas" (each a labor market area, usually a single county, with high unemployment), the districts frequently must be gerrymandered. Thus, the bistate New Hampshire-Vermont EDD was formed by uniting New Hampshire's only redevelopment area—its northern three counties—with the only such area in Vermont. Since the eligible Vermont county lay near the western edge of the state, several intervening Vermont counties had to be included and the resultant sprawling district is neither an economic unit nor a political community. In Massachusetts, economic development districts could not be created to conform to the state's planning regions—which had been carefully drawn to define natural economic areas—and the governor was therefore compelled to sponsor legislation that would reorganize six of the twelve planning regions to conform to the artificial boundaries of the EDDs. Other states were similarly forced to cut across natural planning regions to create artificial ones.

THE PROBLEM OF AUTHORITY

Throughout the year 1966, the formation of an economic development district in the anthracite area of northeastern Pennsylvania was delayed while two competing segments of the "power structure" struggled for recognition by the federal and state governments as the area's economic development district and its Appalachian local development district. One group had strong support from business and civic leadership, the other the backing of prominent political figures. One was centered in Wilkes-Barre, the other in Scranton. Confronted by the conflict, state and federal officials reacted by telling them to get together. But nothing happened. Representatives of the governor invited the competing groups to the state capital to negotiate the merger, but after five hours they adjourned in deadlock. Eventually, at the end of the year, the state recognized the business-backed group—which had reorganized meanwhile to achieve a more balanced representation—as the local development district for Appalachia, and six months later the EDA certified the same group as the area's economic development district.

Such an open struggle for recognition was unique. "Ordinarily, the problem is to find someone in an area to take an interest," observed a consultant active in the formation of EDDs. Yet the Pennsylvania rupture is indicative of the conflict that is always potential in a multicounty area and the difficulty in creating an entity that will be able to speak with authority for the *entire* community.

As we noted in the discussion of community action agencies in an earlier chapter, for an organization to become an effective central coordinator of governmental and private efforts it must have either *power* or *acceptance*. Of the five types of multicounty agencies examined in this chapter, none has significant power. The Georgia area commissions are created by and responsible to the participating local governments; they have no power to coordinate state or federal programs, and any authority they may be granted by the local governments is conferred voluntarily and may be withdrawn at any time. The concerted services coordinators may have influence on federal agencies but they have no power to approve or disapprove projects. The resource conservation and development and the rural renewal project coordinators may recommend the allocation of special funds for projects, but the assistance is limited in amount and restricted in purpose, and they have no authority of any kind outside the Agriculture Department's areas of operation. The economic development districts have a limited indirect financial power, because projects eligible for Economic Development Administration grants that are located within districts and "consistent with" the OEDPs are eligible for a bonus of 10 percent of the aggregate project cost above the grant EDA would otherwise make. But they too have no authority over projects financed by other agencies.

When they move into fields outside those of their sponsoring federal agencies, then, the multicounty bodies must rely for coordinating authority upon a voluntary acceptance by other institutions of that authority, in a consent-of-the-coordinated relationship. Yet the achievements of the agencies as coordinators show that they have succeeded in winning a considerable degree of acceptance. That acceptance appears to rest upon a series of intangible factors that contribute to an agency's "image":

The acceptance of the executive director as an individual. In large degree, the organization in the eyes of the community *is* the executive director; people tend to speak not of the organization's program but of Mr. X's program, not of the organization's accomplishments but of Mr. Y's accomplishments. If he has high standing in the community, if he is respected for his professional qualifications and skill, then the organization has standing, respect, and acceptance.

The experience of the other institutions in the area with the organization's ability to render service. If the agency director has succeeded in finding sources of federal assistance for the community, if he has been able to obtain outside experts to attend community meetings, if he has helped a community to fill out application forms or provided data for applications, if he has succeeded in expediting applications, then his acceptance as a coordinator will be enhanced.

These first two factors are interrelated. At the time the director assumes office, his initial standing is important. That standing will give him opportunities to render service. But as time goes on, the value of the service will be the determining influence upon his standing as an individual. A keen public relations sense is important here, because the director must find ways of letting his usefulness be widely known without appearing to take credit away from the organizations he may have assisted.

The standing of the organization's board members as individuals and their representativeness as a group. A broadly based organization has more acceptance as a coordinator than a narrowly based one. Equitable geographical representation is essential. An organization representing both the political leadership and the civic and business leadership of an area is stronger than one dominated by one or the other segment.

The "legitimacy" that is conferred upon the organization by the manner of its creation. An agency partakes of the authority and acceptance of the body or bodies that established it and is likewise limited by that authority and acceptance. Thus, a federally created agency has the advantages and disadvantages of a federal image—specifically, the image of the agency that created it—and a body established by local governments has the acceptance accorded to bodies that are locally created and responsive to local control.

In terms of these four factors, the five kinds of multicounty organizations fare differently. The Georgia area commissions have the greatest degree of legitimacy; they are created voluntarily as extensions and servants of the participating local governments, who are free to withdraw support at any time. In contrast, the federally sponsored agencies have, initially at least, something of a foreign image, appearing not as native institutions but as structures conceived in

Washington and imposed upon areas as conditions of federal assistance—and often, especially in the case of economic development districts, in unnatural geographical patterns. The agencies strive to modify this image by finding local sponsors and organizing local steering committees or boards of directors and otherwise obtaining local support. The fact of federal backing, however, cuts both ways: at the same time that it may arouse suspicion and hostility among those who are ideologically opposed to federal intervention in local affairs, it also enhances respect on the part of those who look favorably upon federal expertise—or who sense that somewhere behind the agency lie the limitless financial resources of the federal government.

The image of a resource conservation and development or rural renewal project is heavily influenced by the image in the area of the Agriculture Department as a whole. Both types of multicounty body are staffed by Agriculture career employees who may be guided by local citizen groups but are selected by and ultimately responsible to their superiors in the department. If we can generalize about the image of the department's personnel in the field, they are seen as dedicated professionals who are expert when they are dealing with their specialties but not necessarily equally expert when they enter broader fields. These are some comments that reflect the Agriculture Department's image:

A private planning consultant:

The small towns need to get their advice from people who have suffered through the problems of the larger urban areas, because it is these problems that are the problems of the small town in the future. The Agriculture Department, by contrast, is equipped only to deal with the problems of the past. These new programs are the Department of Agriculture trying to justify its existence. Moreover, all of its people—the extension service, the FHA, and so on—have been trained to deal with individuals, with the individual farmer, not with communities.

A university faculty member:

The RC&D project would work better if Mr. W [the director] were divorced from the Soil Conservation Service in order to give the project and its staff a broader image.

A state development official:

The planning process in rural areas must be a comprehensive one, embracing the whole range of governmental interests. Heretofore, it has been deficient in that it has been too heavily dominated by the U.S. Department of Agriculture, even in those areas where agriculture has become an insignificant part of the economy.

A university official:

No matter how broad they make the scope of RC&D, it will still be regarded as an SCS operation. The project does not have people with broad enough training or representing enough disciplines—even for its resource development objective.

A director of a private regional development group:

The Agriculture people are just not in the mainstream in this area, and they are not aggressive. They are always planning at the expense of doing anything. Nobody discusses the idea; they discuss the bureaucracy of it.

A state planning official:

The prospect of USDA officials giving advice on planning makes about as much sense as me giving advice on crop rotation.

The RC&D citizen leaders, it should be noted, thought of the agency as a local rather than a federal organization—whatever the agency's image in the rest of the community. Said one:

The director works for us, not for the Soil Conservation Service as a federal agency. We could fire him or any of his staff any time we wished. We could not recruit his successor in the open market but we would have a controlling voice in his selection. We were instrumental in getting [two specialized staff members] assigned to the project.

The strength of the economic development districts was their broader and firmer base of representation. Not just the federal government but the state government participated in their creation. The governing body was required by law to be broadly representative of the area, and it had full authority over the agency's activities. It hired the director and his staff. But subjection of the agency to local control meant its subjection to local politics, too. In some cases the aura of political patronage that surrounded the appointment of the district directors had severely—perhaps irretrievably—damaged the potential of the districts as coordinating bodies. Following are comments about particular economic development districts (some, of course, escaped this kind of criticism entirely):

A citizen leader:

We are very happy that the steering committee of the RC&D has always been completely out of politics. This is a weakness of the economic development district. It's involved in politics.

A private development organization spokesman:

The EDD here has obvious political leanings. You'll notice how their projects are being spread out geographically without any real consideration of regional priorities.

A citizen leader in another area:

There are some misgivings which stem from the fact that undoubtedly the political climate around EDD is much stronger than around RC&D.

A federal field official (and former state politician):

A major problem could develop in this state if the state tries to turn these districts into political units. Washington has got to exercise its authority to insure that the appointment of the directors is legitimate.

In terms of representativeness, both the economic development districts and the Agriculture-sponsored agencies suffered in some segments of the community from their unabashed identification with the community's power structure, which left them vulnerable to charges that they did not represent, or seek to represent, the entire community. The Economic Development Administration requires representation of minorities and of the unemployed and underemployed on EDD governing boards, but the representatives of those groups are appointed, rather than elected by the constituencies they represent, and their influence is not enough to modify significantly the fact or image of power-structure control. Agriculture has no requirement for representation of minority groups or of the poor on RC&D steering committees. The RC&Ds and most of the EDDs avoided any close official relationship with the community action agencies. As noted earlier, even when they indicated a broad range of concern they tended to exclude CAA programs from that range. Partisans of the CAAs returned the compliment; the following comments illustrate the image of the power structure agencies among the spokesmen for the poor:

A community action director:

The EDD represents the vested interests and is definitely not interested in rocking the boat. There is absolutely no connection between it and the CAA.

A state economic opportunity office director:

If you ask a middle-class person in this state what must be done to alleviate poverty he will usually respond "economic development." But economic development and social development don't always fit together. Very often the poorest people are relatively untouched by some of these economic development projects.

A community action leader:

> We're needed because the established agencies have a record of paying no attention to the poor. That's particularly true of the Department of Agriculture, which is not doing a thing for the poor. The kind of projects promoted by the RC&D bring nothing to the poor people at all. The big industries they bring in import their labor, and they put our local small industries that employ local poor people out of business. And remember, they don't want the poor to be educated or organized, because they want to keep wages down.

We do not suggest that specific allegations such as these are necessarily accurate, but the prevalence of the *belief* among responsible spokesmen for the poor that the power structure does not represent their interests is significant. As in the cities, the hostility between the community action agencies and the established agencies is often acute, and the EDDs and the RC&D organization are recognized— by supporters and critics alike—as establishment, or power structure, agencies.

The multicounty agencies had detractors, occasionally, among previously existing organizations engaged in developmental work. Industrial promotion groups made up of business leaders often spoke caustically of the new economic development districts, even in cases where they had acquiesced in their creation as a prerequisite for additional federal aid. Spokesmen for these groups talked of "politics" in the EDDs and of the "inexperience" of the new staffs. In much the same way that established agencies watched for mistakes made by the community action agencies and publicized them, as reported in Chapter 2, the industrial development groups sometimes appeared to be lying in wait to catch their new rivals in miscues. "We all know what needs to be done to develop this area; why do we need another planning agency?" complained a spokesman for one such group. "More of the same," a spokesman for another group said of the new EDD; "a different name, starting out big, everybody will be enthusiastic, then it will fizzle." "It seems like it's just another governmental layer that we'll just have to work with," sighed a utility executive. "The jealousy of established organizations has been a monumental hurdle, and so we have had to play down what we're doing," said an EDD director.

Similarly, opposition to the new Agriculture-sponsored multi-county agencies came from the department's field personnel and agencies who felt threatened or superseded. We met some Agriculture employees who expressed the view outright that the resource conservation and development, rural renewal, and concerted services structures should all be eliminated, in the interest of coordination and simplification, and the entire job given to the established Agriculture agencies and their technical action panels. One multicounty agency director said he had been instructed not to use a county rural areas development committee in his planning efforts after the county extension agent complained that the committee "belonged to him." In an area where an RC&D project was being organized, fear was expressed by RAD committee members that the new program would lead to elimination of their committee. In another area, officials of the established USDA agencies were bitter at the multicounty agency director for claiming credit for what, they said, they had accomplished.

Occasionally, a departmental field official would express objection to the authority exercised by the RC&D citizen leaders over the individual Agriculture agencies. One cited the absence of a continuing framework of citizen organization as an advantage of the technical action panels over the department's multicounty structures. "When TAP gets ideas," he said, "it is usually able to organize citizen committees to help carry them out."

Perhaps the most serious opposition to the multicounty agencies came from county politicians and public officials. Often these critics expressed fear that the agencies would become regional governments responsible for some or all of the current functions of the counties—a fear abetted by some of the advocates of multicounty agencies who were careless enough to say openly that regional governments were indeed their ultimate objective. "What I'd like to see the federal government do," said a county commissioner who opposed inclusion of his county in a multicounty agency, "is to finance a $15,000 man on the staff of the county commissioners to do that kind of work; then we could really pull together the county program and resources along with those of the state and federal governments." Then came an afterthought: "But I guess that really wouldn't work either, because I would have to appoint a politician to the job." A county planner insisted that regional planning should be strictly limited to intercounty matters. An economic development district director said his greatest problem was local jealousies—what he called "city by city chauvinism." In Georgia, legislation to make the area planning and development commissions creatures of the state rather than the counties, and to give them certain state administrative functions, was defeated by the combined opposition of the counties. One observer in another state thought that the counties' suspicion of a new economic development district was heightening and that "the honeymoon period" of the new structure might be near an end.

Aware of all of these sources of potential or actual opposition, the directors of the multicounty agencies were typically moving with caution—building their standing by rendering service, involving local government and citizen leadership to the maximum extent possible, and responding to that leadership in setting priorities and determining programs. Even where an agency conceived its role as comprehensive, it would avoid moving in fields where other organizations were active. "We don't step on anybody's toes," said an EDD director; "our functions are in the cracks." Two other EDD directors made the point that they would not want to have the same authority and responsibility to approve or disapprove proposed projects in their areas that metropolitan planning bodies are given by federal law. "I don't want to have any clout," explained one. "If I can't succeed by persuasion, I'm not going to get results anyway."

On balance, the multicounty agencies appeared to be able to win enough acceptance to be effective in the absence of legal power. It is noteworthy that in Georgia, where counties are free to withdraw from the area commissions at any time, none has done so. Nor has any federally sponsored multicounty agency run into any serious local pressure to disband. Some of the older agencies were well established as leaders and coordinators. The newer ones may still have been in the "honeymoon" stage, but most of them were proceeding carefully to win acceptance and appeared to be on their way to succeeding. The crucial factor seemed to be the widespread recognition in the nonmetropolitan areas of the vacuum of leadership and professional expertise. The multicounty agencies—whichever the type—were well designed to fill the vacuum and were proceeding skillfully to do so, and the communities were giving them the benefit of any doubt.

CHAPTER SIX

A Model
for Nonmetropolitan Coordination

MORE THAN A DECADE of intensive experimentation is now behind us. Thousands of planning and development structures have been created in nonmetropolitan America—rural areas development committees, overall economic development program committees, technical action panels, economic development districts, resource conservation and development projects, rural renewal programs, concerted services projects, state-sponsored area planning and development commissions, and most recently federally aided nometropolitan districts. Out of the experience of this jumble of approaches, is it possible to construct a theoretical model to guide federal, state, and local authorities as they organize for planning and development? What, exactly, are the functions that need to be performed? How should an organization be defined around those functions?

We begin with a basic suspicion of model-building. The preceding pages of this volume are strewn with the debris of broken models—the community action agencies that were designed in Washington but did not work as intended, the rural areas development committees that were initiated and promoted from Washington but later virtually abandoned, and so on. They foundered because, among other reasons, they could not be fitted uniformly to the diversity of American communities—not alone the physical and economic differences among communities but, what is even more important for model-building, the institutional diversity. A new governmental organization—whether a multicounty coordinating body or something else—takes its place in each locality not as a lone institution but as a member of a family of institutions, and its role depends upon the roles played by all the other members. The new organizations created over the past decade have been developed to fill vacuums in the institutional structure at the community level for the leadership, planning, and coordination of the many facets of community development; and the size, shape, and character of the vacuums differ from state to state and from area to area. The difference among areas is not in the functions to be performed by the community institutions collectively; the needs are basically the same everywhere. The difference lies, rather, in the capacity of the existing institutions to perform each of the functions. The shortfalls in institutional capacity in a state or area define the vacuum to be filled by structural innovation. The functions that are being least successfully performed by the existing institutions, in relation to the importance of those functions, become the focus and the emphasis of the new organization that needs to be created. Any model, then, needs to be adapted to local circumstances in the light of these considerations.

The Functions

The functions to be performed by a coordinating body in a nonmetropolitan area must be examined from the vantage point of each level of government. To make federal programs work as intended, the federal government has certain requirements. To make state programs—and federal programs administered through the states—work as intended, the states likewise have certain needs. Finally, the local communities have requirements for assistance in the development and execution of their own projects and programs. To some extent these requirements are the same, because all levels of government have a mutuality of interest, but they are seen from each vantage point in a different light. In any case, a listing of the requirements as seen from the three levels is the first step in the construction of a model. At the risk of some repetition of conclusions expressed in the preceding chapter, this listing attempts to present systematically the community-level functions in the intergovernmental system whose inadequate performance has given rise to the new organizations discussed in the preceding two chapters. Each of the functions has been performed by at least some of the organizations we visited—not always successfully, but successful in enough cases to demonstrate that the function is one that commonly needs to be, and can be, carried out.

FUNCTIONS IN FEDERAL-LOCAL PROGRAMS

A federal program of direct aid to a community activity is only as good as the community follow-through. If the local communities learn about the program, respond to it, and produce sound and well coordinated applications, then the program can succeed. If the communities fail to learn about the program, fail to respond to it, fail to produce applications that qualify for assistance, or produce poorly coordinated and poorly planned applications, then the federal program itself must fail. The functions required at the community level for the effective execution of federal programs can be identified under seven headings, which represent a perhaps arbitrary division of an interrelated progression of activities.

Communication. The basic federal need in direct aid programs is for a simple and reliable channel of communication between Washington and nonmetropolitan America. The scores of separate federal grant programs[1] are administered at nearly as many different points in Washington—different departments, bureaus, divisions, units, and subunits. From each point of origin the information on the program must be gotten to all of the potential beneficiaries, large and small alike, that the Congress intended should be served. If the potential applicants are communities, they may be some or all of the 30,000 units of general government, or they may even include some or all of the additional 45,000 functional jurisdictions, such as school districts. The number of effective communication links that need to be established between individual points in Washington and individual communities, even if one allows generously for the fact that not every community is eligible for every program, clearly is in the millions. And then, if one adds the programs whose beneficiaries are not communities but individual businessmen or farmers or private

1. The analysis of grant-in-aid programs in effect at the end of 1966 made by the Advisory Commission on Intergovernmental Relations showed 68 separate programs of assistance directly to local governments for planning, operating, and construction purposes (exclusive of those for research, demonstration, and training). *Fiscal Balance in the American System* (October 1967), Vol. 1, Table 25, pp. 166–68. Since the total number of grant programs has risen since then by an estimated 15 percent, the number of direct grant programs to local governments is probably proportionately higher.

groups, the number of communication links that need to be established is almost limitless.

Each federal agency that is responsible for a new program, or an expanded program, or a revised program, faces an enormous—at times, insuperable—problem of communication. Of all the federal agencies, only one—the Department of Agriculture—comes close to having a representative in every one of the country's nearly three thousand nonmetropolitan counties, and even Agriculture is represented not by a departmental agent but only by one or more representatives of individual bureaus. Some federal agencies, such as the Economic Development Administration or the Small Business Administration, have field offices in most states. Others, like Health, Education, and Welfare (HEW) and the Office of Economic Opportunity (OEO), seek to communicate through counterpart state agencies. But some do neither. As was pointed out earlier, for example, a department administering as many programs of assistance to communities as the Department of Housing and Urban Development (HUD) has no representative of some of its major assistance programs in a state as large as New Mexico nor any state counterpart agency to work through.

This circumstance has given rise to the insistent demand from communities everywhere for "a one-stop service"—a single point of contact where information could be obtained on the entire range of federal programs. We heard the demand repeatedly in our field interviews. It has been voiced persistently on Capitol Hill. In response to this demand, the Senate subcommittee on intergovernmental relations in 1964 made the first systematic attempt to come to grips with the information problem in its *Catalog of Federal Aids to State and Local Governments*. The Economic Opportunity Act, passed later that year, directed OEO to establish an "information center" on aid programs; under that authority, OEO has issued a 700-page *Catalog of Federal Assistance Programs*. Vice President Humphrey, as liaison between the Johnson administration and the cities, issued a 300-page *Handbook for Local Officials* in 1967. A large part of the work of senators and congressmen is making introductions—establishing communication links—between communities making inquiries about federal aid, often in the vaguest terms ("please tell us how to get the money for the new program"), and the federal agencies administering the programs in question. But none of these is a substitute for a competent organization, near at hand *at the community level,* to serve the communities by answering their questions and to serve the federal agencies by getting the word out to the potential applicants. In the absence of such a central channel of communication available to serve them, the federal agencies can only fall back on their own devices. They use general media of communication and whatever specialized channels they can find and then wait for the communities that are alert enough, and well organized enough, to respond—which usually means the larger communities that can employ specialized "grantsmen." By the time the smaller communities learn about the program, the funds available are often fully committed. The first requirement, then, is for a central channel of communication available to serve all the federal agencies that need to use it.

Promotion. From the standpoint of the federal government, mere communication is often not enough. If the national purpose is to be served, someone representing the federal government may need to seek out potential initiators of applications and encourage them to participate.

It may be objected that promotion is not a proper function of a federal agency—that if the potential beneficiaries of the program are not sufficiently interested in the program to come to the federal government as applicants, once they learn about the program's existence, then they are not entitled to, or do not deserve, its benefits. But such an argument ignores the national interest that gave rise to the program in the first place. If the Congress adopts, as it did in 1964, the national objective of eliminating poverty and chooses as a means to that end the community action program, then community action agencies have to be created wherever poverty exists—and that is almost everywhere—or the national objective is defeated. The same can be said about the economic development of depressed areas, the prevention of stream pollution, the improvement of education, or any other program where the failure of one community to act may have adverse effects upon other communities and hence upon the nation at large. Federal grant programs, as we noted in Chapter 1, are not just financial assistance to local communities for the advancement of *local* interests; they are *national* programs of assistance for the purpose of serving *national* interests that, usually, coincide with local interests.

Given this premise, there is need at the community level for an instrumentality that can undertake to promote those federal programs where response is lagging. In 1964, for example, when the Office of Economic Opportunity was created, the formation of community action agencies in the nonmetropolitan areas lagged for weeks and sometimes months because there was no general-purpose promoter to whom OEO could assign responsibility for making contact with the likely leaders of the effort in each community, giving them the information, and getting them organized. OEO tried to work through rural areas development committees or county agents or whatever institutional device was at hand, but the results were spotty until the OEO-financed state technical assistance offices were established to take responsibility for promotion of the community action program.

Again, upon passage of medicare legislation in 1965, HEW faced the problem of finding the eligible beneficiaries in rural areas and getting them enrolled. For that purpose, the Agriculture Department's technical action panels were enlisted in a nationwide promotional effort called "Medicare Alert."

At a time when funds for federal programs are restricted, promotion may be something to be avoided. But over the long run, if it is to be accepted that the federal government means business when it establishes its national objectives, then promotion may be crucial.

Technical Assistance. In the planning and initiation of projects, only the larger communities are self-sufficient. Smaller communities need help in the conception of projects, in the refinement of the conceptions, and in the preparation of plans, and provision of such help is an extension of the communication and promotion functions. Part of the need for technical assistance can be met through the employment of consultants, but smaller communities need aid even in locating qualified advisers. For all these purposes, a source of technical assistance, near at hand at the community level, is invaluable. In the simpler cases a local technical assistance agent can provide the needed service directly—he can write the application, rewrite it if necessary, get it into the proper channels, and continue to advise the sponsor until the project is approved and underway. For more complex and sophisticated projects he can bring in more specialized talent from the outside—from a federal or state agency, a university, a private consulting firm, or some other source. As part of the technical assistance function, the assistance agent can train local public officials and citizen leaders in project planning and development, particularly in rural areas where talent is thinly spread.

Design of Development Strategy. In order that federal programs may produce the best developmental result for the money expended, the projects aided should reflect sound development strategy. Each nonmetropolitan area needs a mechanism for determining priorities for the investment of funds, based upon an analysis of problems and resources that is both realistic and imaginative. The priorities need not only to choose among types of projects but also to express a spatial strategy that identifies the area's growth centers and locates the expenditures effectively in relation to those centers. The strategy then needs to be explained to, and accepted by, the public, so that the individual projects and their priorities are supported by a community consensus.[2]

Mobilization of Resources. Frequently a project to be well conceived from the standpoint of the federal purpose needs to be developed by two or more sponsors. These may be separate jurisdictions, as in the case of an area water or sewer system, or they may be separate institutions within the same jurisdiction. To mobilize multiple sponsors of a single project requires an organization with the authority and status to convene meetings and the skill to obtain effective cooperation among the participants. The mobilization of a community's resources may require leadership in bringing about the creation of new institutions for particular purposes—a community action agency for the war on poverty, a development corporation for industrial promotion activity, a joint authority to operate a multijurisdictional airport or other utility, or a specialized educational institution. It may also require the building of morale and initiative in areas that have become defeatist as the consequence of economic setback.

Coordination of Projects. Separate projects and programs often need to be related—as education and training with job development; or water supply with recreation, flood control, and soil conservation; or industrial site development with access roads and utility development. Like the mobilizer of resources, the coordinator of projects

2. See comments of Peter Stern, director of regional studies, Tennessee Valley Authority, in Council of State Planning Agencies, *Substate Districting,* Proceedings of a Technical Seminar (U.S. Department of Commerce, 1967), pp. 6–7.

needs to have the status and authority necessary to convene meetings that may involve multiple jurisdictions as well as separate institutions within the same jurisdiction. Frequently, coordination follows automatically from the simple exchange of information at such a meeting between persons who had previously not been in communication. Beyond that, the coordinator needs the technical competence to discern the relationships between projects and programs so that malcoordination can be detected and coordination achieved. This is the particular skill of the professional planner, and his plan—whether a land-use scheme or an overall economic development program—is an instrument of coordination.

Expediting. Once a project has been submitted to the federal government, questions invariably arise. Unless these are promptly and efficiently answered, projects are delayed. As in the preparation of a project, so in the course of its review and approval it is in the interest of the federal government that project sponsors have available at the community level a source of technical assistance to interpret federal requirements, assist the sponsors in providing the information that the federal government needs, and in general act as a go-between and expediter.

In summary, when the federal government is ready to extend financial assistance, the local communities must be ready to receive it. For that purpose, the federal government requires a network of expert grantsmen at the community level no less than the communities themselves require it.

FUNCTIONS IN STATE-LOCAL AND FEDERAL-STATE-LOCAL PROGRAMS

Each of the functions that must be performed at the community level to make federal programs effective is required also to make state programs effective, including those that are financially assisted from Washington but administered by the state. The problem of communication between the state capitals and the communities is a simpler one, of course, but the differences are of degree rather than of kind. For state as well as federal purposes, the institutional structure at the community level must be competent to design a development strategy, mobilize community resources, coordinate projects, and assist the communities in responding to state program initiatives.

It is for these reasons that the states as well as the federal government have been promoting the formation in nonmetropolitan areas of planning and development bodies, of which the Georgia system of area commissions is the most elaborate.

The interest of the states in the formation of regional organizations was well summarized by the West Virginia economic development office when it divided the state into nine multicounty regions and proposed establishment of a nonprofit development corporation in each:

> The State of West Virginia has been delineated into nine development regions. This delineation was necessary for the following reasons:
>
> 1. To provide a geographical framework for regional planning, analysis and action which is required by several new Federal Programs and desired by the State so that a rationalized investment strategy would maximize the effect of expenditures of both levels of government.
>
> 2. To provide a common set of State administrative districts for various departments and agencies.
>
> 3. To provide a geographical sub-system of West Virginia for analysis of the unique problems and development opportunities in the preparation of State-Local development policy.
>
> 4. To provide a standard framework for multi-county and regional cooperation in development to give guidance to joint efforts by local units of government.
>
> 5. To provide the basis for an information system on development activities within economic subregions of West Virginia.[3]

State universities and land grant colleges have been active in many states in promoting substate districting and in assisting the state planning offices in developing the districting plans. As the director of one university center for technical assistance to communities explained to us, the effectiveness of the university's own assistance program depends upon vigorous and better staffed community organizations to serve as contact points and channels for organizing the utilization of the university's resources.

FUNCTIONS IN COORDINATION OF LOCAL PROGRAMS

For all the reasons that the federal and state governments want the community projects they finance to be well planned and well coordinated, local communities want good projects, too. And if a

3. West Virginia Economic Development Office, "Subject: Regional Development" (memorandum distributed with invitations to local leaders to participate in forming regional development corporations, October 1967).

sound development strategy for each nonmetropolitan area serves the federal and state purposes, it serves even more immediately and directly the purposes of the area itself.

From the local vantage point, however, some of the seven functions enumerated above have even broader and more significant dimensions. The mobilization and coordination of separate jurisdictions in the planning of federally or state aided projects, for instance, may represent only a minor segment of the range of activities where joint agreements and cooperation among the jurisdictions may need to be organized. Many communities have entered into cooperative arrangements with neighboring communities in various fields of strictly local responsibility—police operations, fire protection, hospital services, school administration, libraries, and so on. About two-thirds of the states now have enacted broad legislation permitting interlocal contracting and other cooperative arrangements. An instrumentality that has the function of promoting interjurisdictional coordination—as, say, the Georgia area commissions—can find an unlimited potential for improvement of area public services.

Moreover, resources can be mobilized and coordination fostered in fields of activity that are nongovernmental in character. A development strategy that grows out of the systematic analysis of problems and resources will point the way for private as well as public projects—enterprises to develop timber, agriculture, mineral, recreational, or other resources—and coordination may consist of bringing together one entrepreneur with another or with a private lending agency.

Strictly local sources of technical assistance can be developed, too, in local colleges, state university branches, or elsewhere, and the assistance can take many forms. Several development experts emphasized to us the importance of improving the competence of an area's businessmen through organizing special training at local institutions—in accounting, purchasing, inventory management, market analysis, personnel management and labor relations, and so on.

The function of expediting projects, which the higher levels of government may look upon as something of a nuisance, may be crucial from the standpoint of local sponsors. If delays occur, the most important service of all may be that rendered by the man who makes the trip to Washington, to the federal regional office, or to the state capital, identifies the bottleneck, and then figures out the steps necessary to break it. This is often no job for an amateur; it is the expert "grantsman" who can find his way through the tangles of bureaucracy, knows whom to talk to, and understands the language of administration and of politics.

One community leader listed as follows the general services that a multicounty agency should render to its communities, apart from the development of specific projects:

Provide specialists who will do much leg work, who will help direct leadership of local groups and who will aid in funding and implementation of the plans already made.

Provide consultation with highly qualified persons, available either as formal Technical Panels . . . or as consultants brought in as needed. . . .

Help develop latent local leadership, particularly in rural areas where such leadership is traditionally weak.

Cause local communities to take a long, hard look at themselves, their problems and their opportunities and . . . encourage the communities to evaluate themselves critically.

Encourage a help-your-neighbor attitude, even to the point of crossing state lines.

Place projects in a time schedule which will help to bring many to fruition where formerly they might have remained dormant for a long time.

In launching regionwide attacks on regionwide problems, set in motion the old billiard ball or chain reaction effect—the well-known fact that solution of one problem automatically leads to solution of others.[4]

The Model

In the construction of a model organization to meet the requirements for community-level functions outlined above, three propositions are fundamental.

First, each of the functions can best be performed on a multicommunity basis, which in most areas means a multicounty basis. It is the fragmentation of governmental jurisdictions that is the root cause of the administrative problems of the nonmetropolitan areas discussed in this and the two preceding chapters. There are too many local communities to establish effective communication with the federal government—and frequently even with their state governments. Tiny jurisdictions lack expertise: their elected officials are

4. Address by Daniel Hale at a soil conservation society meeting, Jackson's Mill, W. Va., Sept. 9, 1967.

part-time amateurs, and the communities lack the resources individually to employ professional personnel with skill in planning
and in grantsmanship. They are deficient in capacity to conceive,
plan, design, and expedite projects. They lack the population base
individually to support projects important to development—industrial parks, medical centers, vocational schools, colleges, airports,
programs of industry and tourism promotion. Individually, they are
weak in their influence on state policy. Finally, a strategy for economic development must be based upon an area broad enough to
contain one or more growth centers where public investment can be
concentrated.

Small communities must combine, then, for the planning and
execution of development programs. In most parts of the country
this means organizing on a multicounty basis—creating, in effect, a
new level of government intermediate between the states and the
counties or towns. Two exceptions to this generalization may be
noted: in the smallest states—such as Delaware, which has only
three counties—the multicounty organization may be the state itself.
And in states or parts of states that have large and populous counties—as northern New Jersey or southern California—individual
counties may have attributes corresponding to those of multicounty
areas in other states and may be suitable bases for organizing most
planning and development functions, although a multicounty regional organization may still be desirable for some purposes.

The recommendation for development of the multicounty area as
a significant level of government in nonmetropolitan America is consistent with, and analogous to, the proposals in Chapter 3 for development of the neighborhood as an urban governmental level under
the model cities program. Both these new levels of government serve
the purpose of strengthening the chain of relationships that extends
from the federal and state capitals to the citizen in his primary community group—in other words, the federal system. Each is designed
to strengthen that federal chain at the point where it is weakest. In
the cities the gap has been between the citizen in his neighborhood
and the remote city government; in the countryside the gap has been
between the well established governmental units in jurisdictions that
are analogous to urban neighborhoods in size and sense of community—small counties, small cities, and towns—and the higher
levels of government. In the cities, therefore, decentralization of

planning and initiative to the neighborhood level rectifies the imbalance while in rural areas development of leadership and expertise above the neighborhood level is essential for the same purpose. Creation of multicounty agencies in nonmetropolitan areas gives those areas the essential structure for performing functions requiring a broader population base than the neighborhood that in the urban setting the city itself (or the city in cooperation with its suburbs through metropolitan area instrumentalities) provides.

Second, all of the functions can best be performed by a single multicounty agency responsible both for planning and for project promotion in all fields relating to the area's development. All of the functions are interrelated. Indeed, as suggested at the outset, the seven functions represent a somewhat a bitrary division of a continuum of services that need to be performed at the community level. Communication of information about a program blends into promotion, and promotion blends into technical assistance in the planning and initiation of projects, and these blend into expediting. Individual projects depend upon a development strategy, and the strategic planning leads to the mobilization of resources and the coordination of projects involved in the execution of the strategy, and these in turn lead back to communication with the federal and state governments and to promotion, technical assistance, and expediting. All of the functions require the same, or related, professional skills— the skills of the planner and community organizer. All require the same body of knowledge—an expertise in government programs and especially in intergovernmental program relations.

The contention that the planning function will suffer if it is combined in the same agency with project promotion and grantsmanship can be met by an internal division of responsibility in the multicounty organization. Many federal agencies, like many corporations, have staff units removed from operations and specifically assigned to program analysis and program planning. By the same token, a multicounty agency headed by a generalist can have at least one key assistant with planning skills assigned to planning responsibilities. But to place planning and promotional responsibilities in separate organizations is likely to defeat the purpose of the planners themselves. Planning has value only if it guides the changes that take place in the communities as development proceeds. To assign the planning and promotional responsibilities to the same organization is to provide the planners with the leverage to influence action that they often lack; meanwhile, federal and state influence can be exerted to protect the planning process from being sacrificed to the demands of promotion and grantsmanship. Actual program operation, however, is something else. As will be brought out later, while the planning and promotional functions are compatible, both are likely to suffer if placed in an organization that has responsibility for administering governmental services.

A strong case can be made, likewise, against a division of responsibility among two or more multicounty planning and development agencies assigned to different fields of development. The present division between *economic* development (assigned to economic development districts) and *resource* development (undertaken by resource conservation and development projects) seems particularly illogical. That separation of responsibility did not result from anybody's conscious judgment that a divided approach by the federal government was superior to a unified approach, or that resource development is not an aspect of economic development. It is the result, rather, of accidents of legislative history: the concepts evolved separately, in separate corners of the executive branch, and were enacted after consideration by different committees of the Congress. In the legislative history of the act that authorized the economic development districts there is not even any reference to the preexisting Agriculture-sponsored agencies and the inevitable overlap of functions.

In the program of any economic development district, resource conservation and development are basic. No OEDP (*overall* economic development program) could omit the subject of resource development and be worthy of the name. The need for an interdisciplinary approach to the complex problems of development suggests that the limited supply of professional talent should be brought together rather than divided. Yet now that the economic development districts and the resource conservation and development projects do coexist in the same areas, the pluralism is sometimes defended, as was noted in Chapter 5. More centers of initiative, it is argued, will result in more accomplishment; the competition will keep both agencies alert and aggressive, and any conflicts and overlap can be resolved through interpersonal relations. We would agree that *if* the two multicounty agencies have the same boundaries, *if* their offices are in the same city, *if* there is a clear delineation of relationships, *if* there is some overlapping of board membership to ensure liaison, and *if* the professional staffs and board members of the agencies get along well together, then the case for pluralism can be argued. But nowhere in our field surveys did we find all of these "ifs" satisfied, nor any indication that they are likely to be.

On balance, it seems to us that the stronger case is for a pooling of leadership and professional talent in a single agency in each non-metropolitan area, particularly in the more rural areas where leadership resources are limited. Even if separate agencies have interlocking boards, that imposes upon the board members the burden of "too many meetings" and places on part-time leaders the responsibility of coordinating the work of the separate full-time professional staffs. But instead of the citizens' being able to pull the agencies together, it is more likely that the agencies will pull the citizens apart, dividing them into factions supporting the separate and competing federally sponsored bodies. It is only by unification at the community level that the inevitable fragmentation of federal programs can be overcome and coordination accomplished.

Third, all of the functions need to be performed in all nonmetropolitan areas, not just in some of them. Unlike the states, the federal government until 1968 had taken only a partial and selective approach to multicounty organization. Economic development districts were confined to areas that met certain criteria of unemployment and underemployment. Department of Agriculture projects were strictly limited in number by budget ceilings. Yet the broad problem of communication exists in all of nonmetropolitan America; so do the problems of promoting federal and state programs, providing technical assistance for the development of worthy projects, and expediting the projects. Every nonmetropolitan area needs a developmental strategy to which individual projects can be related, and it needs machinery for the mobilization of resources and the coordination of projects.

The fact is that virtually all of nonmetropolitan America is suffering from underdevelopment. Not only are rural or semirural counties losing population, but many small cities and towns and some middle-sized urban centers are decaying as well. Economic opportunity is limited. Resources are underdeveloped. It makes no sense to suggest that organizing to combat these circumstances should be encouraged only in a few areas that are most depressed. In a very real sense, all of nonmetropolitan America is *relatively* depressed, and its revival is a matter of national interest for many reasons—to maximize employment and production, to give people living outside metropolitan areas—particularly young people—sufficient economic opportunity and adequate community facilities and amenities so that they have a genuine option to remain there if they so desire, and thus to take some of the pressure of in-migration off the metropolitan centers.

Certain program benefits, like those of the Public Works and Economic Development Act, may of course be limited to areas most in need,[5] and the scale of benefits may be varied according to need. Yet it can be noted that most federal programs of assistance to nonmetropolitan communities, including those enacted most recently, are based upon the principle of universality. The loan and grant programs of the Farmers Home Administration, for example, are not limited to depressed areas, nor are the programs of HUD, Labor, HEW, or OEO. Communities benefiting from these programs are as much in need of improved organizational devices to enable them to develop plans, design worthy projects, and communicate effectively with the federal government as are the beneficiaries of the Economic Development Administration program.

The Department of Agriculture holds that *every* nonmetropolitan county—not just some of them—needs the services of a technical action panel. The Economic Opportunity Act likewise accepts the need for community action agencies as universal. Most states are proceeding on a statewide basis with their multicounty planning and

5. While this study was concerned with the administration of programs rather than their substance, it is worth noting that the criteria written into the Public Works and Economic Development Act for designation of areas eligible for benefits was widely—and, we think, soundly—criticized by our interviewees. Exclusive reliance upon unemployment rates as the measure of eligibility (except in the very poorest counties, where median income is also a criterion) means that a county whose unemployment rate falls below the minimum level becomes ineligible for assistance even though its fundamental economic weaknesses have not been overcome. Its tax base may be still too low to support a satisfactory level of public services, its physical facilities still obsolete and deteriorating, and its economic prospects as bleak as before. In the rural areas, unemployment figures are unsatisfactory measures of need because the basic economic problem is not unemployment but underemployment. As Ralph R. Widner, executive director of the Appalachian Regional Commission, has observed: "Economic development is a very long-term process. You cannot base your approach on the roller coaster of unemployment rates and expect solid, permanent results. Counties fall off the unemployment lists and climb back on again." Speech delivered at American Institute of Planners conference, Washington, D.C., Jan. 25, 1969.

development structures. In 1968, finally, the legislation authorizing aid to nonmetropolitan districts for the first time recognized the need for federal support of a universal system of multicounty agencies as these are created by the states.

The model that federal, state, and local governments should adopt, therefore, is a universal system of multicounty agencies with responsibility both for planning and for facilitating action programs covering the entire range of community activities relating to economic and community development. We repeat, however, that what we are presenting here is a *model*. The exact nature of each multicounty agency, and its program priorities and emphasis, will depend upon the structure of the local institutional complex into which it fits.[6] If strong private industrial development groups exist, the new agency may put its stress upon research and planning and community development. If area functional planning agencies have been established in such fields as resource conservation and development, health, manpower, education, and antipoverty programs, then the multicounty agency may incorporate their products in its planning without duplicating their staff resources—although, ideally, area boundaries should be made to coincide. The multicounty agency should have its broad range of responsibility, but a principle of flexibility would govern whether, and when, an individual agency would exercise any particular phase of that responsibility. With that word of caution, then, we can proceed to a further description of the model.

A JOINT FEDERAL-STATE-LOCAL STATUS

One of the more perplexing questions relating to the model multicounty agency is how it can be designed to serve with equal effectiveness the corresponding, yet differing, requirements of all three levels of government—federal, state, and local. It seems clear that the interests of all cannot be served if the agency is conceived as belonging exclusively to any one level of government.

6. Pierre Clavel and his associates at Cornell University have developed a methodology for analyzing the differences in institutional structures among multicounty areas and have suggested adaptations that may need to be made in establishing multicounty organizations to take account of those differences. *Design of Organizational Models to Implement Comprehensive Planning and Development in Multi-County Districts* (unpublished manuscript, 1968).

Certainly a *local* image and some degree of local responsibility are essential. Communities would be slow to gain confidence in a federal or federal-state agency that they did not regard as subject primarily to local influence and control. Such an agency would therefore not be in a position to coordinate activities financed by the local communities themselves. Yet if the agency is created exclusively by the participating counties and cities, like the Georgia area commissions, it may not be a reliable mechanism for the federal and state governments to use in communicating information about, and promoting, their programs. It may pick and choose among federal and state programs and boycott or deemphasize some of them, as has been the case in Georgia. It may neglect its responsibility to organize "outreach" for the federal government. In that case, federal and state agencies would be compelled to bypass the multicounty body and establish their own communication channels and their own local organizations, and the goal of a unified and fully coordinated process for planning and for project promotion at the local level would be defeated.

The federal government needs to protect itself, too, against the possibility—apparent now in a few of the economic development districts—that in areas where state and local governments are ruled by old-fashioned systems of patronage the multicounty agencies created by those governments might be treated as part of those systems. Not only must selection be based on merit if staffs are to be fully competent but salary scales and tenure conditions would probably have to approximate those of the federal government more nearly than those of state and local government.

These considerations point to some kind of joint federal-state-local procedure for establishing the multicounty agency, and joint financing of its operations. The exact pattern in each state and area should come under the principle of flexibility, but perhaps as a general proposition the agencies should be established by local governments pursuant to state law and under state administrative guidance, or by the state and local governments jointly, but with the proviso that the qualifications of key personnel be subject to federal review as a precondition for the payment of the federal share of the administrative costs of the agency. In return for the federal financial assistance, the agency would have to be responsive to demands made upon it by the federal government, but the federal influence could not be allowed to become so pervasive as to destroy the image of the agency as a home-grown institution with strong local roots. Maintenance of the appropriate balance in each area probably would depend, in the long run, on the development of a corps of professional agency administrators attuned to the needs and interests of all three levels of government and adept at working in an intergovernmental role.

The determination of boundaries of the multicounty areas should be a joint state-local responsibility. In drawing the boundaries, two alternative approaches are available. One relies upon objective planning criteria, the other upon the preferences of local leaders. West Virginia, using the former approach, identified fourteen criteria—including sales areas, banking service areas, labor market areas, service areas of public institutions and public utilities, transportation and communication patterns, topographic features, homogeneity of agriculture and other resource bases, and commonality of development problems and needs—to be used in delineating its nine areas. Kentucky, on the other hand, depended primarily on local opinion to determine which counties had a "sense of community" with one another. "Our process for determining this was not scientific," explained Robert M. Cornett, the administrator of the state's area development office at the time. "It consisted essentially of asking leaders what counties could work well together. Surprisingly, a clear consensus existed except in one or two borderline cases. Not surprisingly, this consensus was not greatly at odds with what would have come out of our computer. . . . An area which already views itself as a community makes much easier the identification of public consensus and of appropriate public policy."[7] Pennsylvania used a combination of the two approaches. A regional map was developed by the state planning office, based upon planning criteria, but then subjected to review by local leaders at a meeting in each county. The only significant problems encountered in those meetings, according to state planning officials, concerned the allocation of several border counties that are logically part of regions centered in cities in other states, and the state plan remained unchanged as the result of the county meetings.

7. Robert M. Cornett in Council of State Planning Agencies, Substate Districting, p. 50. See also Robert M. Cornett, "Multi-County Administration," State Government, Summer 1967, pp. 182–86.

Our interviews in West Virginia, conducted shortly after the state plan was promulgated, revealed some local dissatisfaction with the state's delineation of regions. Apart from the substantive objections, local leaders complained of the absence of consultation. On the other hand, the system of districting cannot be left wholly to the voluntary federation of counties if the system is to be universal, as Georgia has learned. There, 6 of the state's 159 counties are still holding out against affiliating with any of the commissions. Moreover, while it has never happened, Georgia counties may at any time withdraw from their structures. The Pennsylvania procedure, which has been followed in other states as well, therefore appears to be the most satisfactory. It permits the product of the computers and the judgment of the planners to be checked against the "sense of community" in making the final determination.

A REPRESENTATIVE GOVERNING BOARD

The question of how the governing board of a multicounty planning and development agency should be constituted came into sharp focus in the drafting of guidelines for designation of nonmetropolitan districts under the 1968 legislation.[8] HUD's eventual directive requiring that at least two-thirds of the board members be public officials—which would require many economic development districts to reorganize in order to qualify as nonmetropolitan districts—was issued without the concurrence of the Economic Development Administration.

The argument for participation of elected local public officials on a board of directors is that only through the public officials can the strategy and planning of the agency be carried into effect. The cities and the counties have the taxing power and the zoning power, and they are the sponsoring bodies of many of the projects. A body directed entirely or predominantly by private citizens may therefore be in the position of kibitzing from the sidelines while decisions are made without reference to it. Moreover, public officials are chosen by and are accountable to the citizenry and therefore give political legitimacy to the decisions of the multicounty agency.

Nevertheless, to require that the agency be directed by public officials does not guarantee breadth of outlook, strong and imaginative leadership, or even representation in a real sense of the whole

8. See pp. 165–66.

community. As we observed earlier, the most dynamic leaders on multicounty agency boards whom we encountered were, in virtually every case, nonofficeholders. In some localities the politicians of the majority party—or even of both parties—comprise a patronage-oriented faction within the community. They may be at odds with the leadership of the business community, as was the case in the Pennsylvania controversy recounted in Chapter 5. They may fail utterly, especially in the South, to represent minorities within the electorate. The turnover rate among elected public officials is high. Moreover, local elected and appointed officials are likely to have a local rather than a regional outlook, and they may overemphasize investment in municipal public works and other public services for which they are responsible, to the neglect of a strategy for industrial, agricultural, and general economic development and even to the neglect of such functions as education that, while publicly supported, have been administered by state agencies or independent school districts.

We believe that the strongest boards are those comprised both of local public officials and of private citizens who are regional in their outlooks and who effectively represent the sources of private power as well as minority groups. We are not at all sure what the balance should be; we would invoke the principle of flexibility and say that much depends upon the strength, the representativeness, and the traditions and character of the local governmental structure in each state and area. But HUD's nationwide requirement that two-thirds of the members *must* be public officials seems too rigid and appears likely to result, in many areas, in agencies that are narrow in concept and lacking in the leadership and vitality that would be possible with a higher proportion of nonofficeholders.

The problem of political legitimacy and accountability can be met if members of the board are appointed by elected officials— either by local officials exclusively or in part by the governor. Self-constituted groups who become official agencies by winning recognition from federal and state authorities are rightly suspect, but the solution does not necessarily lie at the other extreme of requiring that officeholders dominate the board.

Finally, what is the application to our model of the principle incorporated in the community action and model cities programs of representation of the poor in the policy-making process? In a few areas we found a close relationship between the multicounty planning and development body and the community action agency, but the general pattern was otherwise. A startlingly high proportion of the citizen leaders of multicounty agencies with whom we talked—and even some of the professional staff members—were openly contemptuous of the community action concept and objectives. A common view among spokesmen for the agencies that emphasize industrial development was that the problem of poverty would be solved by simply bringing industry into the area to create jobs. Community action spokesmen, it should be added, were often equally hostile to the agency leaders as representatives of a power structure that, in their view, was unconcerned with helping the poor.

Certainly, poverty will not be eliminated without economic development, but we found little appreciation in some multicounty agencies of the opposite view that economic growth would be retarded without intensive efforts to improve an area's education, training, health, welfare, and antipoverty programs in order to develop the area's human resources—or that these were ends in themselves worthy of the best of the community's leadership.

If a comprehensive planning and development agency is to embrace human resource as well as economic resource development, provision should be made for appointment to the board of persons who represent the human resources segment of the community's leadership and institutional structure—the community action agency, for example, or groups concerned with health, education, and welfare. The guidelines issued by HUD to govern the nonmetropolitan districts require a specific plan for citizen participation corresponding to that required by the model cities program and expressly calling for participation of low-income and minority groups. Nevertheless, as we recommended in the case of the urban coordination structure proposed in Chapter 3, it is important that community action agencies be kept in being as a counterweight to the central coordinating bodies that are always liable to be dominated by the community's power structure.

A NEUTRAL COORDINATING ROLE

If the multicounty agency described in this model is to concern itself with the *entire* range of planning and development activities in its area and maintain a balanced perspective in relation to all those activities, then it must occupy a neutral position among the agencies and functions with which it deals. It cannot have any area of *primary* concern. It will set priorities for action, based upon analysis of an area's problems and potential, but it should not start out with a pre-assigned orientation or field of concentration.

As noted in Chapter 5, the tendency of each of the existing types of multicounty agency, whatever its initial orientation, has been to broaden its scope and perspective—particularly in those areas where other multicounty agencies had not been established. Some of the resource conservation and development projects, in particular, were noteworthy for the way in which they had moved from their initial relatively narrow field of interest to fill vacuums of leadership in other fields. Nevertheless, they remained specialized in outlook, in the composition of their boards, and in the competencies of their staffs. The economic development districts began with a more inclusive concept; while "economic" appears as a limiting adjective to the noun "development," it is the kind of adjective that can be stretched to cover almost any field of activity. Consequently, while an economic development district may have started with an orientation toward payroll-building, if its leaders and staff were imaginative they were quick to see that a basic obstacle to job development might lie in the inadequacy of public services that in turn might be rooted in the weakness of local governmental structure, or it might lie in the failure to develop human resources through education, health, welfare, and antipoverty programs. Accordingly, most of the districts appear to be so conceived that they could evolve, perhaps with some reorganization, into agencies along the lines of the model presented in this chapter. Some of them have already been able to assume an "umbrella" role in relation to the functional planning agencies in their areas; some have been designated, for example, as the comprehensive health planning agencies and as the planners for the law enforcement assistance programs authorized in the 1968 legislation. In some Appalachian states the local development districts that are the Appalachian counterparts of the economic development districts have prepared comprehensive public investment programs as part of the Appalachian planning process. The potential of the economic development districts for a broader role is recognized in the nonmetropolitan district legislation of 1968, which authorized their designation as nonmetropolitan districts. The latter, presumably, will be unspecialized and comprehensive from the outset, and could readily be designed on the pattern outlined here.

As a corollary to the principle of neutrality among functions and agencies, the central multicounty planning and development body must avoid accepting responsibility for the administration of any programs. The experience of the Georgia commissions in acting as community action agencies is indicative—besides embroiling the commissions in controversy and staking their prestige upon the success or failure of a particular program, assumption of community action responsibilities overwhelmed the comprehensive planning function with the pressures and burdens of program operation. Observers in many states hope that the multicounty area may evolve into an administrative level of local government, through the consolidation of individual functions if not through the outright consolidation of counties. But while the multicounty agency might conceive plans for functional or governmental consolidation and even design the appropriate administrative agencies, if it were itself to become a special purpose administrative district or seek general governmental status its usefulness for its original purposes would be impaired.

As the comprehensive multicounty agency is developed, the specialized functional planning agencies would come under its umbrella—gradually, no doubt, and at different rates. They would produce the functional components of the comprehensive plan and, at best, would serve as an element of a professional staff that worked as a unified group whether or not they were assigned to different agencies. Thus, where the economic development district did not itself become the comprehensive agency, it would be absorbed into it as the economic development component. The resource conservation and development projects are readily convertible into the resource development component. The concerted service project coordinators would find their places quite readily as specialists in grantsmanship on the staffs of the new agencies, while the rural renewal authorities that exist in a few counties would continue as sponsors and administrators of specific projects. The district technical action panels would take their place as the agriculture element of the unified staff. The comprehensive area manpower planning system would function under the umbrella of the multicounty agency and so would the regional health planning agencies now being created with federal aid. Prototypes for these relationships already exist—for example, the designation of some economic development districts as health planning agencies, referred to earlier, and the organization of a resource conservation and development project under the auspices of the Georgia Mountains area commission. As new functional planning efforts are promoted by the federal and state governments, they would be assigned to the comprehensive agencies either for execution or for supervision.

The community action agencies would contribute to the human resources segment of the antipoverty plan but they would also have a role, if necessary, in representing the interests of the poor before the multicounty agency as before other agencies. They would be a means for offsetting the potential overweighting of the multicounty agencies on the side of the power structure.

The multicounty body would need to concern itself with developing the capability of the local institutions that carry out the actual developmental projects. It would foster the development of expertise in planning and coordination within the county governments, particularly those of the larger jurisdictions. It would encourage the formation of county and municipal planning bodies and develop working arrangements to insure that county, city, and multicounty plans were consistent with one another and complementary. It could detail persons from its own staff for service to the county and municipal planning bodies, either for special projects or on a continuing basis—an arrangement preferable to the use by smaller communities of consultants from many miles away. It could serve, as is the case with some of the Georgia commissions, as a consulting and training service over a wide range of local government administrative functions. It might develop plans for multicounty administration of particular governmental services, or perhaps even of jurisdictional consolidation.

To give metropolitan planning agencies a degree of authority and leverage, applicants for federal aid for locally sponsored projects within the metropolitan areas are now required by law to submit their proposals to the planning agencies for review and comment.[9] A similar review authority for the city demonstration agencies and the neighborhood organizations is incorporated in the model cities pro-

9. Section 204 of the Demonstration Cities and Metropolitan Development Act of 1966.

cess. The same authority should be extended to the multicounty agencies in nonmetropolitan areas, and the states should confer a corresponding authority for the review of plans for state projects. Such a requirement would not only protect the federal and state governments against applications for ill-conceived projects but it would strengthen the nonmetropolitan agencies by assuring them the right of participation in the approval of all projects in their areas. Thus it would give meaning and effect to the function of coordination.

A Postscript on Metropolitan Areas

While we did not delve deeply enough into the problems of coordination in metropolitan areas to present a detailed analysis, we are confident that the model sketched in this chapter for nonmetropolitan areas is applicable to metropolitan areas as well, subject to the general qualification that in all cases the model must be adapted to the particular institutional structure of the area to be served. In Georgia the area commission for the Atlanta region was organized under the same authority and on the same pattern as those for smaller metropolitan areas like Savannah and Macon and those that serve nonmetropolitan areas. The planning of substate regions in other states, similarly, does not distinguish between the two kinds of areas. In fact, the districting schemes being developed by the various states for their nonmetropolitan areas are patterned largely after the councils of governments and area planning bodies that were established first in the metropolitan areas. And our model is not inconsistent with most of the state districting plans.

The difference between metropolitan and nonmetropolitan planning and development agencies is in program emphasis and priorities rather than in structure and general responsibility. The metropolitan agency will deemphasize technical assistance and grantsmanship service to its central city and its metropolitan counties, which are likely to be self-sufficient in these respects. But it may need to render those services to smaller jurisdictions within the metropolitan area, whose needs for help may be as great as those of jurisdictions of the same size anywhere else. The metropolitan agency will not place the same emphasis upon stimulating economic development, probably, because most metropolitan areas are thriving and the problem is not to induce growth but to guide it. On the other hand, the metropolitan agency will place a far greater emphasis upon the coordination of projects—the development of regional plans for functions of government whose costs and consequences spill across municipal boundaries, such as water supply, sewage disposal, air and water pollution control, and transportation. It would probably be limited to such high-consensus areas as these, however. No council of governments or other metropolitan multijurisdictional body that we know of has attacked the crucial problem of fiscal imbalance between the central city and the suburbs—the concentration of poverty in the central city and the relative inadequacy of the city's tax base to support governmental services for the poor. Nor have they confronted the need for metropolitan solutions to problems of housing and education. In structure, they tend to overrepresent suburban jurisdictions and underrepresent the central city.

Perhaps it would be enough to say that the existing metropolitan planning agencies and councils of government in each state would take their places as the metropolitan elements of the statewide system of multicounty agencies. We suspect, however, that in the design of a statewide system, using the criteria set forth in this chapter, the need for some modifications to broaden and strengthen existing metropolitan bodies to make their representation more equitable, and in some cases to combine them, would be identified.

CHAPTER SEVEN

To Make
the System Work

To COORDINATE is not necessarily to simplify. The innovations that
have been introduced over the past decade for purposes of coordination have given us a more complicated federal system—one with five,
six, or even seven levels of government where three or four sufficed
before. Added to the traditional federal-state-local or federal-state-
county-town structure of federalism are new bodies with jurisdiction
over new areas—multicounty bodies interposed between the states
and their local governments, and neighborhood bodies acting as a
link between the people and their local governments within the
larger cities. And it may be that the experimental multistate regional
bodies, like the Appalachian Regional Commission, will also become
increasingly significant as an intermediate level between the federal
government and the states.

Though the new bodies are diverse in origin—created at different
times, by different authorities, in response to different sets of concrete problems—they are remarkably similar in function. They are
not created to administer substantive programs but rather to act as
general agents of the governments that do. Their purpose is to make
the federal system itself work better. They are planners, coordinators,
expediters, facilitators, communicators. They bridge the vertical and
horizontal gaps in the federal structure; they narrow the span of
communication; they act, so to speak, as the intermediate pumping
stations along the federal-state-local-citizen pipelines through which
demands flow upward and funds flow downward.

For two of these new types of structures, we have drawn models. For the multicounty district organizations, our model was sketched in Chapter 6. For the neighborhood structure, we accept the design in the model cities program, subject to the qualifications set forth in Chapter 3. But how are these models to be put in place, and how are they to be supported? What are the implications for the federal government of the new coordinating systems at the community level? How should the federal government organize for intergovernmental relations in the changing federalism? What should be its guiding policies? What are the implications for state government, and what bearing do these have in turn upon federal organization and policy?

In this chapter we offer the outlines of a model of organization for the federal system as a whole, from the presidential level through the federal regional centers and the states to the city and multicounty coordinating bodies.

Federal Organization for Intergovernmental Relations

Federal organization for the new federalism can best be considered if we restate—at the risk of repeating some of what was said in Chapter 1—the theoretical premises on which the new organizational departures in the federal structure rest.

The central premise is that the effectiveness of the execution of federal programs depends crucially upon the competence of community institutions to plan, initiate, and coordinate. The federal contribution of money and ideas and leadership to community programs is indispensable, but it is still only a contribution—a range of offerings—and it is at the community level that the offerings must be accepted, applied, combined with the contributions offered from other sources, and turned into concrete undertakings. It is at the community level that projects and activities are planned. It is there that goals and priorities are set. It is there that applications are originated. It is there that resources from many sources are mobilized for specific purposes. It is there that programs are administered. It is there, consequently, that programs must be related together into coordinated systems. Where federal projects are well planned and well coordinated, it is because the community-level planning and coordination processes have worked well—and the federal regulations have encouraged and permitted them to work. If they do not work well, then no amount of review by, and coordination among, federal agencies is a satisfactory substitute for what must be done properly in the first place within the community itself.

The recognition of the importance of community-level planning and coordination is what gave rise to all of the federally sponsored structures discussed in this study. What remains for the federal government is to reconcile its competing strategies and settle upon a unified approach to perfecting the design of the community-level machinery, getting it established, and then supporting its coordinating efforts. To attain that unified approach to community-level coordination by all of the agencies of the federal government working in concert is the heart of the problem of coordination at the Washington level of federal assistance programs.

If the community-level coordinating structures described in our models—or any other models—are left to the sponsorship of individual federal agencies, it is doubtful that any of them will prove effective in knitting together in the communities the programs of many federal agencies. To be effective as coordinators, their status as such has to be recognized and accepted by all of the agencies whose programs would be affected. But that would mean recognition and acceptance by those same agencies of a corresponding status within the federal government for the sponsoring department. Neither the Office of Economic Opportunity, the Department of Housing and Urban Development, the Economic Development Administration, nor the Department of Agriculture has been accorded that kind of recognition, and that accounts in part for the weaknesses as coordinators shown by all of their community-level creatures—community action agencies, model cities structures, economic development districts, resource conservation and development projects, technical action panels, and all the rest. The facts of bureaucratic life are that no Cabinet department has ever been able to act effectively, for long, as a central coordinator of other departments of equal rank that are its competitors for authority and funds. Nor does coordination spring readily from the mutual adjustment of Cabinet-level equals within the federal hierarchy. It must be induced, overseen, managed, and directed from the supra-Cabinet level—in other words, from the Executive Office of the President, where the authority exists to identify problems that need settlement, expedite discussion, referee disputes, make binding decisions, and issue orders. Voluntary bar-gaining among Cabinet departments of equal rank is no substitute for a decision-making structure led by a presidential staff officer who carries the authority and the governmentwide perspective of the President. Where a structure for central coordination exists, coordination through bargaining and voluntary mutual adjustment remains an option but it ceases to be in effect the only one.

Two conclusions are suggested, then. First, the sponsorship of the community-level planning and coordinating structures should be assigned ideally not to any of the competing agencies with program responsibilities but to a *neutral* agency. Second, the problem of coordination of federal departments and agencies in support of the community structures should be taken in hand by a presidential staff organization in the Executive Office of the President.

Those two purposes could be served simultaneously if the same Executive Office agency were made responsible for both. That agency would then be the central—and neutral—source within the federal structure for technical assistance to governors, mayors, and others engaged in forming and operating the community-level mechanisms. And it would be the channel of federal aid to those mechanisms. This proposal is consistent with that of the President's National Advisory Commission on Rural Poverty, which recommended that assistance to state and local comprehensive planning programs "be consolidated in the Executive Office of the President under one basic authorization."[1]

Such a scheme has the disadvantage, however, of locating in the Executive Office operating responsibilities that would require a staff of substantial size. It may be argued that the size of an agency should not be the controlling consideration; if, by the nature of its function, it should have supradepartmental status then it should be located in the Executive Office of the President no matter what its size. OEO, a large operating agency, was placed in the Executive Office in order

1. The commission explained that "the Executive Office has the authority required for getting departments to cooperate." *The People Left Behind* (1967), p. 156. See also Niles M. Hansen, "Public Policy and Regional Development," *Quarterly Review of Economics and Business*, Vol. 8 (Summer 1968). Hansen (p. 60) emphasizes that the coordinating agency must "be truly independent" of all departments with program responsibilities and therefore suggests an independent agency be created "to coordinate and watch over comprehensive regional policy formation and implementation."

to give it status for the exercise of the coordinating authority assigned to it, and its location damaged neither the Executive Office nor OEO.

The failure of OEO to develop its coordinating role is attributable in large measure to its absorption in operating problems—primarily those associated with the sponsorship of community action agencies throughout the country and the administration of grants to them. An Executive Office agency that assumed responsibility for sponsoring community-level coordinating mechanisms—which would mean, logically, the transfer of the model cities program from HUD as well as the area planning and development programs from HUD, EDA, and Agriculture—would have an immediate operating burden that would, in all probability, similarly prevent its development as a governmentwide coordinator.

On balance, it would appear preferable to leave the administration of assistance funds to the departments. But if a model for community-level organization is to be adopted—whether ours or another—and the competing and conflicting strategies of the separate agencies thus reconciled, the Executive Office of the President must assume the clear responsibility for defining that model and initiating the steps necessary to move toward it. Somewhere in the Executive Office, in other words, must be fixed the responsibility for developing and recommending to the President an organizational philosophy that will govern the administration of assistance programs and, once he adopts it, monitoring its application in the conduct of the executive branch as a whole. Somewhere in the Executive Office must be centered a concern for the structure of federalism—a responsibility for guiding the evolution of the whole system of federal-state-local relations, viewed for the first time as a *single* system.

In the Executive Office of the President as now organized, the Urban Affairs Council would appear to be the most suitable location for those responsibilities. However, the council and its staff might find themselves concentrating upon legislative proposals and policy questions to the neglect of systematic attention to structure and to management; moreover, an office restricted to *urban* affairs is obviously too narrowly conceived to handle the broad range of intergovernmental programs that affect urban and nonurban areas alike. A new element of the Executive Office of the President designed specifically to assist the chief executive in the operational coordination of programs (and perhaps extending beyond the range of intergovernmental programs alone) would be an alternative.[2] In any case, the responsibility for intergovernmental program coordination—or intergovernmental systems development—should be clearly assigned.

A Governing Policy for Federalism: A Policy of Deference

In the absence of a central point of concern in the federal government for the federal system as a whole, each agency develops its own policies and doctrines of intergovernmental relations, and the result—not surprisingly—is a system full of contradictions. Some agencies deal primarily with states, some bypass the states to deal directly with cities and other local governments, and some bypass all general-purpose governments to deal with special-purpose agencies of their own creation. Some programs are tightly controlled from Washington; in others, decisions are delegated to federal regional or field offices or to the states.

The absence of doctrine is particularly apparent in the relations of the federal government to the new community-level coordinating mechanisms. As the various types of structures were created, none was clearly established as the chosen instrument of the federal government *as a whole* in any locality. Nor were the long established habits and practices of federal agencies altered so that their planning would fit within the new comprehensive planning processes, their actions would be subject to coordination by the new mechanisms, and their funds would be made available as called for when the comprehensive plans received official federal approval.

It makes little sense for the federal government to encourage the communities to construct elaborate coordinating systems that the federal government's own agencies are then left free, individually and

2. President Nixon on Feb. 14, 1969, established an Office of Intergovernmental Affairs in the office of Vice President Agnew, but the Vice President's assignment appears to be that of a liaison man and complaint-handler in a role comparable to that given by President Johnson to the director of the Office of Emergency Preparedness (for governors) and Vice President Humphrey (for cities). Dwight A. Ink, assistant director of the Bureau of the Budget and former HUD assistant secretary for administration, has proposed a unit in the White House, backed up by Bureau of the Budget staff, to be responsible "for monitoring that group of departments concerned with human resources and ensuring coordination among them." "A Management Crisis for the New President: People Programs," *Public Administration Review*, November/December 1968, p. 549.

collectively, to ignore. It makes little sense to foster complicated and laborious planning processes unless the government—and that necessarily means all of its agencies—supports the plans and projects that come out of the community processes. When they do not, the authority of the planning agency that the federal government itself has fathered is vitiated, and local leaders become chary of expending time and energy on activities that depend on the federal government's making good upon its actual or implied commitments.

An economic development district director posed the problem this way:

> We spent the better part of a year putting together an overall economic development program. We involved the whole area in it. EDA requires that the OEDP set forth a listing of priorities, so we laid out our priorities. It was published, and widely distributed throughout the district. Pretty soon the word came through that EDA had approved our OEDP, and the local papers played up the good news. The whole area interpreted that to mean that the priority projects were approved as priority projects and would therefore be funded. But now they find out that isn't the case at all. They have to struggle to get acceptance of the very projects that were contained in the approved OEDP, and EDA feels free to upset the priorities that the OEDP sets.

"Many mayors have been hesitant about getting out in front politically and engaging in a comprehensive planning process with citizens because of skepticism about the federal commitment," said H. Ralph Taylor, assistant secretary of HUD in charge of model cities, in the fall of 1968. The mayors questioned whether the federal government would respond promptly to local initiative, whether it would make resources available to support the plans, and whether the federal assistance would be coordinated. "I really don't blame those mayors," Taylor added.

A state planning official expressed the same view:

> Federal programs often raise great expectations. But then they produce interminable delays and not enough results. The delays produce fairly violent antifederal reactions on the part of the local people who resent all the planning requirements in the first place—their attitude being that they know what's wrong and what needs to be done. When their efforts are not followed up by federal grant money for projects, local patience is exhausted.

For obvious reasons, however, the federal agencies cannot be bound absolutely by whatever the local planning process comes up with. They must guard not only against waste and extravagance but against proposals that may distribute the benefits of federal programs unfairly or in other ways inconsistent with the national purpose. "If we left welfare to the localities we might as well have genocide," one federal official remarked in defense of federal review and supervision of welfare programs—and there is wisdom in that view, too. Federal officials must guard against proposals by one community that may have adverse effects upon others—the pirating of industry, for example. Finally, federal funds may not be available to support all of a community's planned projects on the timetable that the community proposes, and the federal government must reserve the right to limit its financial commitments.

Yet it is one thing for federal officials to draw the line against a local proposal on grounds of illegality, waste, inequity, discrimination, spillover effects, or unavailability of funds and quite another for them to substitute their judgment for that of local communities on matters that do not involve these considerations. Our field interview notes are filled with assertions by local officials that federal decisions are being made on matters that should be wholly within the competence of the communities. Local urban renewal administrators, for example, universally complained that the processing time for urban renewal applications—which was measured not in months but in years[3]—is devoted to the most minute review of the local plans, and that federal officials repeatedly supersede the community's judgment as to what constitutes sound planning for that community. Community action directors protested that the earmarking of Economic Opportunity Act funds for "national emphasis" programs in effect determined the content of local antipoverty programs without regard to community views as to needs and priorities. Six years after enactment of the Manpower Development and Training Act, every individual training course still had to be submitted for federal approval; one training center was operating on thirty-two budgets at the time of our visit—one for each course—and a request that these be consolidated into a single budget had been rejected by the Department of Labor. And the division of funds between on-the-job and institutional training was made each year in Washington, with that

3. A presidential directive to all agencies to reduce processing time by 50 percent within a year is being met in HUD programs (of which urban renewal is one), according to Ink, *ibid.*, p. 547.

division applied uniformly to each of the fifty states regardless of differences in need among the states.

The tendency of federal officials to retain power in their own hands must be recognized as natural and inevitable. It is they who must defend their programs before congressional committees. It is they who are held accountable if things go wrong. They are experts confident that they have the best perspective of the country's needs. They are impatient for results. Rather than defer to thousands of independent community decisions on a given question, some of which by the law of averages will be wrong, they prefer to make the one "right" decision themselves and impose it by regulation. And the regulations incorporating those decisions grow ever more detailed, complex, and rigid.

Yet the principle of decentralization is sound. Decisions on community problems made at the community level are *potentially* better than those made at the national level, because only at the community level can the community be seen whole, only there can all the community programs be interrelated, only there can the systems of comprehensive planning and program coordination be established and operated, and only there can widespread citizen participation be organized and the contributions of the citizens blended with those of the professionals in the decision-making process. The object of the federal government must therefore be to realize the superior potential of the community-level processes. The overriding aim must be to perfect the planning and coordinating machinery in the thousands of communities that comprise the country. Then, *as the machinery begins to measure up to its promise and gains in competence,* the conscious policy of the federal government as a whole—and, hopefully, the state governments as well—should be *to defer increasingly to local judgments.*[4]

A policy of deference is one that must be carried out in a differential manner. The organizations that develop the comprehensive plans and the individual projects will vary widely in their competence, and some communities may deliberately flout the national intent as expressed in law. But decisions as to the differentials themselves cannot

4. Section 401(c) of the Intergovernmental Cooperation Act of 1968 expresses the objectives of such policy: "To the maximum extent possible, consistent with national objectives, all Federal aid for development purposes shall be consistent with and further the objectives of State, regional, and local comprehensive planning."

be left to the individual federal departments and agencies, or there will be no *national* policy of deference. When operating agencies lag in applying that policy, there should be the equivalent of a system of appeals to the agency in the Executive Office of the President responsible for oversight of the operations of the federal system, and the reasons for delay should be reviewed. Aided by technicians from the Bureau of the Budget and the departments, that agency should also review, on a regular and systematic basis, regulations and practices throughout the executive branch that restrict the discretion of local communities in the use of federal funds or that lead to delay in the processing of applications—as a counterweight to the inevitable tendency of program administrators to centralize authority. The review should also develop proposals for consolidation of categorical grants, as advocated by President Nixon.[5] In short, a policy of deference cannot be established through exhortation alone; that has been tried, occasionally, by presidents and their representatives, but without enforcement it has proved fruitless. To give the policy meaning, it must be the subject of continuous governmentwide management from the presidential level. But exhortation should continue, too, for a policy of deference cannot be reduced simply to a series of procedural regulations; it will remain in great degree a matter of attitude, expressed in intangible ways, in the tone as well as the substance of administration.

There are many examples, within the federal government, of a policy of deference—but not all are models for emulation. In the case of many programs where funds are distributed among states by formula, deference has meant a virtual abdication of any federal influence at all—a quiet glossing over of inadequate state and local performance. Much is lost, obviously, if the federal government fails to exert leadership. The federal government can assemble expertise that individual communities cannot hope to match. It can collect and evaluate data from many communities. The information and insight of the federal experts must be brought to bear upon the community plans, and the advice growing out of evaluation must be

5. A series of specific proposals in relation to the administration of categorical grants is contained in section 2 of "New Directions in Federal-Aid Policy" (staff study for the Committee on State and Local Revenue to the 59th National Governors' Conference, October 1967), pp. 29–49. The various reports of the Advisory Commission on Intergovernmental Relations contain many other recommendations that would be appropriate for the attention and initiative of the new Executive Office agency.

made available. These purposes require an aggressive federal approach but an aggressive attitude is consistent with a policy of deference if the federal influence is achieved primarily through consultative relationships while the plans are being formed, rather than through review and modification or disapproval of the community's proposals afterwards. The one approach is calculated to stimulate local initiative; the other tends to stultify it.

Among the factors bearing upon local competence to assume decision-making responsibility in the use of federal assistance is preeminently that of personnel. In sponsoring model cities and multicounty coordinating mechanisms, the federal government must concern itself with the development of a whole new profession of planners-coordinators—or group of related professions—to man them. The recruitment of the planners-coordinators, their training, their career development, their assignment, their compensation—all these become matters of national concern as the national government comes to rely upon them for the effective execution of its programs. Systems of interchange of personnel among jurisdictions, and among levels of government, are essential. The intergovernmental personnel bill that passed the Senate in 1967 but died in the House—and has been reintroduced in the current Congress—would provide the framework for a national effort to upgrade state and local personnel.[6]

Organizing in Support of Model Cities

The specific implications of a policy of deference can be traced most clearly in the model cities program. Here the federal government has proclaimed its bold promise of an all-embracing coordinator at the community level, but it has failed to modify all of the other programs and organizational schemes of the government so that they fit into place as "coordinatees." Model cities is *an* instrument of the federal government—but not yet clearly *the single chosen instrument*—for federal relations with the neighborhoods covered by the program. The projects contained in model cities plans are as-

6. George Bennett and Peter Cove have presented an imaginative proposal for a new federal organization that would have the specific responsibility of upgrading local competence in program development through training and technical assistance at the time that programs are being designed, using the approach suggested in this section. National Association for Community Development, *Community Development*, February 1969, pp. 6, 10.

sured no special status. Each project that qualifies for direct federal aid must still be the subject of a separate application to the agency that holds the funds, and that agency may process it in the usual manner, subject to the usual timetable and criteria. It is true that HUD has been able to work out agreements with some agencies whereby they set aside funds for model cities projects and assign priority to their processing, but the arrangements are far from universal. And set-aside arrangements hardly exist at all for any part of the billions of dollars that are distributed by the federal government through the states.

As the model cities legislation was being written, the National League of Cities suggested the creation of a special revolving fund of perhaps $500 million that could be used to finance model cities projects regardless of where they stood on agency priority lists, the fund to be reimbursed when the projects were reached on those priority lists in the regular order. The proposal, however, was not adopted. An alternative would be to set aside, within each appropriation for a categorical grant program, a sum that would be exempted from regular priority criteria to be used to fund model cities projects. To avert protests that the funds for the model neighborhoods were being diverted from other areas, any exempt pool of money would probably have to be provided through additional appropriations. But only in the urban renewal program have additional funds been authorized by Congress especially for model cities. With that exception, and with the further exception of projects that can be financed through the limited HUD supplemental fund for the model cities program, the cities face the prospect that the end product of all their labors—even after their plans are given the official seal of approval by HUD—will be a series of applications to be processed in essentially the same manner as would have been the case if there had been no model cities program.

A vital element of coordination is the synchronization of the planned activities in the model neighborhoods. The provision of services may depend upon the construction of facilities, and that in turn may depend upon site clearance through urban renewal, which may in turn depend upon provision of relocation housing. Unless federal agencies adhere to the priorities and time schedule set in the plan, the planning process can be invalidated.

The logic of the model cities concept calls for a procedure whereby the local plan that is developed as a coordinated, integrated document is reviewed, approved, and funded as a single undertaking. Ideally, the model cities plan should be accompanied by a single application for federal assistance to support the plan as a whole, and the funds made available as a single block grant, even though they might be assembled from various appropriations. Again ideally, state funds should be applied for, and granted, in the same manner, through arrangements worked out between each state and the federal government.

The revolutionary change that such a procedure would introduce in the federal system can be appreciated if it is accepted that, before long, the area coverage of model cities will have to be expanded to include all the slum neighborhoods of the participating cities.[7] The federal block grant (and, hopefully, the state block grant as well) would be a substantial segment of a city's annual budget. Incidental to such a change would be a revised formula for distributing model cities supplemental funds, removing the present arbitrary relationship between the amount of the block grant and the volume of categorical grants. Also incidental would be a unification of information requirements, so that the same data would not have to be presented separately, in different forms, to various agencies, as is now the case in the present fragmented review and approval system.

Conversion of the model cities program into a genuine block grant is, of course, a general goal to be approached gradually. Present procedures are fixed not only in regulations but in innumerable statutes and administrative understandings overseen by various committees and subcommittees in the decentralized structure of the Congress. The functional alliances among specialized community agencies, specialized federal agencies, and specialized congressional committees and subcommittees will be formidable barriers to con-

---

7. As noted in Chap. 3, the planning and coordination processes of model cities could ultimately be extended citywide, particularly in smaller cities, with perhaps some modification of the participation processes in the more affluent neighborhoods. A community's entire aid budget for a particular year would, then, be presented in a single planning document and, ideally, processed as a single application. Robert A. Aleshire developed a specific proposal for such a system when he was director of the model cities program in Reading, Pennsylvania. "The Community Performance Standard: Incentive Approach to Intergovernmental Program Relations" (unpublished manuscript, 1968).

solidation.[8] The Secretary of HUD obviously does not have enough clout, by himself, to combat them. The incorporation of the categorical aid programs within the model cities system will be a slow process at best, but it will be wholly dependent upon leadership and discipline over the entire executive branch by a presidential staff that knows exactly where it is going and has the full support of the President himself in getting there.[9]

In the meantime, a first step would be to establish procedures to assure that federal projects within the model neighborhoods will not be allowed to bypass the model cities coordinating process. At present, projects may go forward that are initiated outside of—or even in conflict with—the model cities plan. A project prepared by a county health department, for example, might be substantially modified in the course of its review by the chosen representatives of the model neighborhood, the city demonstration agency, and the mayor and city council, yet there is no prohibition in law or regulation to prevent its being submitted to and approved by the state and federal health authorities without any such review. The danger may be more theoretical than real, but in any case the loophole should be closed by extending to the city demonstration agencies a right of review and comment upon all projects in the model neighborhoods corresponding to the authority conferred by law upon metropolitan planning bodies in regard to federally aided projects within their areas.[10]

Most important of all, the administration will have to resist the temptation to impose its views upon the content of the model cities plans. The middle-level personnel in HUD, like those in any other

8. An indication of their strength was their ability to defeat the modest proposal submitted by the Johnson administration in 1967 to provide a general authorization for agencies to enter into arrangements for joint funding of projects drawing upon more than one appropriation.

9. HUD Secretary Romney announced on April 28, 1969, that the Council on Urban Affairs in the Executive Office of the President "will assume direct responsibility for inter-departmental policy affecting Model Cities" and that the secretaries of the government departments involved would reserve funds specifically for the funding of model cities proposals. "This will ensure the availability of departmental funds for Model Cities, and will give local authorities a better idea of the amount and kinds of funds they can expect from the various departments for their Model Cities plans," the secretary said. Department of Housing and Urban Development, No. 69–0321, April 28, 1969.

10. In section 204 of the Demonstration Cities and Metropolitan Development Act of 1966.

agency, have ideas as to the best expenditure of model cities funds. Some of these may indeed be superior to those developed by the communities themselves. It would be a simple matter for HUD, perhaps in concert with other agencies, to move in the direction taken early by the Office of Economic Opportunity in prescribing the content of local community action plans through "national emphasis" programs. So far, fortunately, HUD's approach has been consistent with the policy of deference described above.

But, to repeat, deference depends upon the soundness of the planning process in the communities. Accordingly HUD, supported and overseen by the Executive Office of the President, will have to be continuously concerned with monitoring that process in each community—which means, crucially, the exertion of federal influence to maintain (or reestablish) a truly balanced structure whereby the resources of the model neighborhood residents and those of the public and private agencies serving the neighborhood are effectively combined. In the early months of the program, imbalances in both directions have been evident. At one extreme have been the cities where the voice of the neighborhood has been heard only through persons appointed or co-opted by the city demonstration agency. At the other have been those where the residents have seized control—or the city has relinquished control—of the entire planning process, with resulting proposals that are unacceptable to local, state, and federal agencies. No uniform structure can be imposed, and HUD has been wise in not prescribing one. But the effectiveness of the processes now employed throughout the country must be continuously appraised, and federal authorities must be prepared to intervene on a case-by-case basis, to help improve these processes where they are not producing results that serve the national purpose.

Organizing in Support of a "Model Countryside" Program

The principles that apply to organizing in support of the model cities program apply, in analogous form, to organizing in support of nonmetropolitan development. The problems are comparable: both urban and rural areas need comprehensive planning, and they need machinery for coordination of plans and operating programs. The model sketched in Chapter 6 for nonmetropolitan multicounty areas therefore corresponds in many respects to the model cities structure discussed in Chapter 3. And the federal government is assisting in the establishment of coordinating structures along the lines of each of the models.

There is, however, a major difference. There is yet no "model countryside" program that offers the benefits conferred upon model cities. The states are encouraged to set up comprehensive multi-county planning bodies with the promise of federal aid for their administrative costs. But that is all. There is no rural counterpart to the supplemental funds made available to the model cities to enable them to carry out projects not eligible for regular categorical assistance. It is the supplemental funds that give the mayor, the city council, the city demonstration agency, and the neighborhood leaders and planners the leverage to bring a diverse array of public and private agencies under their coordinating sway. Both as a matter of equity and as an essential means for giving strength and substance to the coordination process, a model countryside fund should be established comparable to the supplemental fund made available for the execution of model cities plans.

Similarly, the other recommendations made above to guide the evolution of the model cities program would apply to the model countryside program—the unified review of the model countryside plan, the eventual funding of the plan as a whole through what amounts to a block grant, and the right of the multicounty planning and development bodies to review and comment upon applications for federal assistance originating from within their areas.

The question remains as to where in the federal structure the sponsorship of the multicounty bodies and the model countryside program should be assigned. Assuming that a neutral agency in the Executive Office of the President cannot or should not be assigned a responsibility that has a heavy burden of operating routine, a choice needs to be made among federal departments or agencies for assumption of the central role corresponding to that of HUD in the model cities program. At the time our survey began, two agencies were vigorously competing in the sponsorship of multicounty planning and coordinating machinery—the Agriculture Department in all of rural America, and the Economic Development Administration in the depressed areas. Late in 1968, the Department of Housing and Urban Development obtained its authority to sponsor multicounty planning bodies and so became the third federal agency in the field.

Perhaps the 1968 legislation will turn out to have provided a satisfactory framework for the unification of federal efforts for coordination in nonmetropolitan areas. Under its terms—as amplified by the interdepartmental agreement negotiated during 1968—HUD has the central responsibility for relations with the states in the establishment of the nonmetropolitan districts and will supply the federal assistance for the districts' administrative expenses. Agriculture will provide technical assistance to those planning bodies that do not cover any part of a metropolitan area (that is, a standard metropolitan statistical area). And EDA's economic development districts can qualify as nonmetropolitan district planning bodies provided they conform to HUD's requirements that at least two-thirds of the members of the governing body be public officials.

Whether HUD can give the same quality of leadership to a model countryside program that it has given to model cities is, however, highly conjectural. Heretofore, its programs have been directed primarily to metropolitan areas, and the most insistent pressures upon HUD have always come from the larger cities whose mayors look upon it as *their* department. True, HUD has administered programs designed particularly for small communities—notably the section 701 planning program and aid for community facilities—but these have been incidental to the department's main concerns. The explosive problems of the metropolitan centers are bound to continue to demand HUD's principal attention. Even the title of the Department of Housing and *Urban* Development implies a limitation on its concern—it has no programs that penetrate the rural countryside, and it has no roots there. As for small towns, it was their neglect by HUD and its predecessors that led the Congress to extend, step by step and reluctantly, the lending programs of the Farmers Home Administration to cover housing and community facilities in small urban centers (with an upper limit of 5,500 population).

Moreover, HUD has not concerned itself with *economic* development, which is the primary motivation behind the creation of multicounty planning and development bodies. While HUD has officially adopted a comprehensive concept of planning, its assistance under section 701 still goes primarily to official planning agencies whose interests have traditionally been limited to land use and to the development of public facilities. HUD has little experience with the kind of comprehensive agency, described in Chapter 6, that is concerned with social and economic development as well as land use and that has responsibility for action as well as planning. HUD resisted the amendment to the 1968 legislation authorizing designation of economic development districts as nonmetropolitan planning districts, and its circular listing the functions of the nonmetropolitan districts does not even mention economic development planning among the planning activities that the department will support.

But if HUD is not an altogether satisfactory choice as the lead agency for nonmetropolitan development, either of the alternatives has disadvantages too. If HUD is too urban in its orientation, the Department of Agriculture is too rural, and like HUD's, its very name implies a limitation of its concern. Traditionally, it has been devoted to the interests of farmers, and the farmers in return have looked upon it as *their* department. Yet, most of the people in rural America no longer live on farms or draw their livelihood directly from the land. If employment opportunities are to be increased in nonmetropolitan America, they must be increased *outside* of farming, and the leadership must come from the small towns and cities that have not traditionally identified their interests and concerns with the Department of Agriculture. Most multicounty districts would cover mixed urban-rural, rather than strictly rural, areas.

The Department of Agriculture has by far the strongest field organizations of the federal government in nonmetropolitan areas. In most counties it has three offices—those of the Farmers Home Administration, the Soil Conservation Service, and the Agricultural Stabilization and Conservation Service—and it also helps to finance (but does not control) the county agents of the federal-state extension service. But in terms of dealing with small towns and cities, this field force brings disadvantages as well as advantages. The names of the agencies identify them with "farmers," "soil," and "agriculture," and their clientele until recently has been so limited. As their functions—particularly those of the Farmers Home Administration—have been gradually extended to small towns, the new functions appear to have been grafted uncomfortably upon a basic mission centered on the needs of farmers. Finally, in terms of training and interests, most Agriculture field employees are still farm-oriented and less than ideally equipped to deal broadly with the developmental problems of urban centers of any size.

The Department of Commerce, as currently organized, has severe limitations also. The most obvious weakness is geographical: its jurisdiction over regional economic development extends only to "depressed areas," and communities move in and out of eligibility status with every fluctuation in employment levels. The Department of Commerce as a whole has no tradition of concern with community development, either urban or rural. Its programs affecting regional development date back only to 1961 and have never been more than a secondary concern of the department. Outside of the Economic Development Administration, Commerce has few resources for the purpose. Much of the professional expertise that needs to be drawn upon is concentrated elsewhere—the natural resource development experts in Agriculture and to a lesser extent Interior, the professional planners in HUD, the human resource development talent in HEW, OEO, and Labor.

Even though HUD sponsors and provides administrative funds for the nonmetropolitan planning bodies, much of the substantive aid in support of development projects will continue to flow through Agriculture and EDA. Regardless of what other changes are made in organization, a strong case can be made for combining the resources that those two agencies are now devoting separately to the task of stimulating general economic (that is, nonagricultural) and community development. Such a combination would provide a single agency in the government with a broad mandate to develop and administer, on a nationwide basis, programs designed to reverse the economic decline of nonmetropolitan America and thereby check the mass flow of population to the cities. This is not the place to argue the case for a stronger and more determined national policy for development of nonmetropolitan areas, but if the rapidly rising support for such a policy[11] leads to the enactment of strong measures, such as tax incentives, to supplement present rural development pro-

---

11. See, for example, Advisory Commission on Intergovernmental Relations, *Urban and Rural America: Policies for Future Growth* (April 1968), particularly Chap. 4; President's National Advisory Commission on Rural Poverty, *The People Left Behind*, especially Chaps. 2 and 10; and Republican Coordinating Committee, *Revitalizing Our Rural Areas* (Republican National Committee, July 1967). Both major party platforms in 1968 endorsed proposals to accelerate rural development. The Republican proposals were presented, anomalously, under the heading, "Crisis in the Cities."

grams, then an agency with such a broad mandate will be needed even more than it is now.

The new agency could be housed in either department, but either would have to be reorganized for the purpose. If the Department of Agriculture were selected, the department's name should be changed to "Agriculture and Rural Development" or something similar (as Secretary Freeman proposed several times) and the department reorganized to give its nonagricultural development programs a status equal to that accorded its agricultural programs. If Commerce were chosen, the perspective and interests of the top leadership of the department and of the organization as a whole would have to be reoriented to give nonmetropolitan development an emphasis comparable to that which Agriculture would be prepared to give. If neither department could be so reorganized, an independent agency would be a third alternative.

A National Problem: Upgrading State Government

The creative innovations in community-level programs to meet the problems of the 1960s have arisen predominantly from two levels —from the communities themselves, and from Washington, D.C. Rarely have they come from the fifty state capitals. There have been conspicuous exceptions, of course, particularly in the larger states: California had initiated a program of compensatory education for disadvantaged children before the Elementary and Secondary Education Act of 1965; Pennsylvania's program of retraining of the unemployed was the model on which the Manpower Development and Training Act was patterned; New York has introduced notable housing programs, and so on.[12] But these were isolated undertakings in individual states, and they were almost totally eclipsed by the massive innovative wave of Kennedy's New Frontier and Johnson's Great Society. The Kennedy-Johnson programs stimulated the initiative of community organizations of all kinds, and as the creative impulse flowed back and forth between Washington and the communities, the states seemed stranded on the sidelines, watching. In our interviews with state officials we encountered little of the excitement of

12. Terry Sanford (former North Carolina governor), *Storm Over the States* (McGraw-Hill, 1967), Chap. 7, offers a long list of state innovations and accomplishments, from the turn of the century to the present time.

new policy and program ideas and experimentation that infused the comments of federal and local administrators alike. The states were making little contribution to new policy for community-level programs: policies were made in Washington. And they were contributing little to the implementation of those policies: administration was a local responsibility.

Why is this? Roscoe C. Martin, in his unsparing critique of the failure of the states to cope with urban problems, describes what he calls the "state mind"—compounded of "rural orientation, provincial outlook, commitment to a strict moral code, a philosophy of individualism"; characterized by a "spirit of nostalgia"; and enjoying only "intermittent and imperfect contact with the realities of the modern world."[13] The state mind is reflected in "a hard bitten and almost uniform conservatism," a distrust of big government and especially the federal government, and a dislike of cities and especially big cities. It accounts for the failure of the states to modernize their constitutions and to rally the leadership and find the revenues for the solution of urban problems. Politicians who have risen to power in the states are those who have succeeded in this conservative milieu, and they do not intend to risk losing power by entertaining new and different ideas.

Our study did not focus upon state governments as such, and we do not attempt here a definitive appraisal of their weaknesses. But we found much to confirm Martin's observations—acknowledging, as he does, that there are inevitable exceptions to his generalizations. In our interviews in the state capitols we expected—and heard—criticism of the federal government for its refusal to give the states a larger role in administering federal assistance programs. But when we talked with state officials who were advocates of innovation, we were surprised to find (particularly in the smaller states) the criticism more often turned inward upon the state itself. The complaints were familiar: legislatures were hopelessly conservative; they met infrequently, and adjourned before the members could become familiar with emerging problems and come to grips with them. The state leadership of both parties lived in a world of political maneuvering and jockeying; governors were absorbed in their political role—exercising party leadership and running for reelection or aspiring for

13. *The Cities and the Federal System* (Atherton, 1965), p. 77.

higher office—to the neglect of program and administrative leadership. Where they were limited to a single term, they had little time to establish leadership, even if they had the interest; sometimes, old statehouse hands would go back twenty years or more to identify a governor who had shown any deep concern with the mechanics of state government or taken any leadership toward modernization of the state's constitutional structure.[14]

Governors in some states were chief executives in name only, sharing their power with other elected state officials (in one state, we never heard "the governor acted"; it was always "the governor-and-council acted") or with independent administrative boards and commissions, usually bipartisan and with members appointed for fixed terms overlapping that of the governor. Governors lacked staff assistance ("I'm trying to create a budget examination staff; all we have are account clerks, more or less," said a state director of administration). It was difficult to hire and retain professional personnel on pay scales fixed at clerical levels ("As soon as one of my planners gets a couple of years experience, he's gone, either to work with a private consultant or a local planning commission," said a state planning director). Even the merit system for state personnel was not everywhere established ("In this state we still have a spoils system," said a state senator; "to turn a federal program over to this state is a waste of time." "We have political planning," said a state planner, "and all appointments are made on a political basis"). State officials who were most conscious of state weaknesses did not necessarily repeat the official position of the National Governors' Conference that federal responsibilities should be devolved upon the states. "The federal government already keeps loading things on the states that the states are just not able to handle," said a state planning official, and a gubernatorial aide in another state used almost identical language.

14. Several appeals for modernization of state government, with summaries of the specific measures that need to be taken, have recently been published—all of them in essential agreement. They include U.S. Chamber of Commerce, *Modernizing State Government* (1967); Research Policy Committee, Committee for Economic Development, *Modernizing State Government* (1967); John P. Wheeler, Jr. (ed.), *Salient Issues of Constitutional Revision* (National Municipal League, 1961); Martin, *The Cities and the Federal System*, Chap. 3; Sanford, *Storm Over the States*, Chap. 4; and Advisory Commission on Intergovernmental Relations, *Fiscal Balance in the Federal System* (October 1967), Vol. 1, pp. 200–62.

The larger states had stronger governors, more competent gubernatorial staff agencies, higher salary scales, civil service protection for state employees, more progressive legislatures, and more all-around administrative capability. Since they were the more urbanized states, they also paid more attention to city problems. That attention was often symbolized by a new and vigorous department or staff office of "community affairs" or "urban affairs," a type of administrative unit that has now been created in more than half the states. But while those departments were helping prepare model cities applications, for example, and sometimes paying part of the nonfederal share of federal programs, they were introducing few major innovative programs of their own.

For the larger states shared with the smaller ones the most decisive barrier of all to innovation—financial stricture. State tax rates have been steadily rising, and new tax levies have been regularly introduced, just to meet demands for upgrading existing services, for raising state pay scales to keep abreast of private industry, and for coping with workload increases.[15] Small wonder that the states have been slow to accept the challenges of new community-level problems for which the federal government and the communities seem to have accepted a joint responsibility.

"The flexibility for new programs in state government is zero," said a gubernatorial aide. "Even with a large tax increase, we have not been able to fund any new programs." Among the demands upon each state is the requirement that it provide a share of the costs of of those new federal programs that are administered through the states, on pain of losing the state's share of federal assistance. New revenues are thus absorbed in response to federal initiatives, and while the states participate in launching the federal innovations they have no margin for their own. "There is a constant juggling of priorities, taking dollars from the general service areas and putting them toward federal funds in order to double them," observed a state budget director. "I'm not so sure that it should be the federal bureaucrats' aspirations that set the course of our state. But you can't expect political leadership to say no to a handout. They simply can't

15. For a listing of tax increases and enactment of new taxes, by state, 1959–69, see Advisory Commission on Intergovernmental Relations, *State and Local Finances, Significant Features, 1966 to 1969* (1968), Table 21, p. 48. That report shows that state and local tax revenue for all states, as a percentage of total personal income, rose from 8.27 percent in 1957 to 9.80 percent in 1967 (Table 1, pp. 10–11). During the same period, federal income tax rates were reduced.

take the heat." "Every single new activity of state government in our state in quite a few years has been the direct consequence of federal grant programs," said a state university professor in a small state. "The result is that it's people in Washington who are deciding in what direction our state government moves—but then, if the federal government didn't move us, we wouldn't be moving at all."

On those occasions when a state did try to insert itself into what had been a direct federal-local channel it was liable to be welcomed neither by Washington nor by the larger of the local communities. We found the attitudes of mayors toward the states to be at best ambivalent and at worst downright hostile. Following are comments made by eight mayors of large or middle sized cities or by their top staff assistants speaking for them:

Everything we've gotten in this city is from the federal government. The state has not done one d——d thing for us.

What we really want is to have our cake and eat it too. We'd like state money, and we need their help. But we don't want them in the direct channel between the federal agencies and the city, where they'd just be another layer of supervision and review and another group of bureaucrats we'd have to satisfy.

In principle, I'm a believer in channels, and in theory I think the federal money should flow to the state and then to the local community. I'm a Republican. But if you ask me, as a practical matter, would it be useful to the city right now for the state to be in the channel, I have to say that I don't see how it would be. I'm afraid of the delay and the red tape.

It's very handy to be able to deal directly with the federal agencies, and relations with all of them except OEO have been excellent. Of course, if the state were allowed to make the decisions, that would be another matter.

The larger, more competent cities must deal as much as possible with the federal government and the states should keep out of the way, performing services for the less able rural areas.

If the need is in the city it should be met in the city. Passing the money through an extra pair of hands is wasteful. I would ten times rather go to the federal government than the state government. Washington programs are directed to urban areas. State programs are different.

Ideally, the state government should be involved but up to now they have had little to offer. They are always counting votes. They are much more involved in politics than is the federal government.

Our most satisfactory federal relations are with the departments which deal directly with the city. In the case of HEW, and some of the

Labor Department programs, where we deal with Washington through the state capital, communications take six times as long.

These representative comments reflect what appears to have become a vicious circle. When the rurally oriented states failed to respond to the growing needs of the cities for assistance, the cities turned to the federal government and obtained a positive response. Beginning in the 1930s, direct federal-local relationships developed— in emergency public works and work relief projects, in airport development, in financing of sewage treatment plants and hospitals, in urban renewal and other housing measures—and when the community action and model cities programs were launched in the 1960s they followed the same direct federal-local channel. But as the federal government assumed responsibility for urban problems, the states were under even less pressure to concern themselves with those problems; indeed, they were under the opposite pressure, in the words of the mayor quoted above, to "keep out of the way." The mayors might press for state funds, but not for state responsibility. So the capacity of the states to cope with urban problems remained undeveloped. The more the states lagged in that area of concern the tighter became the alliance between the federal government and the cities and the more jealously their direct channel was guarded against intrusion by the states. The more the states were excluded the more they lagged in developing competence, and so the circle progressed. We found no one in our interviews who thought that the recent reapportionment of state legislatures on a one-man-one-vote basis had, as of late 1967, made any significant difference; it had strengthened the suburbs at the expense of rural areas, but that shift had not altered the conservative outlook of the legislatures.

The hostility toward the states so often expressed by mayors of the larger cities was not matched in the comments of community leaders in the rural areas and small towns we visited. To them, Washington was remote. They had no direct channel to the national capital. They were accustomed to looking to their state governments for assistance in community projects, and they welcomed state help in their communication with federal agencies (other than with the omnipresent Department of Agriculture, whose offices were at the county seat). The states had taken a more active role in the formation of planning and coordinating bodies in rural areas than in the promotion of such bodies in the cities and their metropolitan areas. The states had, for example, taken the initiative—through state offices financed by OEO—to get community action agencies organized in their rural counties while the cities were organizing their own. The rural leaders, clearly, had not experienced the frustration of the larger cities in dealing with their states; the rurally oriented state governments were, by definition, oriented *toward* them. But the states, Martin suggests, have been not so much *rurally* oriented as *conservatively* oriented, and the rapport with the rural leadership perhaps rested mainly on a common attachment to the status quo. For the states were not vigorously pursuing rural development any more than urban development; most of the creative new programs for rural areas too were being generated out of Washington.

What is the answer? Martin, like many of his academic colleagues, simply gives up on the states. The "promise of positive action on metro-urban problems," he concludes, lies in "increased direct cooperation between the federal government and the cities."[16]

But that answer is not good enough. The problem of coordination that we have discussed in this book demands that the states be brought effectively into the federal-state-local chain of relationships. The functions on which the federal government and the cities can cooperate directly comprise only part of the whole that must be brought together. Locally administered functions for which the states are the traditional channel for federal funds (particularly education, health, and welfare) and state-administered functions (such as employment services, regional vocational schools, correctional systems, vocational rehabilitation, specialized health services) have to be brought into the coordination system, too. Moreover, the state's legal powers must frequently be brought into play to make it possible to solve community problems. As an Urban Coalition task force concluded in regard to housing and urban development programs:

> The states have abilities and legal authority unavailable to other levels of government. If these resources are withheld from national programs, the federal government, the cities and the private sector will be seriously hampered in carrying out their roles. If the states apply their authority and abilities creatively, they can enhance the effectiveness of the other partners in programs aimed at providing a decent environment for the residents of our communities.[17]

16. *The Cities and the Federal System*, p. 82.
17. Urban Coalition, Task Force on Housing, Reconstruction and Investment, *Agenda for Positive Action: State Programs in Housing and Community Development* (November 1, 1968), p. v.

If the model cities coordination process is to succeed, state agencies will have to be directed by their governors and their legislatures to enter without reservation into that process and to conform their programs to the model city plans, and it will require state leadership—and perhaps coercion at times—to bring counties, school districts, and other independent governmental bodies into that process also. Without the unstinting support of governors and legislatures, the mayors and city demonstration agencies will find it a hopeless task to attempt to mobilize all available resources and to unify the planning and administrative efforts.

And the same applies to the problems of the nonmetropolitan areas. "Direct cooperation between the federal government and the cities," in Martin's phrase, is no solution at all for smaller communities. The federal government cannot establish effective communication with them except through an intermediate multicounty mechanism which it is incumbent upon the states to create. Martin's treatise was written before coordination came to be recognized in the middle 1960s as a crucial necessity. Once that problem is recognized, it is no longer possible to dismiss the states or any other source of authority and program leadership as one that can be isolated and bypassed. All of them must be brought together, and ways must be found to do it.

One way to bring the states into the community-level coordination processes is the very device of the grant-in-aid that has been used to accomplish so many other federal objectives. Federal funds are now being made available to state planning offices for the purpose of developing nonmetropolitan multicounty districts. A similar approach was used by the Appalachian Regional Commission to stimulate state planning of local development districts, which have now been established throughout the region. HUD is now extending that approach by authorizing section 701 grants to the states to finance the staff services necessary for coordination of the participation of state agencies in model cities. By these means, the states can be helped to develop a significant technical assistance capacity in relation both to model cities and to nonmetropolitan development. Staff assistance can be financed without putting the state in the channel of review of the plans and disbursement of the funds, which would result in the delays and red tape the cities fear.

The problem is, of course, broader. As the federal government continues to establish national objectives that can be executed only through state and local initiative and participation, the stake of the country in the upgrading of state government—and the upgrading of local government through the exercise of state legal powers—becomes ever greater. The inability of state governments to assume their necessary role in the solution of national problems must itself be recognized as a national problem, and one that must be approached and solved through national action like any other national problem. As in so many other cases, the first step toward a solution must be to remove the issue from the realm of ideological combat; relations among the federal government, the states, and the cities must be discussed in terms of practical administrative problems rather than in the language of constitutional law and power struggles. Then the problem can be treated like any other practical problem; it can be broken into its elements and specific measures dealing with each element then assembled in a comprehensive national program for the upgrading of state government.

The measures will consist of a judicious selection from many approaches that have been used with some success already. Grants-in-aid can be used to build a governor's capacity for leadership by building the instrumentalities he needs for leadership. The federal government can facilitate the training and interchange of state personnel. It can continue to experiment with regional multistate cooperative approaches like those pioneered in Appalachia. It can extend the requirement for merit systems of personnel administration where federal funds are involved. It can attach many other kinds of administrative conditions to grants-in-aid. It can reform its own practices where these result in the dilution of state leadership—the "single state agency" requirements in many federal statutes, for instance, that severely limit a state's freedom to organize its own executive branch to suit its own needs.[18] It can simplify financial relationships where these interfere with initiative and effective management at the state level—through consolidating categorical grants, for example, and committing assistance funds in advance of, or during an early stage of, the state's planning cycle. Matching requirements can be removed where they serve primarily to encumber rather than facilitate the effective administration of grant-in-aid programs. Finally, an imaginative approach is incorporated in a bill introduced by Representative

18. The Intergovernmental Cooperation Act of 1968 gives federal department heads blanket authority to waive the requirement upon a state's request.

Henry S. Reuss, Democrat of Wisconsin, who proposes that revenue sharing with the states (or block grants to them) be made contingent upon the development by the states of broad plans for constitutional modernization that would be submitted to, and approved by, regional committees created by the regions' governors.[19]

The range of possible content of a national program to upgrade the states as participants in the federal system is infinite. The important thing is not what goes into the program, but that such a program be deliberately put together. Once more, central leadership within the federal government is required. One more task is identified for the unit in the Executive Office of the President concerned with management of the federal system, proceeding with the assistance of the Advisory Commission on Intergovernmental Relations and organizations of state and local officials.

A Differential Approach to Federal-State Relations

One of the great difficulties in evolving a pattern of federal-state-local relations is the diversity of the states. The largest has seventy times the population of the smallest, and financial resources and capability extend over the same range. One state embraces a New York City, while others have no city over fifty thousand population. Some states have concentrations of minorities, others virtually none. Some states have smog; others lack smokestacks. State governmental structures and traditions are equally diverse—strong governors and weak governors, merit systems and spoils systems, high state tax levels and low state tax levels, progressivism and standpattism. Yet the federal government now writes one series of regulations, embodying one set of relationships with all states alike. The consequence is that it fits none precisely. A common complaint we heard in western states was that federal regulations were written with the East in mind. Rural states complained that the rules were drafted to suit the urban states, but the urban states sometimes had exactly the opposite complaint.

In the drafting of federal aid legislation, a drafter's view of the role the states should play is likely to depend upon his estimate of state competence—and that is apt to depend upon which state he is

19. H.R. 2519, introduced Jan. 8, 1969.

thinking about. If his picture is of New York or California, he is likely to write his bill in terms of what the state can contribute. If his picture is of a small and backward state, he is liable to leave the states out of the administrative channel in order to prevent them from impeding progress. In the drafting of the Economic Opportunity Act, an "Alabama syndrome" developed. Any suggestion within the poverty task force that the states be given a role in the administration of the act was met with the question, "Do you want to give that kind of power to George Wallace?" And so, in the bill submitted by President Johnson to the Congress, not only George Wallace but Nelson Rockefeller and George Romney and Edmund Brown and all the other governors were excluded from any assigned role.

Both sides in the argument are right. New York and California do have a contribution to make to federal programs in leadership and administrative capacity, and a program will usually stand to gain in those states if they have authority and responsibility to participate. Other states, where administrative capacity is lacking or where the state's leadership is indifferent or hostile to the objectives of the legislation, can only hamper and delay. Given this diversity, the advantages of state participation can be maximized and the disadvantages minimized only if the federal government can adopt a *differential* approach, working through some states and bypassing others in the same programs. To make such an approach possible, federal-state relations have to be converted from a *legal* concept, in which the states collectively negotiate in the legislative and administrative processes for rights and powers that all of them then possess, to an *administrative* concept, in which the federal government exercises judgment as to how much reliance can be placed upon each state and reaches an individual understanding with that state governing federal-state administrative relationships. At present a state that raises its level of competence substantially above that of its sister states notices no difference in its treatment by the federal departments. But under a differential approach a state that established a strong department of community affairs, for example, could be granted more authority over federal aid projects, perhaps through informal devices whereby its advice was systematically sought and heeded.

A corollary to the abandonment of a legal approach to the states' role in the federal system would be the abandonment of the now customary requirement that the states buy their right of participation in federal programs by the contribution of matching funds. The benefit to be derived from a state's participation comes not from its money but from its ability to make an administrative and leadership contribution, and these bear no necessary relationship to its ability or willingness to pay a share of program costs. The matching requirements have numerous adverse effects: They involve the state's legislative and appropriations processes, which may result in delay and sometimes in conflict between state and federal actions. They distort the state's budget processes if they induce it to divert funds from nonaided programs to what may be lower priority aided programs, or from programs requiring a higher state proportion to those requiring a lesser share. And the program benefits flow to the states that are able and willing to raise the matching funds, which may be disproportionate to need. As recent state programs that have begun with a 100 percent federal contribution have shifted to a 90–10 or 80–20 ratio, no improvement has been discernible in program operation or results; the consequences have been only administrative complications, bookkeeping headaches, and federal-state tensions. A simple and direct way for the federal government to ease the financial pressure on state governments (thus accomplishing the purpose of revenue-sharing) and to simplify the complexity of grant-in-aid relationships would be to refrain from writing matching requirements into new programs and reduce or remove the requirements from existing programs where other controls, such as budget approval and auditing, will assure the proper expenditure of federal funds.

Coordination at the Regional Level

In moving toward a differential approach to federal-state relations, two things seem clear: First, the understanding with each state should be reasonably consistent as among federal programs; if a state is competent for a general leadership and coordination role relating to community-level programs, the competence will extend to all of them. Second, the understandings with the individual states must be reached at, and administered from, the regional level; the regional staffs of federal agencies are the federal government's specialized instrument for knowing and dealing with individual states.

The problem of coordination at the regional level, then, is centrally one of working out—and enforcing—a common approach to intergovernmental relations that will relate the federal government as a whole to each state government as a whole in an individualized way and, consistent with the pattern of federal-state relations in that state, to its communities.

Yet the only mechanism at the regional level for coordination of federal agencies in relation to state and local governments is a system of regional councils made up of agency regional representatives of equal status. In the past, interdepartmental committees at the regional level made up of equals—like their counterparts in Washington—have proved ineffective: "They fall apart as soon as there is some divergence," one regional official said, "yet divergence is the very thing they are supposed to come to grips with." In Washington, if the Urban Affairs Council proves to be an effective decision-making mechanism, it will be because it is chaired by the President and administered by a competent staff reporting to the President. No analogous arrangements have been made for the regional councils.

A coordinated approach to intergovernmental relations requires the introduction of a new force at the regional level—a supradepartmental official with responsibility and authority to speak for the federal government as a whole in matters of intergovernmental relations. In the absence of such a spokesman, there will not be a satisfactory channel of central communication between the federal government as a whole and state and local governments. Regional representatives of individual departments and agencies now speak with governors, but they speak with authority only about the business of their individual agencies, and most of their communication is with the state departments that receive and administer the federal funds— regional education staffs deal with state education staffs, health staffs with health staffs, employment service officials with their counterparts, and so on. We heard from governors and their staffs a repeated demand for "dialogue" with the federal government about the patterns of federal-state-local relations being established in their states— dialogue, that is, with *the federal government,* not with its individual specialized agencies.

The role of a supradepartmental official in a regional center would be analogous to that of the unit proposed earlier for the Executive

Office of the President. He would administer no substantive programs; his concern would be to establish and manage a system of governmentwide coordination, to provide a central channel of communication with governors and mayors, to develop and oversee a general pattern of coordination of intergovernmental programs. He should be, then, a regional representative of the intergovernmental program coordination unit of the Executive Office.

When suggestions for regional representation of the Executive Office of the President have been made in the past by various task forces on governmental organization, they have been met with the response that such a move would be politically impossible. Department heads, it is argued, would resist a presidential agent in the field who had any degree of authority over the departments' field personnel. Even more important, governors would oppose any suggestion of "assistant presidents" stationed in their states who might be political rivals and might come to overshadow the governors themselves. Senators and congressmen would fear such officials for the same reasons.

But, as in other cases, the office is its image. It would be essential that the appointees to the regional positions not be politicians or even public figures. Their primary interest would have to be not in the substance of particular policies but in administrative systems—specifically, systems of intergovernmental relations. They would have to possess, in the oft-quoted advice to presidential aides in the 1938 report of the President's Committee on Administrative Management, a "passion for anonymity" (and because those aides heeded that advice, it may be noted, they largely overcame the fear and distrust with which they were regarded at the outset both by department heads and by members of Congress). The regional representatives would represent the President not in his roles as party leader and policy advocate but only in his role as chief administrator, and in that capacity they would represent the intergovernmental program coordination unit of the Executive Office rather than the President himself. The department heads would then possess the same rights of appeal to the President over the regional representatives' actions that they possessed in regard to any other exercise of authority by that unit. A way to begin the evolution of such a coordinating force in the field might be, indeed, the assignment to the regions on an experimental and temporary basis of members of the staff of the intergovernmental program coordination unit of the Executive Office.

To summarize, the role of the regional representatives of the intergovernmental program coordination staff would be to monitor the workings of the federal system at the regional level in much the same way that the Executive Office unit of which they are a part would monitor the workings of that system in Washington. The regional representative would develop a common approach by all federal agencies to the coordinating machinery established at lower levels—in governors' offices, in multicounty regions, and in cities. In other words, he would organize the entire federal government in support of that machinery. He would supervise the development, in cooperation with the substantive agencies, of unified but diverse patterns of relationships with individual states and their subdivisions. He would convene the interdepartmental meetings at the regional level necessary to mediate disputes and to coordinate the federal position on individual projects involving more than one department; he would make sure that the federal review teams assigned to work with model cities applicants, for example, worked in harmony. If he could not himself bring about coordination, he would alert the Executive Office of the President to unsettled questions of coordination that needed attention there. He would provide a chairmanship and a staff for the regional councils of departmental representatives. As arrangements were worked out at the Washington level for joint funding of projects, he would follow through at the regional level to organize unified review of project applications. He would oversee the processes of decentralization of decision making. To the extent that the Executive Office of the President might assume responsibility in Washington for sponsorship and funding of the community-level coordinating structures—city demonstration agencies and multicounty bodies—he would assume a corresponding responsibility at the regional level. And he could administer the noncategorical grants to state governments designed to upgrade the administrative capacity of the states.

More is required to achieve coordination at the regional level, however, than just the appointment of a coordinator, indispensable as that step is. The federal regional pattern itself needs to be rationalized. Until 1969, it had been difficult to find any two agencies in the federal government with identical patterns of regional boundaries and headquarters cities—even those that administered related programs of grants-in-aid and dealt with the same configuration of states and communities. The state of Kentucky and its subdivisions, for example, were served by the regional offices of HUD in Atlanta, Georgia; HEW in Charlottesville, Virginia; the Bureau of Employment Security (Labor) in Cleveland, Ohio; the Bureau of Work Programs (Labor) and OEO in Washington, D.C.; EDA in Huntington, West Virginia; and state offices of Agriculture in Kentucky. A representative of the Executive Office of the President—or anybody else—could not call an interdepartmental regional meeting to consider a common approach to a problem or project in Kentucky without bringing people in from half a dozen localities—people who, when the meeting was over, would again scatter to cities spread across a third of the country. At not one point in the entire nation did all of the agencies primarily concerned with federal grant programs and intergovernmental relations have their headquarters in the same city, and even when most of them were located together their regional jurisdictions differed. Thus, almost all of the agencies had regional offices in New York City, but the only state these regions had in common was New York. A Bureau of Employment Security regional director in Boston found his OEO and HUD counterparts in New York City, and a two-hour meeting for purposes of coordination cost either the Boston or New York participants a full day of working time—and if flights were canceled the meetings had to be rearranged. The Department of Labor did not even have a uniform pattern for its various bureaus, and the Department of Agriculture bureaus concerned with rural development did not have regional offices at all.

To rationalize this hodgepodge, President Nixon in the spring of 1969 defied the political consequences and boldly ordered into effect a uniform ten-region pattern for five agencies—Labor, HEW, HUD, OEO, and the Small Business Administration.[20] The relocation of regional offices into the same headquarters cities and the reassignment of states as between regions was to take place over a period of eighteen months.

20. The President's plan, as initially announced on March 27, called for eight regions. In response to criticism from Capitol Hill and elsewhere, on May 21 he announced revisions increasing the number of regions to ten.

The President asked all other agencies, also, to "take note" of the new regional pattern and conform to it any changes they might make in their field organization structures. Among the agencies omitted in the March order, perhaps the one in greatest need of a new regional pattern is the Economic Development Administration. When EDA was formed, its regional offices were established in such out-of-the-way places as Huntington, West Virginia; Wilkes-Barre, Pennsylvania; Huntsville, Alabama; Portland, Maine; and Duluth, Minnesota. The clients of EDA in the Southeast point out that it is easier to get to the national capital itself than to Huntsville from almost any point in the region, and the same can be said of EDA's Wilkes-Barre and Duluth offices. Close collaboration between EDA and other agencies of the government was virtually ruled out when EDA was born. The opportunity for redesigning its regional pattern that would follow upon superseding EDA with another economic development organization, as discussed earlier in this chapter, is one of the stronger arguments for doing so.

Coordination at the regional level also depends upon a reasonably uniform pattern of decentralization of decision making to the regions. But here, too, the variations are extreme. HUD and OEO have delegated authority to their regions for project approval; Labor has delegated authority for some programs but not for others; HEW has delegated very little. Joint funding depends upon joint review by the approving agencies, and that is unsatisfactory if the authority resides at different levels. For the regional offices to administer a common pool of money for model cities or model countryside programs, approval authority would have to be delegated to the regions on a uniform basis. This, finally, is still another task for the intergovernmental program coordination unit in the Executive Office of the President.[21]

An Age of Management

In this study we have presented a series of models that, taken together, will constitute a system of intergovernmental program co-

---

21. The President on March 27, 1969, instructed the director of the Bureau of the Budget and the heads of nine departments and agencies to undertake a joint review of headquarters-field relationships with a view to greater decentralization and greater consistency of patterns among departments.

ordination extending from the Presidency through the federal regional centers and the states to the communities.

In a democratic, pluralistic society, no system of intergovernmental relations can be established through a single action, or even a series of actions; it evolves. But the evolution, if the result is to be a *system* of relationships rather than a jumble, must be guided according to a consistent set of principles and governing doctrine. The principles and the doctrine we have sought to outline. The guidance, however, can come from but a single source of authority—the President. It is he who must apply the principles and the doctrine in proposing legislation to the Congress and in directing the execution of the laws.

The 1960s were years of defining new objectives for the nation. The 1970s will see those objectives refined and new ones proclaimed, but it also must be the period in which the federal system is organized to make possible the achievement of the nation's goals.

The 1960s have been a decade of spectacular innovation in policy. What is needed now is a decade of innovation in administration that, while it perhaps can never be as spectacular, will be equally historic.

APPENDIX

Federal Grants-in-Aid
to State and Local Governments,
1966-68[a]

Program and year established	Federal agency administering program, 1967	Amount of grant, in thousands of dollars		
		Fiscal year 1966	Fiscal year 1967 (estimated)	Fiscal year 1968 (estimated)
Established prior to 1930				
Teaching materials for the blind (1879)	HEW	935	953	1,150
Cooperative state experiment station service: Agricultural experiment stations (1887)	Agriculture	50,301	57,000	64,100
Veterans' homes (1888)	VA	8,634	8,957	9,295
Land grant colleges (1890)	HEW	14,500	b	b
Forestry cooperation (1911)	Agriculture	16,526	17,290	17,280
Maritime academies or colleges (1911)	Commerce	972	375	375
Federal extension service (1914)	Agriculture	84,995	87,773	92,017
Federal-aid highways (1916)	Transportation	3,923,743	3,926,800	3,802,700
Vocational education (1917)	HEW	128,938	220,737	227,961
Vocational rehabilitation (1920)	HEW	156,526	256,815	309,688
Subtotal		4,386,070	c	c
Established during period 1931–45				
Agricultural commodity distributions Price-support donations (1933)	Agriculture	114,853	185,465	193,024

Footnotes to table appear on pp. 284–85.

279

Program and year established	Federal agency administering program, 1967	Amount of grant, in thousands of dollars		
		Fiscal year 1966	Fiscal year 1967 (estimated)	Fiscal year 1968 (estimated)
Agricultural commodity distributions (cont.)				
Food stamp program (1933)	Agriculture	65,353	131,399	184,000
Employment service and unemployment compensation and administration (1933)	Labor	469,332	517,546	551,625
Indian education and welfare services (1934)	Interior	10,019	9,452	9,952
Indian resources management (1934)	Interior	862	947	947
Agricultural Marketing Service: Agricultural commodity distribution—removal of surplus (1935)	Agriculture	112,044	139,020	168,137
Aid and services to needy families with children (1935)	HEW	1,215,829	1,299,800	1,368,900
Aid to the blind (1935)	HEW	51,163	52,300	52,700
Child welfare services (1935)	HEW	39,564	154,600	207,300
Community and environmental health activities—general health (1935)	HEW	14,906	d	d
Crippled children's services (1935)	HEW	37,158	e	e
Maternal and child health services (1935)	HEW	36,744	e	e
Old age assistance (1935)	HEW	1,161,029	1,205,100	1,170,100
Low-rent public housing (1937)	HUD	225,516	249,055	277,679
Wildlife restoration (1937)	Interior	15,666	18,421	17,959
Venereal disease control (1938)	HEW	5,194	f	f
Tuberculosis control (1944)	HEW	9,890	f	f
Subtotal		3,585,122	c	c
Established during period 1946–60				
Agricultural commodity distributions—school lunch programs (1946)	Agriculture	194,991	211,370	240,250

Footnotes to table appear on pp. 284–85.

Program and year established	Federal agency administering program, 1967	Amount of grant, in thousands of dollars		
		Fiscal year 1966	Fiscal year 1967 (estimated)	Fiscal year 1968 (estimated)
Agricultural marketing and research services (1946)	Agriculture	3,414	3,443	3,242
Airport planning and development (1946)	Transportation	53,989	54,000	59,000
Basic scientific research grants—Department of Agriculture (1946)	Agriculture	2,950	1,000	1,000
Hospital and medical facilities—construction (1946)	HEW	194,911	219,911	230,400
Mental health activities (1946)	HEW	6,570	112,400	216,100
Disaster relief and repairs (1947)	OEP	131,651	81,100	34,500
Cancer control and demonstrations (1948)	HEW	3,488	f	f
Heart disease control (1948)	HEW	7,249	f	f
Urban renewal (1949)	HUD	316,569	361,254	447,507
Aid to permanently and totally disabled (1950)	HEW	338,272	375,900	416,600
Federally affected public schools Maintenance and operation (1950)	HEW	333,974	360,000	360,170
Construction (1950)	HEW	44,361	31,000	29,830
Fish restoration and management (1950)	Interior	6,168	6,000	6,310
Civil Defense (1950)	Defense	21,231	25,500	30,000
State supervision of schools and training establishments (1952)	VA	267	1,515	1,515
Agricultural commodity distribution—special milk program for children (1954)	Agriculture	96,477	103,350	103,350
Soil Conservation Service: Watershed protection and flood prevention (1954)	Agriculture	69,441	68,166	71,401
State and local preparedness planning (1954)	OEP	897	716	167
Urban planning (1954)	HUD	20,050	22,000	30,000
Health research facilities construction (1956)	HEW	133	g	g
Library services and construction (1956)	HEW	40,915	89,900	107,300

| | Federal agency administering program, 1967 | Amount of grant, in thousands of dollars | | |
Program and year established		Fiscal year 1966	Fiscal year 1967 (estimated)	Fiscal year 1968 (estimated)
Waste treatment works construction (1956)	Interior	81,478	83,000	152,000
Water pollution control (1956)	Interior	6,170	8,960	18,242
Defense educational activities (1958)	HEW	84,860	104,330	32,259
Education of mentally retarded and other handicapped children (1958)	HEW	2,564	6,000	12,968
Forest and public lands highways (1958)	Transportation	40,037	39,427	h
National guard centers— construction (1958)	Defense	3,044	700	2,700
Medical assistance for the aged (1960)	HEW	298,911	19,700	7,300
Subtotal		2,405,032	c	c

Established during period 1961–66

Community health services, particularly for chronically ill and aged (excluding heart, cancer) (1961)	HEW	11,537	f	f
Open-space land preservation (1961)	HUD	7,912	28,500	57,800
Public facilities grants and area redevelopment assistance[i] (1961)	Commerce	6,889	50,600	131,800
Educational television (1962)	HEW	4,402	7,825	19,675
Manpower development and training (1962)	Labor	21,998	30,000	40,000
Public works acceleration (1962)	Commerce	87,033	35,700	–
Radiological health and institutional training (1962)	HEW	1,990	f	f
Air pollution control and prevention (1963)	HEW	622	f	f
Higher educational facilities—construction (1963)	HEW	1,289	b	b
Adult basic education (1964)	OEO, HEW	21,131	13,900	–

Footnotes to table appear on pp. 284–85.

Program and year established	Federal agency administering program, 1967	Amount of grant, in thousands of dollars		
		Fiscal year 1966	Fiscal year 1967 (estimated)	Fiscal year 1968 (estimated)
Low-rent housing for domestic farm labor (1964)	Agriculture	–	6,000	4,000
Communicable disease activities (1964)	HEW	11,680	f	f
Community action programs (1964)	OEO	326,085	568,000	796,000
Mass transportation (1964)	HUD	15,373	55,900	108,700
Neighborhood Youth Corps (1964)	OEO, Labor	239,333	291,000	300,800
Work experience and training program (1964)	OEO, HEW	74,357	124,800	97,000
Water resources research (1964)	Interior	5,403	5,578	8,036
Commercial fisheries research and development (1964)	Interior	422	3,215	4,385
Highway beautification and control of outdoor advertising (1965)	Transportation	2,537	36,901	j
Land and water conservation (1965)	Interior	3,144	28,814	50,982
Appalachian highways (1965)	Commerce	8,877	42,100	80,700
Elementary and secondary educational activities (1965)	HEW	815,099	1,219,900	1,422,841
Administration on aging (1965)	HEW	1,331	4,557	10,274
Medical assistance[k] (1965)	HEW	487,200	768,200	1,244,800
Dental services and resources (1965)	HEW	742	l	l
Promotion of arts and humanities (1965)	NFAH	–	1,000	2,000
State technical services (1965)	Commerce	1,341	3,500	7,100
Rural water and waste disposal grants (1965)	Agriculture	96	40,900	30,000
National Teachers Corps (1965)	HEW	–	3,000	8,500
Higher educational activities (1965)	HEW	3,926	170,300[m]	245,300[m]
Equal educational opportunities program (1965)	HEW	2,651	3,500	15,900

283

Program and year established	Federal agency administering program, 1967	Amount of grant, in thousands of dollars		
		Fiscal year 1966	Fiscal year 1967 (estimated)	Fiscal year 1968 (estimated)
Basic water and sewer facilities (1965)	HUD	–	40,000	110,000
Neighborhood facilities (1965)	HUD	–	3,000	15,000
Metropolitan development (1966)	HUD	–	–	7,000
Demonstration cities (1966)	HUD	–	5,250	147,000
Urban information services (1966)	HUD	–	–	1,500
Highway beauty-safety trust fund (1966)	Transportation	–	–	227,500
Office of Economic Opportunity Special Impact (1966)	OEO	–	75,000	185,000
Adult work training (1966)	OEO	–		
Health grants[n]				
Health manpower	HEW	–	47,510	138,341
Disease prevention and environmental control	HEW	–	72,800	49,600
Health services	HEW	–	33,181	55,650
Mental health	HEW	–	112,350	216,147
Comprehensive health planning and services	HEW	–	3,991	105,686
Subtotal		2,164,400	c	c
Grand total		12,540,624	14,867,219	17,286,017

SUMMARY

Basic program established			
Prior to 1930	4,386,070	–	–
1931–45	3,585,122	–	–
1946–60	2,405,032	–	–
1961–66	2,164,400	–	–

Source: Advisory Commission on Intergovernmental Relations, *Fiscal Balance in the American Federal System* (1967), Vol. 1, pp. 140–44. Data for fiscal 1966: Table 84, Federal grants-in-aid to State and local governments and to individuals and private institutions within the States, fiscal year 1966, Part A., *Annual Report of the Secretary of the Treasury, 1966;* 1967 and 1968 fiscal data: *Special Analysis J, Budget of the United States, 1968,* with subsequent adjustments obtained from Bureau of the Budget Fiscal Analysis Section; public assistance figures for all three years were taken from *Budget of the United States, 1968,* Appendix, pp. 486–87.

a. Excluded are shared revenues and certain minor grants, such as Department of State: East-West Cultural and Technical Interchange Center; grants limited to specific states, such as transitional grants to Alaska; and federal payment to District of Columbia. Total for fiscal year 1968 exceeds that shown in *Special Analysis J, Budget of the United States, 1968,* p. 161, because of difference in figures used for public assistance (see source note above).

b. Included in higher educational activities (1965).
c. Not subtotaled because of account classification shifts.
d. Included under health services (at end of table).
e. Included under child welfare services (1935).
f. Included under disease prevention and environmental control (at end of table).
g. Included under hospital and medical facilities—construction (1946).
h. Reflects transfer to federal-aid highways (1916).
i. Became Economic Development Administration in 1965.
j. Reflects proposed establishment of a new beauty-safety trust fund.
k. Includes "payments to medical vendors—other programs" as follows: 1966—$285,194; 1967—$118,200; 1968—$48,600 (see *Budget of the United States, 1968,* Appendix, pp. 486–87).
l. Included under health manpower (at end of table).
m. Starting in 1967, includes higher education construction (1963) and land grant colleges (1890).
n. This is the account classification for health grants for 1967 and 1968 used by the Bureau of the Budget in *Special Analysis J, Budget of the United States, 1968,* p. 160.

Abbreviations:
HEW   Health, Education, and Welfare
HUD   Housing and Urban Development
NFAH   National Foundation on Arts and Humanities
OEO   Office of Economic Opportunity
OEP   Office of Emergency Planning
VA   Veterans Administration

Index

TYPESETTING   Monotype Composition Company, Inc., Baltimore

PRINTING & BINDING   Garamond/Pridemark Press, Inc., Baltimore